The Tax Collector and the Pharisee

The Tax Collector and the Pharisee

*Exploring the Plausible Origin of
the Parable's Justification Theme*

Peter Tan-Gatue

☙PICKWICK *Publications* · Eugene, Oregon

THE TAX COLLECTOR AND THE PHARISEE
Exploring the Plausible Origin of the Parable's Justification Theme

Copyright © 2022 Peter Tan-Gatue. All rights reserved. Except for brief quotations in critical publications or reviews, no part of this book may be reproduced in any manner without prior written permission from the publisher. Write: Permissions, Wipf and Stock Publishers, 199 W. 8th Ave., Suite 3, Eugene, OR 97401.

Pickwick Publications
An Imprint of Wipf and Stock Publishers
199 W. 8th Ave., Suite 3
Eugene, OR 97401

www.wipfandstock.com

PAPERBACK ISBN: 978-1-6667-0706-9
HARDCOVER ISBN: 978-1-6667-0707-6
EBOOK ISBN: 978-1-6667-0708-3

Cataloguing-in-Publication data:

Names: Tan-Gatue, Peter, author.

Title: The tax collector and the Pharisee : exploring the plausible origin of the parable's justification theme / by Peter Tan-Gatue.

Description: Eugene, OR: Pickwick Publications, 2022 | Includes bibliographical references and index.

Identifiers: ISBN 978-1-6667-0706-9 (paperback) | ISBN 978-1-6667-0707-6 (hardcover) | ISBN 978-1-6667-0708-3 (ebook)

Subjects: LCSH: Bible. Luke, XVIII, 9–14—Criticism, interpretation, etc. | Justification (Christian theology)—Biblical teaching.

Classification: BT375.2 T36 2022 (print) | BT375.2 (ebook)

01/13/22

This book is dedicated to my family—
Jill, Cecilia, Pedro, and Aquene.

I am blessed.

Contents

Preface | xi
List of Abbreviations | xiv

Chapter 1: Introduction | 1
    Literature Review 3
    Research Issue and Thesis 5
    Methodology 6
    Plan of this Monograph 10

Chapter 2: Luke 18:9–14 | 15
    General Background of the Parable 15
    Parable Analysis 16
        Parable Context 16
        Translation 17
        Overall Structure 19
        Major Semantic Features 19
        Relationship to Luke 18:1–8 22
        Issues and Comments 23
            Luke 18:9 23
            Luke 18:10 25
            Luke 18:11 31
            Luke 18:12 33

CONTENTS

    Luke 18:13   35
    Luke 18:14a   37
    Luke 18:14b   40
  The notion of justification/righteousness in this parable   41
Next Step   44

Chapter 3: Coherence of Justification with the Lukan Tradition (L) | 46
  Luke 7:36–50   47
  Special Lukan Parables   53
    Luke 10:25–37   53
    Luke 14:7–14   57
    Luke 15:1–32   60
    Luke 16:14–31   62
    Luke 18:1–8   69
  Luke 19:1–10   71
  The Passion Narrative   74
  Conclusion   77

Chapter 4: Coherence of Justification with Mark and Q | 79
  Mark   80
    Mark 10:13–16 // Luke 18:15–17 // Matthew 19:13–15   80
    Mark 10:17–31 // Luke 18:18–30 // Matthew 19:16–30   83
    Mark 10:46–52 // Luke 18:35–43 // Matthew 20:29–34; 9:27–31   88
  Q Source   91
    Luke 13:22–30 / Matthew 7:13–14; 22–23; 8:11–12; 19:30   91
    Luke 14:15–24 / Matthew 22:1–14   93
    Luke 7:1–10 / Matthew 8:5–13   95
  Conclusion   98

Chapter 5: Jewish Palestinian Background of Luke 18:9–14 | 100
  The Pharisee   101
  The Tax Collector   102
  The Temple Setting   104

The Pharisee Stands Apart   106
The Prayer of the Pharisee   108
The Tax Collector Stands Far Off, Downcast   111
The Tax Collector's Prayer   112
The Notion of Justification   114
Conclusion   114

Chapter 6: The "Inauthenticity" of Luke 18:9–14,
  Other Unique Lukan Parables | 115
A Marginal Jew Volume 5—Probing the Authenticity
of the Parables   118
  Background Overview   118
  Methodology   119
  Seven "Unfashionable" Theses   125
Critique Against the Criteria of Authenticity   134
  Multiple Attestation   137
  Dissimilarity   139
  Coherence   142
  Embarrassment   145
  Conclusion   146
Studies on Oral Tradition, Transmission, Eyewitnesses, Memory   146
  Form Criticism   147
  Rabbinic Model   149
  Informal Controlled Model   151
  Validation of Informal Controlled Model from Genre Studies   153
  Oral and Written Media Contrast Model   155
  Eyewitnesses to the Tradition   157
  Social Memory   159
  Conclusion   168

Conclusion | 170

Bibliography | 173

Ancient Document Index | 185

Preface

THE TAX COLLECTOR AND *the Pharisee* carry forward my main scholarly interests: the parables of Jesus Christ (especially the unique Lukan parables), historical Jesus studies, and the biblical theme of justification and its possible origins. My hope is this work will highlight the parable in Luke 18:9–14 as an important link between Jesus and Paul in the central Christian concept of "justification by faith."

My book argues that the theme of justification mentioned in Luke 18:9–14 plausibly originated from the Jesus tradition. In other words, this theme as expressed in this parable is not so incongruent to Jesus's teaching that the only likely explanation of its presence in the Gospels is that it was an import of Paul's view of justification. On the other hand, this book demonstrates, primarily through the theme's coherence and fit with Luke and other earlier synoptic sources, that it is also possible that Luke derived it from Jesus material. Since this notion of justification in the parable is consistent with Jesus's wider teaching, the possibility also increases that Paul's view of justification by faith comes from Jesus's early teaching instead of it being a purely Pauline innovation.

The main focus of my work is the parable of the Pharisee and the tax collector (Luke 18:9–14) and its idea of justification along with its related themes and motifs. Chapter 1 introduces the thesis and explains the method of using a reformulated and qualified version of the criterion of coherence. Chapter 2 presents an exegetical study on Luke 18:9–14, which sheds light on what justification or righteousness is from the standpoint of this parable. It then derives possible related ideas that can be used to identify their recurrence in other sources and forms in the Gospels. Since the parable comes from unique Lukan material, it is not attested to in other independent sources. Therefore, related themes and motifs are used for determining coherence. In chapters 3 and 4, thematic coherences are noted in special Lukan material L (chapter 3), Mark and Q (chapter 4), and in specific forms (both chapters), such as parables, aphorisms, and pronouncement stories. Chapter 5 explores the contextual plausibility of Luke 18:9–14 by looking at the parable's fit in the first-century Jewish Palestinian environment. Chapter 6 calls into question the charge of "inauthenticity" of Luke 18:9–14 and other unique Lukan parables in general, using John Meier's monograph (vol. 5 of *A Marginal Jew*) that makes a case for their inauthenticity as a case study. It does this first by arguing against Meier's unqualified and minimalist use of the criteria of authenticity. Then it presents recent findings on oral tradition, transmission, eyewitnesses, and social memory that calls into serious question the faulty form-critical assumptions behind Meier's work. The conclusion simply summarizes the findings: Given the coherence of justification in Luke 18:9–14 with the broader gospel tradition, the parable's fit in the first-century Jewish Palestinian environment, and the questioning of the parable's so-called "inauthenticity," these factors provide good reasons to believe that the theme of justification plausibly comes from the Jesus tradition.

I am most grateful to my mentor, Dr. Craig Keener for his guidance and support for this project. I also wish to thank Dr. David Bauer, and Dr. Joseph Dongell of Asbury Theological Seminary for their invaluable input. I could not have finished this book without the support of the Session and members of Praise Community Church for granting me some study leave from my pastoral duties and my family for the encouragement to bring this work to completion.

I also wish to thank those who first taught me the New Testament such as Dr. Marianne Meye Thompson (Fuller Theological Seminary), Dr. Diane Chen (Palmer Theological Seminary), and Dr. Seyoon Kim (Fuller Theological Seminary). Their excellent instruction piqued my interest in the parables, the doctrine of justification by faith, and historical Jesus studies.

Going back even further, I wish to thank some significant people from Woodland Hills Church in Saint Paul, Minnesota which I consider my very first home church. In particular I thank Mary Lynn Christopher, Delores Pappas, and Tyler De Armond. They were responsible for mentoring me directly during my initial years of spiritual formation as a Christian and for helping develop my love for the Scriptures. Many thanks to other members and friends from Woodland Hills who first modeled the Christian lifestyle for me, including my wife, Jill, whom I met in my first church small group. There are also so many others who helped me and supported me in my ministry from churches such as Bel Air Presbyterian Church, Church on the Solid Rock, and Filipino churches in Azusa and Eagle Rock. I also thank my colleagues and mentors from UCLA Medical Center, Mission Hospice, and St. Joseph hospital in Lexington, Kentucky. Of course, I thank Jill for supporting me all this time and enduring with me all the life changes (and many address changes) she never imagined we would make. She deserves a break!

Ultimately, I give thanks and praise to God. Glory to God!

Abbreviations

ABD	*The Anchor Bible Dictionary*. 6 vols. Edited by David Noel Freedman. New York: Doubleday, 1992.
ʾAbot	ʾAbot
ʾAbot R. Nat.	ʾAbot de Rabbi Nathan
Apoc. Ab.	Apocalypse of Abraham
As. Mos.	Assumption of Moses
AThR	*Anglican Theological Review*
b.	Babylonian Talmud
B. Qam.	*Baba Qamma*
Ber.	*Berakot*
BDAG	Walter Bauer, Frederick W. Danker, W. F. Arndt, and F. W. Gingrich. *Greek English Lexicon of the New Testament and Other Early Christian Literature*. 3rd ed. Chicago: University of Chicago Press, 2000.
BECNT	Baker Exegetical Commentary on the New Testament
CBQ	*Catholic Biblical Quarterly*
CD	Cairo (Genizah text of the) Damascus (Document)
CE	Common Era
CGT	Coptic Gospel of Thomas
Cicero	
Off.	*De officiis*

ABBREVIATIONS

2 Clem.	2 Clement
CRINT	Compedia Rerum Iudaicarum ad Novum Testamentum
CTQ	*Concordia Theological Quarterly*
CurTM	*Currents in Theology and Mission*
Demai	Demai

Dio Chrysostom

Disc.	*Discourses*
Or.	*Orations*
DJG	*Dictionary of Jesus and the Gospels*. Edited by Joel B. Green, Scot McKnight, and I. Howard Marshall. Downers Grove, IL:InterVarsity Press, 1992.
DJG, 2nd ed.	*Dictionary of Jesus and the Gospels*. Edited by Joel B. Green, Jeannine K. Brown, and Nicholas Perrin. 2nd ed. Downers Grove, IL:InterVarsity Press, 2013.
DNTB	*Dictionary of New Testament Background*. Edited by Craig A. Evans and Stanley E. Porter. Downers Grove, IL:InterVarsity Press, 2000.
Did.	Didache
1 En.	1 Enoch
ʿErub.	ʿErubin
1–2 Esd	1–2 Esdras
EvQ	*The Evangelical Quarterly*
ExAud	*Ex Auditu*
ExpTim	*Expository Times*
4QFlor	Florilegium (or Eschatological Midrashim) from Qumran Cave 4
Gos. Thom.	Gospel of Thomas
Ḥag.	Hagigah
HALOT	*The Hebrew and Aramaic Lexicon of the Old Testament*. Study ed. 2 vols. Koehler, Ludwig and Walter Baumgartner. London: Brill, 2001.

ABBREVIATIONS

Herodotus
Hist.   *Historiae*

Hesiod
Op.   *Opera et dies*

Int	*Interpretation*
JBL	*Journal of Biblical Literature*
Jdt	Judith
JETS	*Journal of the Evangelical Theological Society*

Josephus
Ant.   *Antiquities*
J.W.   *Jewish War*

Jos. Asen.	*Joseph and Aseneth*
JSHJ	*Journal for the Study of the Historical Jesus*
JSNT	*Journal for the Study of the NT*
JSNTSup	Journal for the Study of the New Testament Supplement Series
JSOT	*Journal for the Study of the Old Testament*
JTS	*Journal of Theological Studies*
L	L (Lukan) special material
LCL	Loeb Classical Library
LNTS	Library of New Testament Studies
LS	*Louvain Studies*

Lucian
Tim.   *Timon*

LXX	Septuagint
Ma'aś.	*Ma'aśerot*
M	M (Matthean) special material
m.	Mishnah
MT	Masoretic Text

ABBREVIATIONS

NAC	New American Commentary
NCB	New Century Bible
Ned.	*Nedarim*
NICNT	New International Commentary on the New Testament
NIGTC	New International Greek Testament Commentary
NovT	*Novum Testamentum*
NT	New Testament
NTS	*New Testament Studies*
Q	Q ("*Quelle*") Hypothetical Document
1QH	*Hodayot* or Thanksgiving Hymn from Qumran Cave 1
1QS	*Serek Hayahad* (Rule of Community, Manual of Discipline)
1QSa	Appendix A (Rule of the Congregation) to 1QS
1QSb	Appendix B (Rule of the Blessings) to 1QS
OT	Old Testament
PNTC	Pillar New Testament Commentary
Pr Man	Prayer of Manasseh
PRSt	*Perspectives in Religious Studies*
Philo	
Praem.	*De praemiis et poenis*
Spec.	*De specialibus legibus*
Pss. Sol.	Psalms of Solomon
Rab.	*Rabbah (following abbreviation for biblical book: Eccl. Rab. = Ecclesiastes Rabbah)*
RevExp	*Review and Expositor*
Sanh.	*Sanhedrin*
SBL	Society of Biblical Literature
SBT	Studies in Biblical Theology
Šeb.	*Shevi'it*
Sir	Sirach
SNTSMS	Society for New Testament Studies Monograph Series
SNTSU	Studien zum Neuen Testament und seiner Umwelt

Soṭah	Sotah
SP	Sacra Pagina
SwJT	*Southwestern Journal of Theology*
Suk.	Sukka
Taʿanit	Taʿanit
T. Ab.	*Testament of Abraham*
T. Gad	*Testament of Gad*

Tacitus
Hist.	*Historiae*

Tamid	Tamid
Ṭehar.	Teharot
TDNT	*Theological Dictionary of the New Testament.* 10 vols. Edited by Gerhard Kittel and Gerhard Friedrich. Translated by Geoffrey W. Bromiley. Grand Rapids: Eerdmans, 1964–76.
TNTC	Tyndale New Testament Commentaries
WBC	Word Biblical Commentary
ZNW	*Zeitschrift fur die neutestamentliche Wissenschaft und die kunde der alteren*

— Chapter 1 —

Introduction

LUKE 18:9–14, THE PARABLE of the Pharisee and the Tax Collector is one of the singly attested Lukan parables in the Jesus tradition.[1] One notable feature of this parable, especially when read together with Luke 18:1–8, is the concentrated use of the δικαιόω word group (i.e., ἐκδικήσω, ἀδικίας, ἐκδίκησιν, δίκαιοι, δεδικαιωμένος—18:3, 5–8, 9, 14). Interestingly, various commentators have noticed that the parable presents a theme or notion of justification/righteousness, and they often try to relate it to the Pauline idea of righteousness. For example, I. H. Marshall suggests that the picture of justification in Luke 18 (and in Acts 13:13–41) is not different from the notion depicted in Paul's writings.[2] He further asserts that both Paul and Luke drew from the Jesus tradition and that the variety in the way these are expressed stems from the different language used by the authors.[3] On the other hand, John Nolland states that Luke 18:9–14 does not provide a picture of justification but instead addresses the Pharisees' concern about their appearance before others. Therefore, he believes that this parable should not

---

1. It is generally regarded as an authentic parable in historical Jesus studies, but the Jesus Seminar designates it as a Lucan composition in the late first century. Funk et al. gave the parable a pink rating. They assert that the parable belongs in the late first century, arising from polemic between Christianity and Judaism. Funk et al., *Parables of Jesus*, 21, 56, 74.

2. Marshall, *New Testament Theology*, 477.

3. Marshall, *Gospel of Luke*, 680. Bruce, "Justification by Faith," 67–68, states that the doctrine of justification in Luke 18 is from the Jesus tradition, the same as the doctrine presented by Paul but not influenced by Paul. Schreiner, *New Testament Theology*, 550, understands Luke's portrayal of justification to be Pauline, as well as that of Acts 13.

be seen through Paul's doctrine of justification.[4] Overall, for those who find it notable to mention the theme of justification/righteousness in this parable, they compare it to Paul's version and then argue that they say and mean the same thing, signify something totally different, or are related in some particular way.[5] In addition, some would conjure up different theories or assumptions about the Gospel author's relationship to Paul, which in their view perhaps influenced the notion of justification/righteousness in the parable. For example, W. C. Van Unnik proposes that Luke's author, as a second-generation theologian, really had no understanding of the concerns of Paul's day and ultimately did not really comprehend the doctrine of justification by faith. He was supposedly an admirer of Paul, and he shared his view of a gospel that had done away with Jewish law. Unfortunately, he did not truly get what Paul was saying in his letters.[6] Likewise, Joseph Fitzmyer believes that the evangelist considered Paul a hero and prominent example of the earlier generation of Christian missionaries, which was why the evangelist highlighted Paul for most of the second half of Acts. However, the Gospel of Luke presents Paul's notion of justification as "forgiveness of sins" because the Lukan evangelist was not well informed about Pauline theology.[7] More recently, John Meier, in his fifth volume of his series on the historical Jesus, proposes that the unique Lukan parables are creative works of the early church or by the evangelists themselves, and that the theology of justification in Luke 18:9–14 was unmistakably imported from Paul.[8]

Did Luke the evangelist co-opt or recast this theme of justification from Paul? Is there a better likelihood that Luke derived the theme from the teachings of Jesus himself? This study is an attempt to find an answer for the second question.

---

4. Nolland, *Luke 9:21—18:34*, 810, 878.

5. See Barrett, "Justification," 1–26. An excellent survey of authors and their various perspectives can be found in his dissertation in pages 1–26. Barrett notes that "most commentaries and theologies give little or no attention to the concept of justification as it is presented in Luke-Acts." Barrett, "Justification," 20.

6. Van Unnik, "Luke-Acts," 26.

7. Fitzmyer, "Pauline Justification," 258, 261–62.

8. Meier, *Marginal Jew*, 5:198–99, 210.

INTRODUCTION

Literature Review

A scarcity of scholarly works deal with the theme of justification or righteousness in Luke. Some early modern sources deal with the topic of justification in various non-Pauline biblical writings of which justification in the Gospel of Luke is but one subtopic. That is the case for F. F. Bruce's "Justification by Faith in the Non-Pauline Writings of the New Testament" and also the work of J. H. P. Reumann, Joseph A. Fitzmyer, and Jerome D. Quinn's *Righteousness in the New Testament: Justification in the United States Lutheran-Roman Catholic Dialogue*.[9] Various other works deal with the presentation of justification by the Lukan author, specifically in the book of Acts.[10] A monograph by Richard Gaffin about the theme of justification in the whole Bible includes a chapter on justification in Luke-Acts.[11] Gaffin comments that "monographs and articles on the theme of justification in Luke-Acts are few indeed" and also notes that there are "numerous relevant materials in various commentaries, New Testament theologies, and monographs and articles on Lucan theology but they are not substantial."[12] The most recent work concerning the topic of justification in Luke is Kyle Barrett's dissertation on justification in Lukan theology. In his work he asserts that Luke has "a conscious and detectable theology of justification which is explicit in the parable of the Pharisee and the Tax Collector, yet subtly permeates the entirety of Luke's work." He also claims that Luke's understanding of justification has its foundation in the Old Testament view of God's vindication of the righteous.[13]

While Barrett and some of the other authors do suggest origins or sources of this theme of justification in Luke, they do not necessarily fully develop their line of thinking to support their claims in a more comprehensive manner. In addition to those who claim that Luke simply copied, reworked, or misunderstood Paul's notion of justification, there are also those who

---

9. Bruce, "Justification by Faith," 67–68; Reumann et al., *Righteousness in the New Testament*.

10. Fitzmyer, "Pauline Justification"; Menoud, "Justification by Faith," 202–27; Scaer, "Resurrection as Justification," 219–31.

11. Gaffin, "Justification," 106–25.

12. Gaffin, "Justification," 108, 271.

13. Barrett, "Justification," 3. Barrett also cites the scarcity of works on the theme of the Lukan notion of justification and offers as one possible reason the domination of more historical concerns in earlier Lukan studies and the tendency of earlier authors to undervalue Luke's theology.

believe that the ultimate source of the theme of justification in Luke is the Jesus tradition. An example is Joseph Fitzmyer who claims that pre-Lukan tradition was used in the parable of the Pharisee and the Tax Collector.[14] Another example is I. H. Marshall who asserts that both Luke and Paul derive their notion of justification from the Jesus tradition, which is ultimately rooted in the Old Testament.[15] In all the other reviewed works of authors who make similar claims, none of them further develops nor strengthens their claim in a manner that would be along the lines of the criterion of coherence as conceptualized by the criterion of plausibility (the method planned in this study) as determined by the continuum approach.[16]

One of the key works that looks for themes and motifs as part of the Jesus tradition using the criterion of coherence is the essay of Gerd Theissen and Annette Merz, which explores the theme of the delay of the Parousia.[17] Theissen and Merz apply this criterion looking at the recurrence of the notion of eschatological delay in different currents of tradition in the Gospels and across different forms.[18] Other examples of authors applying the approach to various themes are in a monograph edited by Tom Holmen.[19] Themes discussed include the mixed genealogy of Jesus, his sexuality, narrative tradition about widows, and the expression Son of Man. In this book, every author applied the approach in his or her own distinctive way while integrating the criterion of coherence.[20] Sean Freyne, Bruce Chilton, and Craig Evans also produced studies that follow

---

14. Fitzmyer, *Luke X–XXIV*, 1185. Fitzmyer cautions against reading Pauline justification into the parable.

15. Marshall, *Gospel of Luke*, 680. F. F. Bruce also has this understanding and claims that there is no Pauline influence in Luke's portrayal of justification in the parable since he believes this comes directly from Jesus's teaching. See Bruce, "Justification by Faith," 67–68. Also see Bailey, *Through Peasant Eyes*, 156; Blomberg, *Jesus and the Gospels*, 380; Ellis, *Gospel of Luke*, 214; Ladd, *Theology*, 78; McKnight and Osborne, *New Vision for Israel*, 205; Schreiner, *Paul*, 472; Stein, *Gospel of Luke*, 451.

16. The method that will be used for this monograph will be defined and explained further in the methods section.

17. Theissen and Merz, "Delay," 49–66.

18. Different currents are Q, Mark, Matthew, Luke, John, Thomas; different forms include beatitudes, cries of woe, parables, and aphorisms. See Theissen and Merz, "Delay," 61–62.

19. Holmen, *Jesus from Judaism*.

20. Chilton, "Mamzerut and Jesus," 17–33; Loader, "Sexuality," 34–48; Merz, "How a Woman," 49–86; Kazen, "Son of Man," 87–108.

in principle the continuum approach.²¹ Theissen and Dagmar Winter give other stock examples in their book that explains the approach on a theoretical level.²² Other authors of historical Jesus monographs (such as Craig Keener and Theissen and Merz) account for coherence of major themes in Gospel sources, but none have explored the theme of justification in the parable of the Pharisee and the tax collector and its coherence with the different currents of tradition in the other Gospels.²³

Research Issue and Thesis

The theme of righteousness in the Gospel of Luke has not been explored much for various possible reasons, one of which is that scholars at one time undervalued Luke's theology.²⁴ However, for many decades now, Luke has been regarded as a theologian in his own right, and the various themes and theology of Luke have been examined and explored.²⁵ Barrett's work explores Lukan theology through the theme of justification, which he claims is made explicit by the parable of the Pharisee and the Tax Collector. However, he does not attempt to answer in a comprehensive way the question concerning the source of this theme.²⁶

As mentioned earlier, for some authors, the basis or defining source of the theme in the parable depends on the relationship between Luke and Pauline thought. Many assert that Luke may have copied and/or reworked Paul's view of justification to fit his own context or, as one author suggests, that Luke did not really fully grasp what Paul meant by justification.²⁷

---

21. See Freyne, *Jesus a Jewish Galilean*.

22. Theissen and Winter, *Quest*, 177–79.

23. Keener, *Historical Jesus*; Theissen and Merz, *Historical Jesus*.

24. See Van Unnik, "Luke-Acts," 19. Van Unnik states that before 1950 Luke was almost exclusively viewed as a historian; see also Tannehill, "Theology of Luke-Acts," 195. He cites the tendency of writers to perceive Paul as the theologian and Luke as the historian.

25. See a discussion of Lukan scholarship with extensive bibliographies on different aspects of Luke: Bovon, *Luke the Theologian*.

26. Barrett, "Justification," 24, 54, makes assertions as to how he believes this theme in Luke relates to the Pauline notion. Barrett claims that Paul's idea of justification by faith is the more explicit and developed notion and that Luke's idea runs parallel but not dependent on Paul. But it is not part of the scope of his dissertation to necessarily assess the plausibility or possibility of his claims.

27. Dunn, *Beginning from Jerusalem*, 428n65; He states that the Lukan author half

Therefore, for some authors, the Lukan source of this notion depends on a particular relationship between Luke's author and Paul.[28] However, some authors claim that the theme of justification in Luke may have been based on sources within the Jesus tradition instead of representing a wholesale dependence on or reaction to Pauline thought.

This study puts forward the thesis that the theme of justification as determined in Luke 18:9–14 possibly originated from Jesus tradition. In other words, this theme as expressed in this parable is not so incongruent to the Jesus tradition that one needs to explain its presence in the Gospels as a Pauline addition. On the other hand, this study will demonstrate, primarily through the theme's coherence and fit with Luke and other synoptic sources, that Luke may have derived it from earlier Jesus material.

Methodology

For many years now, one consideration that scholars use to test whether a saying, a notion, or action of Jesus in the Gospels can be judged as historically authentic is the "criteria of authenticity." This is a set of criteria unique to New Testament studies as a form of historiography that traditionally delineates ways to distinguish the authenticity or inauthenticity of the traditions depicted in sources about Jesus. The early church already practiced certain fundamental criteria, but the height of the development of the "criteria of authenticity" was during the early to mid-twentieth century due to the rise of form critical studies.[29] There was a conviction that parts of the Jesus tradition should be analyzed individually to see whether they originated within Judaism or the early Christian church or if they can be considered as "authentic" tradition from Jesus. A number of criteria exist, and some additional ones continue to be developed, since most of them gain or lose prominence throughout the history of Jesus research (each criterion has its own strengths and flaws), although a select few are considered "traditional" criteria.[30]

---

grasped Paul's notion of justification. In this case he is referring to the passage in Acts 13.

28. Luke most likely knew much about Paul and his ministry. See Keener, *Acts: An Exegetical Commentary*, 1: 221–57 for a more comprehensive discussion regarding Acts and Paul.

29. Porter, "Criteria of Authenticity," *DJG*, 2nd ed., 153–62.

30. Porter cites seven, although he acknowledges that various scholars would count differently depending on what they identify as "traditional." Porter, "Criteria of

The use of the criteria approach was challenged early as this outgrowth of form criticism was applied to the quest for the historical Jesus. Form criticism's main goal is not really to reconstruct "authentic" Jesus tradition but to use the criteria to scrutinize early stages of the tradition. A prominent early skeptic is Morna Hooker who wrote a scathing critique of the criteria approach. In her essay she points out the danger in the criteria approach's movement from "the confines of form-criticism into the wider field of "traditio-historical criticism."[31] She argues that the criteria (especially the criterion of dissimilarity) are the wrong tools because they do not achieve their intended purpose.[32] Much later, other voices emerged and for many reasons continue to express their sincere doubts on the traditional use of the criteria.[33] Some scholars advocate abandoning the criteria approach altogether; others try to rebuild it, reformulate it, qualify it, or use it more responsibly.[34]

Theissen and Winter (and Annette Merz) elected to reformulate and qualify the criteria approach after definitively issuing a thorough critique against the criterion of dissimilarity.[35] It is their approach and creation of a new criterion, the "criterion of plausibility," that is pertinent for the method of this book. This study uses one main criterion—coherence as conceptualized from Theissen and Winter's criterion of Plausibility. Traditionally, the criterion of coherence is normally used in a secondary sense, that is, it is only used to authenticate correspondences to other Jesus material already proven authentic through the criterion of double dissimilarity.[36] But Theissen and Winter reformulated the definition of

---

Authenticity," *DJG*, 2nd ed., 153–58. These include double dissimilarity, least distinctiveness, coherence or consistency, multiple attestation, and embarrassment or movement against the redactional tendency. Theissen and Merz only cite three—double dissimilarity, coherence, and multiple attestation, labeling these as the "trinity" of criteria that gained canonical status in the New Quest, in agreement with Perrin, *Rediscovering*, 39–48. Theissen and Merz, "Delay," 52.

31. Hooker, "Christology and Methodology," 480–87; Hooker, "On Using," 570–81.

32. Hooker, "On Using," 570.

33. A few recent examples are Rodriguez, "Authenticating Criteria," 152–67 and Allison, "How to Marginalize," 1:3–30.

34. Keith, "Fall," 200–201. Chris Keith, Dale Allison, and Rafael Rodriguez are examples of those who vouch for abandoning the criteria approach.

35. Theissen and Winter, *Quest*. A summary of the criterion of plausibility is in Theissen and Merz, *Historical Jesus*, 115–21. Also see Theissen, "Historical Scepticism," 1:54–87.

36. Perrin, *Rediscovering*, 45.

this criterion, making it available for use independently of other criteria. They state, "What is coherent in independent sources or in different currents of tradition or in different genres and forms of the Jesus tradition may indeed be authentic (historical)—regardless of whether or not it can be derived from Judaism or from Early Christianity."[37] Therefore, it does not presuppose that the application of the criterion of coherence is limited to those traditions that have already been authenticated by other criteria, especially the criterion of double dissimilarity.[38]

The overall theoretical foundation or concept that the method falls under is called the "continuum approach." This approach in historical Jesus research seeks to locate Jesus within the context of Judaism but also tries to account for the effect of Jesus on early Christianity. It presupposes that the historical Jesus needs to correspond and cohere with ancient Judaism and the early Christian movement. There is, then, a continuum among Judaism, Jesus, and early Christianity. Within that approach rests an overall criterion of "historical plausibility," which can be broken down into "effective plausibility" (i.e., the impact the historical Jesus had on the early Christian movement) and "contextual plausibility" (i.e., the impact and fit of Jesus within first century Judaism). The criterion of coherence falls under "effective plausibility" as it is a measurement of the effect made by the historical Jesus. In addition to using the criterion of coherence, this study tests Luke 18:9–14 for contextual appropriateness in the Jewish Palestinian environment. This assessment falls under the criterion of plausibility in the category of "contextual plausibility." Theissen and Winter assert,

> The more a Jesus tradition fits into the context of contemporary events, local circumstances, Jewish traditions, and Jewish mentality, the more confidence develops within us that Jesus cannot be the creation of early Christian imagination. How else can a fictitious figure be distinguished from a historical personage except by localizing him in a particular time and place and relating him to other historical figures?[39]

---

37. Theissen and Merz, "Delay," 53.

38. For more information on the criterion's characteristics, see Theissen and Merz, "Delay," 53–55. It is notable that they consider multiple attestation to be a sub-criterion of the criterion of coherence: "It refers to the coherence or the correspondence of the same tradition in different sources. But just as important is the coherence of the same motif and topic in different traditions." Theissen and Merz, "Delay," 55.

39. Theissen and Winter, *Quest*, 246.

INTRODUCTION

This exercise is done to support and strengthen the notion that this parable is a plausible fit within first-century Judaism.[40]

In terms of limits, this study does not comprehensively apply the criterion of plausibility and all its sub-criteria. It only uses the criterion of coherence (of sources) to account for the plausible historical impact or effect of Jesus. For this book, this one criterion is used to gauge if justification in Luke 18:9–14 coheres or fits in with the synoptic tradition as a way of sizing up the possibility that it reflects Jesus material. This book does not use coherence in a negative sense, nor does it label any tradition as "inauthentic." Coherence in this study is simply a tool utilized to look for the plausible historical impact of this theme.[41] Therefore, the use of the criterion is qualified as well as reformulated in its approach. Even a prominent critic of the criteria of authenticity, Dale Allison, agrees with this kind of approach. He similarly uses coherence of sources to focus on deriving memory out of recurrent themes in different streams of tradition where he believes the true memory of the tradition is located. Based on his study of cognitive memory, he believes in looking for tradition in the larger patterns of the Jesus material through themes and motifs rather than at the level of individual sayings because of his skepticism of the ability of early Christians to retain detailed memory.[42]

Chapter 6 of this study deals with the so-called "inauthenticity" of Luke 18:9–14. At certain times in the history of the criteria approach, the unique Lukan parables such as Luke 18:9–14 (not just the theme of justification) are labeled or designated as "inauthentic" in the sense that these did not come from the historical Jesus. A recent book by Meier promotes this assertion, and to proponents of the criteria approach, this claim implies that any theme or motif derived from these parables, such as the theme of justification, is also not "authentic." This charge is not very much different in substance from the allegation that Luke copied Paul's

---

40. For a more comprehensive explanation of the continuum approach and the criterion of historical plausibility. See Theissen and Winter, *Quest*, 172–225; Holmen, "Continuum Approach," 1–16; Theissen and Merz, "Delay," 52–57.

41. Dunn, *Jesus Remembered*, 327–36, similarly asserts that whatever is characteristic of the synoptic tradition comes from the impact Jesus made on his first followers without dealing with any notion of authenticity or lack of authenticity in specific passages.

42. Allison, "How to Marginalize," 1:3–30. Allison calls his criterion "recurrent attestation." For him it is about looking for the gist of the historical events or figures instead of their precise details. See Allison, *Constructing Jesus*, 1–17.

notion of justification and imported it into the parable. In both cases, it is a charge of "inauthenticity."

This book's primary response to this charge is to use the criterion of coherence in a qualified and reformulated manner in contrast with Meier's negative and minimalist use of the criteria. This response is additionally supported by using the contextual plausibility criterion in determining the fit of Luke 18:9–14 with its Jewish environment. Chapter 6 further explains the need to qualify and reformulate the criteria, especially not using it in a negative sense to probe for inauthenticity. The purpose of Chapter 6 is, in effect, to provide the various rationale for the methodology employed in this study while in the process critiquing Meier's work and using it as a case study. This chapter summarizes and analyzes Meier's book and gives reasons as to why his assumptions and conclusions are questionable. What follows after the analysis are (1) a critique of the unqualified use of the criteria of authenticity, including certain methodological flaws of the criteria as a whole and individually (multiple attestation, dissimilarity, coherence, embarrassment) as well as the form-critical assumptions behind the criteria, and (2) a critique of the form-critical assumptions behind the criteria approach as determined from studies in oral tradition, transmission, eye-witnesses, and social memory. Again, the goal of Chapter 6 is to explain the need to qualify and reformulate the criteria (especially the need to prevent the criteria's negative use) and, in the process of doing so, also cast some serious doubt on Meier's charges and conclusions. This chapter gives additional strength to the findings of this book in its use of the criterion of coherence under the continuum approach.

Plan of this Monograph

Theissen and Merz claim that the criterion of coherence is an application of a general historical principle. They state, "Where we have several sources at our disposal which are different enough to permit us to assume their independence, but which are similar enough for us to refer them to the same person or the same event," and if observations of coherence within the plurality of sources, currents of tradition, and forms are established, then there are "strong indications of a historical reality behind our sources."[43] Therefore, for this monograph, it is important to look at a plurality of sources or forms where traits can recur and have coherence.

43. Theissen and Merz, "Delay," 56–57.

INTRODUCTION

The term *coherence* as used in this book needs further clarification. *Coherence* itself is already a misleading word as the criterion works only because the sources contain a combination of coherent and incoherent features. The approach is either to examine the coherent characteristics against the background of incoherent elements and interpret the coherent elements as indications of historical material or to look at incoherent characteristics against the background of more coherent tendencies and see elements of history in those sources. This book concentrates only on the first approach, which is technically called "coherence of sources."[44] The coherence of sources that this book adopts, is comprised of two kinds. One is called "cross-section evidence," which looks for elements of content, motifs and themes, and forms in different streams of tradition. For example, Jesus spoke in parables in different sources, such as Q, Mark, Luke, and Matthew. The other kind of coherence is called "genre-constancy," which looks for features and motifs in different forms and genre. For example, the motif of "seeking the lost" is found not just in Lukan parables (Luke 15:1–32) but also in apophthegms (Mark 2:15–17) and in sayings about Jesus seeking the lost sheep of the house of Israel (Matt 15:24).[45] Both these types of coherence are reflected in this study.

Also important to note is a key assumption that Theissen and Winter emphasize when looking for "cross-section evidence" and "genre-constancy" in different traditions and forms. They state that differences found in the streams of tradition and genre "reflect the 'imperfection' of human beings, their inability to transmit the historical truth in a coherent picture (which is a very creative imperfection, in that it has produced a plethora of 'poetic' images of Jesus)."[46] In other words, human beings are fallible creatures that never simply transmit historical reality by itself but also include elements that reflect "their own interests, tendencies, and intentions."[47] Despite distortions and opposing tendencies, when characteristics do recur, even compared with other tendencies, these features do indicate remnants of history.[48] Therefore, detecting coherence with sources and traditions is an interpretive task that cannot be done in a

---

44. The second approach is called "resistance to the tendencies of the tradition." Theissen and Winter, *Quest*, 235.
45. Theissen and Winter, *Quest*, 178, 236–37.
46. Theissen and Winter, *Quest*, 236.
47. Theissen and Winter, *Quest*, 233.
48. Theissen and Winter, *Quest*, 236.

mechanical way. What is incoherent on one level may be coherent on a deeper level.⁴⁹ Coherence is not limited simply to finding verbal resonances between sources and forms or finding exact parallels. One can argue that finding many vocabulary parallels increase the likelihood that what is pictured is not coherence but, ironically, dependence.⁵⁰ That is why coherence in this study involves themes and motifs in passages that may or may not contain the δικαιόω word group.

In addition, as a caveat, "coherence," per Theissen and Winter, "are not timeless standards of measurement. That which we consider coherent is perhaps incoherent for others, and vice versa."⁵¹ Theissen and Winter believe that "We must thus develop a historical sense for what a particular author in a particular situation would have considered 'consistent' and what he would have perceived as contradictory."⁵² They further comment that just comparing a couple of historical works of Josephus (*Jewish War* and *Antiquities*), show "what amazing divergences can be found in the same author in reporting the same events, using the same sources and traditions!"⁵³ In addition, since the criterion of coherence as reformulated and qualified is applied to sources without having to assume that authentic and inauthentic elements in them have already been distinguished, one can argue that coherent motifs and themes may also be expected in inauthentic material or so called "expansions" supposedly added by the early church or the evangelists. Therefore, this assumption of expansions with coherent elements brings into question how many historical remnants the criterion can really uncover behind the sources. However, Chapter 6 of this book will assert that through recent findings in studies on oral tradition, transmission, eyewitnesses, and social memory, the assumption of the presence of wholesale and inauthentic "expansions" in the tradition is quite questionable. Therefore,

---

49. Theissen and Merz, "Delay," 57.

50. Dependence means these may be "inauthentic" (e.g., Luke copied the notion of justification from Paul).

51. Theissen and Merz notes that "disagreements regarding the extent of legitimate coherence are to be expected; their existence does not of itself constitute an argument against the criterion. The main reasons for such disagreements are the openness of the individual traditions to a variety of interpretations, and our limited knowledge of the historical context. Naturally, the transmitters of the oral tradition and the evangelists created a picture of Jesus, of his historical period, his life and his teaching which was coherent for their specific group of readers." Theissen and Merz, "Delay," 57n15.

52. Theissen and Winter, *Quest*, 236n7.

53. Theissen and Winter, *Quest*, 236n7.

INTRODUCTION

the analysis in Chapter 6 increases the confidence that the coherence of themes and motifs across the sources and forms indicate that these themes and motifs represent historical remnants.

In terms of procedure, the main focus of the investigation is the parable of the Pharisee and the Tax Collector (Luke 18:9–14) and its theme of justification along with its related themes and motifs. After this introduction, Chapter 2 presents an exegetical study on Luke 18:9–14, which sheds light on what justification/righteousness is from the standpoint of this parable. It then derives possible related themes that can be used to identify their recurrence in other sources and forms in the Gospels. Since the parable comes from unique Lukan material, it is not attested to in other independent sources. Therefore, it is important to relate, as Merz indicates, "substantially comparable motifs and texts in the Jesus tradition."[54] The comparable motifs and themes considered are the important aspects in the interpretation of the theme of justification. Merz applies this specific approach of looking for coherence of related motifs and themes in the Jesus material in her analysis of another unique Lukan parable—the parable of the widow and the judge (Luke 18:1–8).[55] This book uses a more stringent version of her procedure. The approach in this study is more rigorous because, unlike Merz's method, it does not merely look for the recurrence of the related themes and motifs of justification in Luke 18:9–14 individually in various sources and forms in the Gospels but looks for the combination of most, if not all, of these themes and motifs in specific passages in various sources and forms of the tradition. The convergence of this particular combination of themes and motifs in other Jesus material makes the selected passages pertinent for this study. Note also that the minimum requirement is that most, if not all, the related themes and motifs needs to recur. In several passages considered in this work, not all the relevant themes and motifs are present. For example, the related motif of faith may be emphasized in one pericope but may be more in the background in others. Deriving theological concepts from narratives such as the parables make certain themes and motifs either less explicit or more obvious given that the themes are portrayed or imaged in stories instead of being stated overtly in a verbal manner. In addition, imperfections and different tendencies and emphases reflect the fallible

---

54. Merz, "How a Woman," 72, applies this principle in her analysis of the parable of the widow and the judge (Luke 18:1–8).

55. Merz, "How a Woman," 49–86.

writers' own interests, preferences, and intentions. Therefore, some of the passages analyzed do not have all the relevant elements and/or have varying degrees of coherence. Rather than disproving coherence, this imprecision and imperfection can strengthen the case for coherence in the midst of incoherent elements, especially since the alternative of having perfect coherences among sources, including exact verbal resonances, may point more towards the likelihood of dependence among the sources. This study highlights these imprecisions as they occur in the analysis.

The independent synoptic sources considered for this book are: Unique Lukan source (L), Mark, and Q. This study uses the L source as a way to test for the theme's consistency within Luke's theology. Mark and Q are considered because these are pre-Lukan sources. The coherence of the theme of justification in these two early gospel sources increases the probability that the theme comes from early Jesus material. Again, the search for coherence is not limited to passages that belong to the δικαιόω word group. In the next two chapters, thematic coherences will be noted in L (Chapter 3), Mark and Q (Chapter 4) and in specific forms (both chapters), such as parables, aphorisms, and pronouncement stories. Chapter 5 explores the contextual plausibility of Luke 18:9–14 by looking at the parable's fit in the first-century Jewish Palestinian Environment. Chapter 6 will look Meier's charge of "inauthenticity" of the unique Lukan parables. Finally, Chapter 7 is the conclusion with a note on possible areas of future research.

― Chapter 2 ―

Luke 18:9-14

General Background of the Parable

THE PARABLE OF THE Pharisee and the Tax Collector and three other parables, namely, the good Samaritan (Luke 10:30-35), the rich fool (Luke 12:16-20), and the rich man and Lazarus (Luke 16:19-31), are classified as "example stories," a category popularized in scholarly circles by Adolf Jülicher.[1] It is one of the few famous parables attributed to Jesus found in the Gospel of Luke belonging to Luke's *Sondergut* (called "L"). It is not narrated anywhere else in the Synoptic Gospel tradition, nor are there any parallels in works such as the Gospel of Thomas or the Gospel of John.[2] Kim Paffenroth, in her study and analysis of the L tradition, regards the parable source as pre-Lukan.[3] In addition, she also notes that L does not

---

1. See Tucker, *Example Stories*, 14, where Tucker cites Jülicher, *Gleichnisreden*, 1:112. The precise term is "example narratives" *Beispielerzahlungen*. Other examples of modern interpreters who follow suit are Fitzmyer, *Luke X-XXIV*, 1183—"an *exemplum*"; Hultgren, *Parables*, 120—a "Parable of Exemplary Behavior"; Forbes, *God of Old*, 211. Tucker, *Example Stories*, 13-24, esp. 19-30, argues that the separate categorization of these parables in Luke created a tension and tendency to view parables overall as either the parables of Jesus or the parables of Luke. In addition, he reports that this breakdown also creates ambiguity in interpreting those considered parables or those considered in the separate category of "examples." Finally, he said that for others, the categorization instills an artificial notion that some parables are authentic and some are not. From another perspective, Keener, *Historical Jesus*, 494n36, (citing Johnston) notes that Jesus's and rabbinic parables, specifically Tannaitic parables, are divided into groups, including example stories, short similes and metaphors, and parabolized fables.

2. See Fitzmyer, *Luke I-IX*, 83-87, for an overall write up of L and a list of L passages.

3. Paffenroth, *Story*, 64, evaluates the source origin of various passages in L by examining factors such as vocabulary and style, formal characteristics such as the use of

indicate or say something about the destruction of Jerusalem, not to mention that Luke 18:10–14a makes reference to an existing temple. She claims that these are evidence that support dating the pre-Lukan source earlier than 70 CE.[4] The majority of the pericopae, which she considers as part of the L tradition, consists of parables.[5] For Arland Hultgren, the presence of Semitisms and the portrayal of the customs of Jesus's day support the judgment that it is an authentic parable of Jesus.[6]

Parable Analysis

Parable Context

Within the Gospel of Luke, the parable is in Luke's central section, which is the so-called "travel narrative" (Luke 9:51—19:27). This section contains short narratives and accounts of teachings of Jesus with an overall backdrop of Jesus's "journey" from Galilee to Jerusalem. Throughout this journey he addresses various groups of people, including his disciples, the crowds, and his opponents such as the Pharisees and scribes. This section contains a high concentration of teaching with seventeen parables present.[7]

The previous chapters are addressed to his disciples (16:1; 17:1), though the Pharisees are able to listen in (16:14–15). The teachings of Luke 16 focus mostly on wealth and the kingdom, while Luke 17 teaches about the need for forgiveness and faith and expectations of the kingdom of God and the end times (17:22–37). Luke 18:1 and 18:9 seem to indicate that this parable is mainly addressed to the crowds and/or Jesus's disciples. What strengthens this notion is the use in 18:9 of the conjunction "also," which links it to the parable in 18:1–8.[8] In addition, Luke 18:9 gives a very general statement, portraying an audience that "trusted in themselves and disdained others."[9]

---

dialogue/monologue and content (e.g., the use of numbers and general themes).

4. Paffenroth, *Story*, 155.

5. Paffenroth, *Story*, 96–98.

6. Hultgren, *Parables*, 125; Jülicher, *Gleichnisreden*, 2:608; Jeremias, *Parables*, 139–40; Marshall, *Gospel of Luke*, 678; Hendrickx, *Parables*, 243.

7. Bock, "Luke, Gospel of," *DJG*, 501.

8. Green, *Gospel of Luke*, 645.

9. Snodgrass, *Stories*, 470; Green, *Gospel of Luke*, 644.

Translation: Luke 18:9-14

⁹ Εἶπεν δὲ καὶ πρός τινας¹⁰ τοὺς πεποιθότας¹¹ ἐφ᾽ ἑαυτοῖς ὅτι¹² εἰσὶν δίκαιοι καὶ ἐξουθενοῦντας τοὺς λοιποὺς τὴν παραβολὴν ταύτην.¹³

And he also told this parable to certain ones who had trusted in themselves that they were righteous, and who disdained the others.

¹⁰ Ἄνθρωποι δύο ἀνέβησαν εἰς τὸ ἱερὸν προσεύξασθαι,¹⁴ ὁ εἷς Φαρισαῖος καὶ ὁ ἕτερος τελώνης.¹⁵

Two men went up into the temple to pray, the one a Pharisee, and the other, a tax collector.

10. It is possible to translate πρός τινας as "against some," which gives the parable a more polemical notion. But "to" is a better translation similar to other passages in Luke with a dialogue beginning with πρός (4:21, 43; 5:10; 6:3; 7:24; 9:3, 13, 14; 11:1; 12:1; 14:3; 15:3; 16:1; 17:1); Bock, *Luke 9:51—24:53*, 1461n2; also Fitzmyer, *Luke X-XXIV*, 1185.

11. Barrett suggests that πεποιθότας should to be understood as either "persuaded" or "convinced" as opposed to "trust" or "rely" to avoid any sense of "overt legalism." Barrett, "Justification," 28n2. Other commentators who render this word as "trust" or "rely" do expound further on the meaning of this word as, for example, one who is self-possessed or able to live honorably before God. Green, *Gospel of Luke*, 645–46. Bock mentions another rendition which relies on the meaning of πέποιθα + ἐπὶ in Luke 11:22 and 2 Cor 1:9 puts the meaning as having a "misdirected state of self-confidence," convinced that they are acceptable to God "on their own merits." Bock, *Luke 9:51—24:53*, 1461.

12. ὅτι introduces a clausal complement of τοὺς πεποιθότας. In this sense, "that" states the content of their self-confidence. See Culy, Parsons, and Stigall, *Luke*, 567. Forbes, *God of Old*, 212; Hultgren, *Parables*, 118; Barrett, "Justification," 28n4; Bock, *Luke 9:51—24:53*, 1460; Stein, *Gospel of Luke*, 449. As another option, Nolland claims that ὅτι actually introduces the reason or cause ("because") of the self-confidence instead of a complement. Nolland, *Luke 9:21—18:34*, 875. See also Green, *Gospel of Luke*, 111. Jeremias concludes that it is also translated as "because" comparable to its function in 2 Cor 1:9 where those who trusted in themselves were contrasted to those who trusted in God. Jeremias, *Parables*, 111. Others such as Johnson and Fitzmyer prefer to leave the use of ὅτι as ambiguous ("as being righteous" or "as upright"). Johnson, *Gospel of Luke*, 271. Fitzmyer, *Luke X-XXIV*, 1185.

13. τὴν παραβολὴν ταύτην accusative direct object of the verb Εἶπεν.

14. προσεύξασθαι infinitive of purpose.

15. ὁ εἷς, ὁ ἕτερος same structure as 7:41, 17:34.

THE TAX COLLECTOR AND THE PHARISEE

¹¹ ὁ Φαρισαῖος σταθεὶς πρὸς ἑαυτὸν ταῦτα¹⁶ προσηύχετο· ὁ θεός¹⁷, εὐχαριστῶ σοι ὅτι¹⁸ οὐκ εἰμὶ ὥσπερ οἱ λοιποὶ τῶν ἀνθρώπων, ἅρπαγες, ἄδικοι, μοιχοί¹⁹, ἢ καὶ ὡς οὗτος ὁ τελώνης.²⁰

The Pharisee stood by himself and prayed these (words): "God, I thank you that I am not like other men (people): robbers, unjust, adulterers, or even like this tax collector."

¹² νηστεύω δὶς τοῦ σαββάτου²¹, ἀποδεκατῶ πάντα²² ὅσα κτῶμαι.

"I fast two times a week, I tithe with respect to all things that I get."

¹³ ὁ δὲ τελώνης μακρόθεν ἑστὼς οὐκ ἤθελεν οὐδὲ²³ τοὺς ὀφθαλμοὺς ἐπᾶραι²⁴ εἰς τὸν οὐρανόν, ἀλλ' ἔτυπτεν τὸ στῆθος αὐτοῦ λέγων· ὁ θεός, ἱλάσθητί²⁵μοι²⁶ τῷ²⁷ ἁμαρτωλῷ.

16. Of major note, 𝔓75 ℵc B Θ Ψ favor an alternative word order of ταῦτα πρὸς ἑαυτὸν instead of πρὸς ἑαυτὸν ταῦτα. The prepositional phrase was thought to modify προσηύχετο as opposed to modifying σταθείς. The more difficult reading is "standing by himself," which parallels the tax collector's description in 18:13 as "standing from a distance." Additional support for this reading is Codex D, which states καθ ἑαυτὸν ταῦτα. Please see Metzger, *Textual Commentary*, 143; Culy, Parsons, and Stigall, *Luke*, 568; Barrett, "Justification," 42–43n50.

17. Nominative functioning as vocative. In the LXX, according to Wallace, *Greek Grammar*, 57n71. God is primarily addressed with an articular nominative.

18. Introduces the clausal complement of εὐχαριστῶ.

19. ἅρπαγες, ἄδικοι, μοιχοί nominative in apposition to οἱ λοιποί.

20. Jeremias and Snodgrass note that part of the Semitic flavor of the parable can be seen with the occurrences of asyndeton in (18:11, 12, 14) according to Jeremias, *Parables*, 111 and Snodgrass, *Stories*, 467, 740n137.

21. τοῦ σαββάτου genitive of time.

22. πάντα per Bock, *Luke 9:51—24:53*, 1463, an accusative of reference. "I gave . . . with respect to all I get."

23. A compound negative comes after another negative in the same clause, reinforcing the prior negative force per Culy, Parsons, and Stigall, *Luke*, 569.

24. Complementary infinitive of helper verb ἤθελεν.

25. From the verb ἱλάσκομαι aorist, deponent, imperative second person singular; Bauer et al., "ἱλάσκομαι," BDAG 473–74. Meaning given—"to cause to be favorably inclined, to propitiate." The translation "God be merciful to me," should be avoided as it mutes the verb's focus on propitiation and makes it a synonym for the verb ἐλεέω; Culy, Parsons, and Stigall, *Luke*, 570. However, in agreement with Bailey, *Through Peasant Eyes*, 154, and Forbes, *God of Old*, 212, both notions of propitiation and expiation are reflected here. The tax collector overall is yearning for the benefits of atonement.

26. Dative of advantage.

27. The article τῷ is an example of a par excellence article. The tax collector is proclaiming from his point of view that he is the worst of all sinners. See Wallace, *Greek*

But the tax collector, standing from a distance, was not even willing to lift up his eyes to heaven, but was beating his breast saying: "God, make an atonement for me, a sinner!"

¹⁴ λέγω ὑμῖν, κατέβη οὗτος δεδικαιωμένος²⁸ εἰς τὸν οἶκον αὐτοῦ παρ' ἐκεῖνον²⁹· ὅτι πᾶς ὁ ὑψῶν ἑαυτὸν ταπεινωθήσεται, ὁ δὲ ταπεινῶν ἑαυτὸν ὑψωθήσεται.

I say to you, this man went down to his house justified instead of the other; for anyone who exalts himself will be humbled, but he who humbles himself will be exalted.

Overall Structure

The passage begins with an introduction explaining the intent of the parable (18:9) followed by the story itself (18:10-13), which first presents the two characters of the parable (18:10) and then the parallel descriptions of the prayers of the Pharisee (18:11-12) and tax collector (18:13). The last verse contains a pronouncement of judgment on the two characters (18:14a) and a rationale for that pronouncement (18:14b).

Major Semantic Features

In terms of its major semantic features, quite noticeable for this parable is the use of *synkrisis*, or comparison between the two characters, which, in this case, is one positive and the other negative. The two men represent opposite personalities in first-century Jewish culture. Pharisees were regarded as the most pious, and tax collectors were highly reviled.[30] The

---

Grammar, 223.

28. From the verb δικαιόω, perfect passive participle (manner), nominative, masculine, singular. Bauer et al., "δικαιόω," BDAG 249; "to be vindicated, to be found in the right by God."

29. παρ' ἐκεῖνον is an attempt to translate the Aramaic *min*, which is used in the comparative sense. The comparative *min* is used either with an exclusive sense or merely comparative sense. In agreement with Jeremias, *Parables*, 112-13, it is used here in a more exclusive sense (God justified him and not the other) because a mere comparative force (one justified than another to a higher degree?) is less comprehensible. Also see Snodgrass, *Stories*, 467, 740n137.

30. Bock, *Luke 9:51—24:53*, 1461. The next sections will explore further the reasons why the two characters contrast each other.

same type of juxtaposition is employed in the parable of the rich man and Lazarus (16:19–31) and the good Samaritan (for example, between the Samaritan and the priest/Levite—10:25–37).

A chiasm or inverted parallelism can be discerned from 18:10 to 18:14a. Bailey describes the structure as seven "stanzas" that invert with a climax at the center. In 18:10 the story begins with the two men going up to the temple, and then it ends in 18:14a with the men going down from the temple but in reverse order. Then 18:11a describes the Pharisee's exterior appearance and opening prayer, which corresponds to 18:13b that likewise shows the tax collector's exterior manner (beating of his chest) and opening prayer. The verses that are close to the center describe the tax collector's image (18:11b) and self-perception (18:13a). Finally, 18:12 is at the center of the chiasm or climax and describes the Pharisee presenting his qualifications for his own righteousness.[31] The chiasm looks like the following:[32]

> A Two of them go up to the temple: first the Pharisee, then the tax collector (18:10).
>
> > B The Pharisee stood by himself and prayed (18:11a).
> >
> > > C The tax collector is compared to robbers, the unjust, and adulterers (18:11b).
> > >
> > > > D "I fast two times a week; I tithe with respect to all things that I get." (18:12).
> > >
> > > C' The tax collector is standing from a distance with eyes down (18:13a).
> >
> > B' The tax collector was beating his breast and praying (18:13b).
>
> A' Two of them go down: first the justified tax collector, then the Pharisee (18:14a).

Bailey admits that the parallelism is not quite precise since the verses that describe how each of the characters was standing do not match up with each other. But rearranging the structure in such a way that B (18:11a) is matched with C' (18:13a) results in losing the prominence of the Pharisee's depiction of his grounds for self-righteousness (18:12). In addition, if the climactic center is eliminated, it is more noticeable that the prayer of the

---

31. Bailey, *Through Peasant Eyes*, 142–43.
32. Bailey, *Through Peasant Eyes*, 142.

Pharisee is significantly longer than the prayer of the tax collector, which reveals an imbalance in the overall structure. This option, however, simplifies the movement of the parable:[33]

    A Two went up (Pharisee, tax collector).

    B The Pharisee stood and prayed.

    B' The tax collector stood and prayed.

    A' Two went down (tax collector, Pharisee).

Craig Blomberg asserts that there is a structural interchange pattern of A-B-A-B-B-A-A-B with A standing for the actions of the Pharisee and B as the actions of the tax collector.[34] This pattern of alternation seems to strengthen the contrast between the characters. The inversion of the fifth (18:14a) and sixth positions (18:14b) in the structure underscores a reversal of status between the characters.[35] This reversal also adds an element of surprise or twist at the end of the parable.[36] For the pre-Gospel audience, the Pharisee would normally have been perceived initially as the hero of the story instead of the tax collector,[37] but with the way Luke structures the account, using a "point-for-point polarization" between the two characters throughout the whole parable, the tax collector, and not the Pharisee, will be looked upon as the positive model in the story.[38] The characterization of each person, including the description of his actions in the temple, in addition to what each says in his prayers, provides content and color for the point-by-point polarization.[39] A generalizing

---

33. Bailey, *Through Peasant Eyes*, 143.

34. Per Blomberg, *Interpreting the Parables*, 341, the arrangement is as follows: (A) Pharisee (v. 10a), (B) tax collector (v. 10b), (A) Pharisee (vv. 11–12), (B) tax collector (v. 13), (B) tax collector (v. 14a), (A) Pharisee (v. 14b), (A) Pharisee (v. 14c), (B) tax collector (v. 14d). Bailey, *Jesus*, 343, sees an A-B, A-B structure with the reader told how the Pharisee stands and prays, and then likewise displays how the tax collector does the same.

35. Blomberg, *Interpreting the Parables*, 341. Snodgrass notes that the parables of Jesus "often contain the element of reversal," a characteristic of his parables that forces listeners towards unexpected decisions and associations. Snodgrass, *Stories*, 19.

36. An element of surprise in the end is also characteristic of many of Jesus's parables per Hultgren, *Parables*, 10. In addition, Snodgrass states that this ending material functions like "the punch line of a joke." Snodgrass, *Stories*, 19.

37. Blomberg, *Interpreting the Parables*, 341.

38. Green, *Gospel of Luke*, 645.

39. For example, although both are standing apart from others, the tax collector is portrayed in a motif of repentance ("beating his breast") as opposed to the Pharisee.

summary concludes the parable at 18:14b, which is also the climax of the parable and informs the whole story.[40]

Relationship to Luke 18:1–8

The parable is certainly linked to Luke 18:1–8 because of the motif of prayer and the use of the δικαιόω word group (i.e., ἐκδικέω, ἀδικία and ἐκδίκησις—18:3, 5–8). Although prayer is present in both parables, 18:9-14 is not primarily about prayer but more about the nature of fitness for entering the kingdom of God.[41] The depiction of what qualifications are needed for kingdom entry continues beyond 18:9-14. The following verses also depict the characteristics needed, such as childlike faith (to enter into the kingdom) portrayed in 18:15-17, and the appropriate attitudes concerning wealth, faith, and repentance in 18:18—19:10 and their impact on being able to belong to the kingdom.[42] Luke 18:8 forms an *inclusio* with 17:20, with the unit of 17:20—18:8 reflecting an eschatological focus, describing the nature of the kingdom as opposed to the following unit of 18:9—19:27 that deals more about one's fitness in the kingdom.[43] On the other hand, Barrett rightly cautions against making a sharp distinction between the two parables on the basis that one is eschatological and the other is not. He asserts that in Luke 18:14b, a theme of eschatological exaltation can be detected that is also present in the first parable (18:1–8). Barrett argues that the parable temple setting represents a courtroom scene where God as the judge delivers a judicial declaration in 18:14b that gives a new status to the unrighteous. It is not a simple declaration in 18:14 about who is right or wrong in a court case but about the granting of a new reality—a status of "righteousness."[44]

---

40. Barrett, "Justification," 58.

41. Forbes, *God of Old*, 211; Marshall, *Gospel of Luke*, 677, notes that where 18:8 asks for who will be found faithful when the Son of Man comes, 18:9 begins the section where it describes which qualifications and characteristic of disciples are required.

42. Forbes, *God of Old*, 211.

43. Green, *Gospel of Luke*, 643–45.

44. Barrett, "Justification," 56, 157–58.

LUKE 18:9-14

Issues and Comments

Luke 18:9

Luke 18:9 serves as the Lukan introduction to the parable.[45] It identifies the purpose or intent of the parable in advance, which is to give a word to the parable's target audience: (1) Certain ones who "had trusted in themselves that they were righteous," and (2) "who disdained the others."

The expression τοὺς πεποιθότας may be read in the milder sense as in "persuaded" or "convinced" as opposed to "trusted in," so that no thought of obvious legalism is implied.[46] However, this term seems to have a stronger or more intense notion as in "trusted in," especially comparing the phrase πέποιθα + ἐπὶ and its use in 2 Cor 1:9; Matt 27:43; Luke 11:22; and Heb 2:13.[47] When the verse says that they had "trusted in themselves that they were righteous," they were so highly convinced to the level that they have placed much confidence in this idea.[48] In its immediate context, the term "righteous" here in Luke's literary frame can be contrasted with those considered as ἄδικοι or "unrighteous" in 18:11 and likewise with other characters described in the same verse such as the ἅρπαγες and μοιχοί (robbers and adulterers).[49] However, in the wider context of the Gospel of Luke itself and in the framing of the parable, the term *righteous*

---

45. Other parables with Luke's introduction at the beginning are the unjust judge (18:1), and the parable of the ten pounds (Luke 19:11); Forbes, *God of Old*, 211; Barrett, "Justification," 28; Jeremias, *Parables*, 116; Fitzmyer, *Luke X-XXIV*, 1183; Bock, *Luke 9:51—24:53*, 1461; Snodgrass, *Stories*, 470. Marshall, *Gospel of Luke*, 678, does mention the possibility that this introduction may come from Luke's source. Some commentators read this parable without this introduction. Farris says that for Luke, "the parable has become a fairly straightforward moral lesson about humility versus arrogance. But as a painting should be studied apart from its frame, so too should this parable be studied apart from Luke's interpretive frame." Farris, "Tale," 23n1. John Dominic Crossan also removes 18:9 as well as 18:14b in his analysis in Crossan, "Parable and Example," 287-307, contra to Bailey who says that to "dismiss it is to reject this apostolic signpost of what the parable is about and substitute our own . . . assumptions regarding its focus." Bailey, *Jesus*, 344.

46. Barrett, "Justification," 28n3.

47. Snodgrass, *Stories*, 742n167.

48. In this sense, one does not need to think of importing overt legalism; Bauer et al., "πείθω," BDAG 792; ("to be so convinced that one puts confidence in something").

49. Forbes associates the meaning of "righteous" as ones who adopt "a sense of lifestyle that makes one acceptable before God." Forbes, *God of Old*, 212. Also see Nolland, *Luke 9:21—18:34*, 875; Marshall, *Gospel of Luke*, 678.

in this verse is meant to be taken in a negative sense.⁵⁰ This negative assessment is also supported by the second description of these people as those who ἐξουθενοῦντας τοὺς λοιποὺς ("disdained the others").⁵¹ Other verses where ἐξουθενέω is used are Luke 23:11 and Acts 4:11. In Luke 23:11, ἐξουθενέω is associated with the mistreatment of Jesus by Herod and his soldiers. Likewise, in Acts 4:11, the word is used in Peter's speech before the Council for describing the rejection or mistreatment of Jesus. The "others" (τοὺς λοιποὺς) is described further in 18:11 as the swindlers, unjust, adulterers, and even the tax collector.

As far as who the "righteous" are, the options include the disciples, the Pharisees, or a much broader audience. In Luke 17:22, Jesus is portrayed as speaking to the disciples after he spoke with some Pharisees two verses earlier in 17:20. While, at first glance, the parable is addressed to the disciples, it is not inconceivable that the Pharisees are within earshot to hear the parable similar to how some of them are portrayed as listening in to the teachings of Jesus in 16:14.⁵² It may also be tempting to think that the parable's primary audience could be the Pharisees (and scribes) as some of them are shown in other verses as "exalting themselves" (10:29; 11:37–44; 14:1–14; 15:1–2; 16:14–17). But the disciples are also warned of similar self-absorbing behavior in Luke 12:1–2 and in Luke 9:46–50.⁵³ In the end, the parable is meant for the disciples or the people Jesus is addressing in 17:20 regardless of whether the Pharisees are present or not. The target audience, therefore, is broader and not just one specific group. Moreover, Luke uses the indefinite pronoun τινας ("some" or "certain ones"), making the target more general. Although the parable portrays a Pharisee as a negative example, it seems to focus more on any type of person who may have the attitude of the Pharisee in the story.⁵⁴

50. Luke 5:32; 10:29; 16:14–17.

51. Bauer et al., "ἐξουθενέω," BDAG 352.

52. Some conclude that the parable is meant for the Pharisees; Johnson, *Gospel of Luke*, 271; Marshall, *Gospel of Luke*, 678.

53. Green, *Gospel of Luke*, 646.

54. Green, *Gospel of Luke*, 646; Nolland, *Luke 9:21—18:34*, 875; Bock, *Luke 9:51—24:53*, 1461; Bock rightly notes that not all Pharisees are addressed. Other Pharisees in the NT are portrayed more positively, such as Nicodemus (John 19:39–40) and Joseph of Arimathea (Luke 23:50–54, "a member of the council"; cf. Matt 27:57; Mark 15:43; John 19:38–42); Snodgrass, *Stories*, 470; Hultgren, *Parables*, 120. Also, Fitzmyer, *Luke X–XXIV*, 1185, cites Ezek 33:13 about the prophet looking negatively on his people for trusting in their own righteousness. Barrett agrees that the parable does not single out the Pharisees but asserts that there is still "a polemical edge" present against them and

While this introduction in 18:9 gives an early signal that the Pharisee is a negative figure, the concluding pronouncement in 14a may still come as a surprise to the reader. On the other hand, there are those who say that that this introduction "lessens the suspense and shock that the original parable would have had without the introduction."[55] The more complex picture of the Pharisees in Luke's Gospel complicates how the reader may initially perceive the Pharisee in this story.[56] However, by the time we get to this point in the Gospel narrative, a number of incidents of tension have taken place between Jesus and the Pharisees due to Jesus's acceptance of the tax collectors and sinners (5:28–32; 7:36–50; 15:1–32). Thus, the reader may see the Pharisee primarily as a negative figure. Overall, the introduction does not necessarily totally negate the impact of the reversal that happens in the end.

Luke 18:10

In Luke 18:10, two men from very different backgrounds are introduced as the characters in the story. The Pharisee was the paragon of the religious and pious person, rigorously observant of the law and traditions.[57]

In terms of the Pharisees' relationship to Jesus and his movement, Luke's Gospel shows a degree of complexity in this aspect, compared to the other Gospels. Throughout Luke, the Pharisees are antagonists to Jesus in their encounters, but their opposition is somewhat tempered by other more positive portrayals that make them seem more sympathetic to Jesus.

The Pharisees are in opposition to Jesus in various stories of conflict. For example, the Pharisees question Jesus's authority in forgiving the sins of the paralytic (5:17–26). They also question Jesus's practice of table fellowship since he dines with "tax collectors and sinners" (5:30). This practice elicits complaining or grumbling on their part (15:2). Also, the Pharisees question Jesus and his disciples' behavior during the Sabbath (6:2), and they look for evidence to accuse Jesus of wrongdoing (6:7). The Pharisees reject God's purposes because they rejected John's baptism (7:30). Negative portrayals continue on as Pharisees are described as "lovers of money" who sneer at

---

that this should not be discounted. Barrett, "Justification," 29.

55. Forbes, *God of Old*, 212; Snodgrass, *Stories*, 470–71.

56. The Pharisees in Luke's Gospel will be discussed in the analysis of Luke 18:10.

57. The Pharisees were "known for surpassing the others in the observances of piety and exact interpretation of the laws." Josephus, *J. W.* 1.5.2 110.

Jesus's teachings (16:14). Two woes are directed explicitly to the Pharisees (as compared to Matthew's six woes). One woe concerns their tithing practice and their neglect of more ethical concerns (11:42). The other accuses the Pharisees of seeking the most important seats in synagogues and greetings in public places (11:43). In addition, Jesus warns the crowd to be on guard against the Pharisees due to their hypocrisy (12:1), as the Pharisees and teachers of the law began to oppose Jesus vigorously to catch him and entice him to say something controversial (11:53).

The portrayal of the Pharisees as Jesus's adversaries is somewhat tempered in Luke in stories that reflect them in a more positive light. There are three stories of Jesus's encounter with the Pharisee where Jesus is a guest in the Pharisee's home. First, in 7:36–50, Jesus is a guest of Simon the Pharisee ("Simon the leper" in Mark 14:3 and Matt 26:6). Second, a Pharisee invites Jesus to eat (no host is mentioned in Mark and Matthew), which eventually leads to a discussion of his ceremonial washing practices (11:37–41). Third, a prominent Pharisee hosts Jesus in another setting (14:1). At least for this Gospel narrative as compared with Mark and Matthew, Luke displays Jesus and the Pharisee in a friendlier setting although, ultimately, the stories themselves are still conflict oriented and picture the Pharisee in a generally negative light. However, one example of a unique and extraordinary story shows some Pharisees warning Jesus that Herod wants to kill him (13:31–33). Taken at face value, this is a rather friendly and positive action. Finally, a more positive image continues in Acts. In Acts 23, Pharisees were in some sense political allies of Paul as he stood before the Sanhedrin. Notable also in Acts 15:5 is the presence of believers who belonged to the party of the Pharisees, in other words, "Christian Pharisees."[58]

Although the Pharisees are portrayed overall as complex antagonists with some favorable affinities towards Jesus, the pattern of the relationship shows a rising hostility between them. In other words, Luke displays a "plausible evolution of hostility" between Jesus and the Pharisees.[59] This

---

58. Zeisler, "Luke," 146–57, comments that the communities of Matthew, Mark, and John knew the traditions of the Pharisees as adversaries of Jesus, unlike Luke who finds much more occasions to portray them more positively. Carroll, "Luke's Portrayal," 604–21, concludes that the more positive portrayal of the Pharisees serves to legitimize the gentile Christian movement, one of whose main leader is Paul who was also a Pharisee. In addition, Westerholm, "Pharisees," *DJG*, 614, suggests that while the tradition of depicting the Pharisees negatively remains, Luke's more positive elements highlights Luke's desire to show continuity from Judaism to Christianity.

59. Carroll ultimately explains the opposition of the Pharisees to Jesus as primarily due to differences in style of ministry associated with a different view or "competing

evolution is clearer in the level of conflict between them as it plays out in the Gospel. In the initial series of encounters (5:17—6:11), the Pharisees question Jesus on his actions, especially in his decision to have fellowship with tax collectors and sinners (5:30) and issues on the Sabbath (6:1–11). In healing the paralytic, Jesus gets questioned by the Pharisees (just in their minds and not verbally) regarding his authority to forgive sins. After healing the paralytic, the Pharisees join in with regards to giving praise to God (5:26). But only after Jesus heals the man with the shriveled hand on the Sabbath do the Pharisees and teachers of the law plot together against Jesus (6:11), although at this point the Pharisees were not antagonizing Jesus openly, and neither Jesus nor Luke have given any spiritual assessment of the Pharisees. In 7:30 the Pharisees reject God's purposes for themselves because they were not (or refused to be) baptized by John the Baptist. Later in his encounter with his Pharisee host (7:36–50), Jesus uses a parable (41–42) and praises the sinful woman (44–46) as a way of distinguishing against his meal host with regards to having fellowship with sinners. In the travel narrative portion, the conflict between Jesus and the Pharisees escalates even more. During a meal with a Pharisee host, Jesus sharply accuses the Pharisees of greed and wickedness (11:39), of neglect of justice and love of God (11:42), and of being self-important pursuers of people's approval (11:43). In response the Pharisees and the teachers of the law begin to oppose him fiercely, asking him questions to catch him if he says something wrong (11:53–54). Mutual antagonism is shown in the incident of the Sabbath healing (14:1–6), on Pharisees seeking places of honor (14:7–11), on inviting guests who can repay or not (14:12–14), and on those who will be present in God's banquet (14:15–24). Incidents after that include conflicts over Jesus's association with tax collectors and sinners (15:1–32), the use of money and greed (16:1–31), and self-righteousness (18:9–14). As Jesus makes his triumphal entry into Jerusalem, some of the Pharisees tell Jesus to rebuke his own disciples for praising his entry (19:39). Therefore, although Luke shows that the Pharisees have a more complex relationship with Jesus (as compared with the relationship shown in other Gospels), overall it is still a contentious one. This is especially true with regards to the matter of Jesus's association with sinners where the Pharisees' negative attitude serves as a foil to that of Jesus's.[60]

---

understandings of the kingdom of God." Carroll, "Luke's Portrayal," 608.

60. See Westerholm, "Pharisees," *DJG*, 614.

On the other hand, Jesus's relationship with tax collectors is not marked with contentiousness. Of the four incidents where tax collectors are depicted (prior to Luke 18), the relationship seems to be positive as evidenced by Jesus's fellowship with them and their favorable response to his ministry and that of John the Baptist's. Luke 3:12–13 shows tax collectors coming to be baptized by John and asking for instruction. Jesus calls Levi, a tax collector, to be his disciple and Levi goes on to make a feast for Jesus in the company of other tax collectors, even as it elicits grumbling from the Pharisees (5:27–31). In response, Jesus states that the purpose of his ministry is to call sinners to repentance (5:32). Tax collectors are contrasted with Pharisees as not rejecting God's purposes because John baptized them (7:29). Furthermore, the perceived closeness of relationship between Jesus and the tax collectors earned Jesus the description as a "friend of tax collectors and sinners" (7:34). Finally, later in the Gospel, tax collectors and others were drawing near to Jesus as he was teaching, which again draws adverse comments from the Pharisees and scribes (15:1–2). Furthermore, one portrayal of the tax collector this time after Luke 18 concerns Jesus's interaction with a chief tax collector, Zacchaeus. He is rich and he is called a "sinner" (19:7) by those who disapprove of Jesus's association with him and who oppose Jesus's plans to be a guest in his house. In response to people's objections, Jesus declares that he came to seek and to save the lost (19:10).

It is best to look at tax collectors as part of the expression "tax collectors and sinners," which is a subcategory of "sinners" in general.[61] The use of the term associates and links the tax collectors with the segment of people regarded as sinners (5:30; 7:34; 15:1; also 19:7 as *sinner* clearly refers to the chief tax collector Zacchaeus).[62] In these instances, Jesus gets criticized for associating with this group. Jesus seeks sinners since his mission and purpose are to save the "lost" (19:10) and call them to repentance (5:32; 15:7; 15:10). Therefore, the presence of tax collectors (as a subcategory) is likewise central to Jesus's ministry and mission of salvation to sinners. In the Gospel of Luke, from a literary perspective, "sinners" is an ideological or religious category representing people who oppose God and are against God's will.[63] The welcoming of sinners in Jesus's ministry highlights the

---

61. ἁμαρτωλός is mentioned in the Synoptic Gospels twenty-nine times with Luke having the most number (eighteen), then Mark (six), and Matthew (five).

62. "Tax collector" is also paired with "prostitutes" in Matt 21:31–32.

63. Neale argues that instead of treating "sinners" as a specifically identifiable social group, "sinner" is an ideological category within the language of a moral universe that contrasts good and evil. Neale, *None*, 15–16, 95–97. He arrived at this conclusion

radical and alternative character of Jesus's ministry and purpose. It also elicits criticism and antagonism from other Jewish groups such as the Pharisees.[64] At this point of the Gospel narrative, tax collectors are already portrayed as receptive to Jesus and his message (3:12; 5:27–30; 7:34; 15:1). However, given their reputation historically, this depiction is not enough to stunt the shocking reversal of having one of them as a positive example, although the reader may be a little predisposed to anticipate a more positive portrayal different from what their reputation suggests.[65]

Historically, tax collectors gather either direct taxes (e.g., land tax or head tax) or indirect taxes (e.g., customs systems tolls and duties). The land tax involved the produce of the land, usually payable in grain and normally fixed by authorities based on a percentage of the land's yield. The head tax was a tribute per person, which was one denarius or one day's wage per year. These taxes were directly due to Rome, and the populace despised the tax collectors for these direct taxes due to their contact and collaboration with the Jewish aristocracy and the Gentile empire. Indirect taxes were systems of tolls and duties collected at ports and offices near city gates of which the rates varied from 2 to 5 percent of the goods. These goods incurred multiple taxes on those doing commercial travel through towns and cities. The collection of these indirect taxes was farmed to bidders who already paid in advance to be a collector at a certain district. Rome received their taxes in advance, and the tax collectors made money from commissions on these tolls and customs. As the highest bidders got the collection duties, the assessments of the value of the goods possibly at times get inflated, resulting in high commissions for the tax collectors. As a result, these tax collectors or farmers were undesired because not only

---

through a study of linguistic evidence of the Greek Psalms and other primary sources after a review of past studies that rely on rabbinic categories and other modern definitions of the sinner and found them inadequate.

64. Neale, *None*, 15–16, 94–95, argues that the role of a "sinner" shifted, beginning from the Prayer of Manasseh and in later pseudepigraphic literature, from a symbol of someone who is irredeemably condemned to that of a penitent sinner who can be shown mercy. Whether the Gospel traditions influenced this shift or not is unknown, but he asserts that this new view of the sinner was familiar before Jesus because of the presence of the Prayer of Manasseh.

65. Hultgren, *Parables*, 121, notes that it would have been a shocking spectacle for any original hearer of the parable to envision a tax collector going to the temple to pray as it is not likely that the tax collector would want to be identified as such in public.

did they collect taxes that could be very excessive, but some were known to make excessive profits from their work.[66]

The story states that two men went up to the temple to pray. The reason for going up is that the temple is on a hill, which makes sense as, correspondingly, in 18:14, the two men are said to be "going down" after their time in the temple.[67] In terms of the specific occasion for praying, Dennis Hamm asserts that this incident may have taken place during the afternoon Tamid service. This service is a whole offering in the temple twice a day, morning and afternoon, which serves as the primary daily liturgy of the temple. The community sponsored the entire event through the temple tax. Therefore, Hamm suggests that this story could have taken place in the context of public worship.[68] If the events did take place in a public worship setting, it actually amplifies the tax collector's plea for atonement as opposed to a plea in a more ordinary private prayer setting.[69] Although the possibility exists that the two men prayed in the temple at any time privately between sacrifices, most hearers of the parable would have thought of these prayers as taking place at the time of sacrifice, specifically either the morning or afternoon sacrifice.[70]

Various authors debate on whether the characters of the story are genuine or true to form, or are these merely caricatures to enhance the story's points. For example, Schottroff asserts that the image of the Pharisee here is such a caricature that it cannot be seen as authentic.[71] She claims that

---

66. See Schmidt, "Taxes," *DJG*, 804–7; Blomberg, *Interpreting the Parables*, 201–2; Snodgrass, *Stories*, 467; Keener, *Historical Jesus*, 210–11.

67. The high elevation of Jerusalem and the temple is also reflected in 2:22, 42, 51; Acts 3:1.

68. Hamm, "Tamid Service," 223–25. Bailey likewise suggests that the two men went up to the temple to participate in public worship to the only daily service with atonement offerings in the temple, which took place at dawn and at three o'clock in the afternoon. A time of prayer is made within the worship after the officiating priest offers the incense (see Luke 1:10). Bailey, *Jesus*, 346–47. Hamm argues persuasively that allusions are made to the daily sacrifice not only in this parable but also in other passages such as Luke 1:5–25, 24:50–53; Acts 3:1; 10:3, 30. Hamm, "Tamid Service," 223–25. Fitzmyer likewise cites the two periods of the day reserved for public prayer, which were at the third hour and at the ninth hour, although he also states that prayer could have also occurred at other times as well. Fitzmyer, *Luke X–XXIV*, 1186. Therefore, there are others who think that the event did not necessarily happen during public worship and instead assume a private prayer setting. See also Hendrick, *Parables*, 214.

69. Forbes, *God of Old*, 212–13.

70. See Snodgrass, *Stories*, 472–73, 744n185, citing Hedrick and Hengel.

71. Schottroff, "Die Erzählung," 439–61; Her point is that the Pharisee's portrayal

in the parable, the Pharisee is an embodiment of self-righteousness and that his prayer is an exaggeration of this quality.[72] However, there seems to be a stronger argument to view the characters as true to form instead of caricatures since an attitude of self-righteousness (as well as other attitudes) among ancient Pharisees is depicted in ancient Jewish literature.[73]

Luke 18:11

Luke 18:11 describes the Pharisee standing by himself and saying a prayer. Externally, the Pharisee adopts the normal standing posture for prayer (1 Sam 1:26; 1 Kgs 8:14, 22; Matt 6:5; Mark 11:25). There is much discussion about whether the prepositional phrase πρὸς ἑαυτὸν is modifying the participle for standing ("standing by himself") or the main verb ("prayed by himself" or "prayed about himself"). If πρὸς ἑαυτὸν modifies the participle, perhaps he was simply standing or he was standing aloof because of his attitude of self-righteousness. If the phrase modifies the main verb, he may have been praying silently, about himself or, seemingly, to God. Given that 18:13 shows the tax collector as "standing from afar," it is better to consider the more difficult textual reading of "standing by himself" as the appropriate parallel.

The verse does not say exactly where the Pharisee stood by himself, but some commentators imagine that he most likely stood in the inner

---

stems from later anti-Jewish polemic.

72. Schottroff, *Parables of Jesus*, 8–9. Holmgren also believes that the parable is hyperbolic because of its use of characters that can be contrasted clearly and definitively. Holmgren, "Pharisee," 253. Downing asserts that the characters in the story are merely caricatures who are self-absorbed and they serve as warnings to hearers. See Downing, "Ambiguity," 80–99.

73. Two examples are 1QH 15.34–35: "[I give you thanks], Lord, because you did not make my lot fall in the congregation of falsehood, nor have you placed my regulation in the counsel of the hypocrites, [but you have led me] to your favour and your forgiveness." Also b. Ber. 28b: "I give thanks to Thee, O Lord my God, that Thou hast set my portion with those who sit in the Beth ha-Midrash and Thou hast not set my portion with those who sit in [street] corners, for I rise early and they rise early, but I rese early for words of Torah and they rise early for frivolous talk; I labour and they labour, but I labour and receive a reward and they labour and do not receive a reward; I run and they run, but I run to the life of the future world and they run to the pit of destruction"; cited from Snodgrass, *Stories*, 463–65. Also, examples of authors who argue against the characters being labelled as caricatures include Marshall, *Gospel of Luke*, 677; Friedrichsen, "Temple," 91–95; Nolland, *Luke 9:21—18:34*, 874–75; Blomberg, *Interpreting the Parables*, 342–43; Snodgrass, *Stories*, 472.

court of the temple as far as an Israelite who was not a priest would have been permitted in the court of Israel. This location is in contrast with the tax collector who was standing far off from the Pharisee.[74]

The Pharisee prays aloud but not in a rude manner.[75] He starts with the vocative ὁ θεός, which indicates that the prayer is directed to God. His prayer begins in a similar fashion to a thanksgiving psalm (e.g., Pss 30; 92; 118; 136; 138) in the way it praises God for God's activity. The Pharisee thanks God first that he is not like other people (οἱ λοιποὶ τῶν ἀνθρώπων) whom he refers to as robbers (ἅρπαγες), the unjust (ἄδικοι), adulterers (μοιχοί), and also, in particular, the tax collector in the temple. In effect, the Pharisee is giving credit to God in that he has been able to avoid the sins or the adverse qualities of the others he enumerated. However, it is also possible to view his prayer as a more self-exalting kind of prayer. Although he starts with thanksgiving to God, he does not thank God's actions but instead cites his own deeds. Thus, he does not associate his moral accomplishments as ultimately coming from the grace of God. His prayer does not focus on God at all but fixates on his self-comparison with those who violate God's laws.[76] Robbers and adulterers can be counted as violators of the Decalogue.[77] The use of ἄδικοι here seems to be in a more general sense as a sinner, an evildoer, or an unrighteous person. This is in contrast with the term δίκαιοι in 18:9. It has been argued that ἄδικοι may refer to "swindlers" or "deceivers."[78] The Pharisee then singles out from among the other people the tax collector (ἢ καὶ ὡς οὗτος ὁ τελώνης) in

---

74. Bock, *Luke 9:51—24:53*, 1462, 1464, speculates that the tax collector was on the outer edge of the court of the gentiles; Fitzmyer, *Luke X–XXIV*, 1186, 1188, sees the tax collector at the outer edge on the court of Israel; Barrett, "Justification," 42.

75. Marshall, *Gospel of Luke*, 679, notes some criticism of rabbis who prayed too loudly. Snodgrass also mentions that "people in antiquity usually prayed aloud." Snodgrass, *Stories*, 470. See the example of Hannah in 1 Sam 1:13. Bailey further speculates that by praying aloud, the Pharisee, through his prayer, is preaching to those around him whom he considers unrighteous by giving them "words of judgment along with some instruction in righteousness." Bailey, *Through Peasant Eyes*, 149.

76. Barrett, "Justification," 44, notes that it is a genuine thanksgiving to God that even highlights the dramatic reversal that Jesus declares in 18:14. Others think the Pharisee never mentions any praiseworthy action from God. Instead, it is mostly about the Pharisee's actions and not God; Green, *Gospel of Luke*, 648; Bock, *Luke 9:51—24:53*, 1462.

77. Exod 20:14-15; Deut 5:17-18; Fitzmyer, *Luke X–XXIV*, 1187. Also see the vice lists in 1 Cor 5:10-11, 6:9-10.

78. Barrett, "Justification," 44; Fitzmyer, *Luke X–XXIV*, 1187; Bock, *Luke 9:51—24:53*, 1462; Marshall, *Gospel of Luke*, 679, argues that ἄδικοι may refer to swindlers or cheats based on 1 Cor 6:9; Lev 19:13.

the parable. The word οὗτος can carry a derogatory impression associated with the tax collector and, in a sense, turns him into a highlight and concrete example of who the Pharisee is not like, unlike the more general references made to robbers, adulterers, and the unjust.[79] It is possible that the Pharisee is merely putting the tax collector in the same category as the rest of the unrighteous group, but a similar pejorative use of οὗτος can also be found in 15:2 and Acts 17:18. Therefore, the use of this term in this instance crosses a line as it seems to distinguish and call out the tax collector from the list of "other people."[80]

Overall, the Pharisee's initial action and portion of his prayer portrays his separation from others in the temple. He is physically separated as he stands by himself, and he also considers himself separated in saying that he is not like the rest. Then he highlights even more particular reasons why he is separate and different from the rest, why he considers himself as an example of someone "righteous" but, unfortunately, also as someone who disdains the others (18:9).

Luke 18:12

In Luke 18:12, the Pharisee enumerates some examples of why he is righteous compared to the others, by mentioning specifically his practice of fasting twice a week and tithing from everything he gets. In terms of fasting, Jews were only required to do a national fast on the Day of Atonement (Lev 16:29–31).[81] Fasting also possibly occurred over four days in memory of the destruction of Jerusalem (Zech 7:3, 5; 8:19). Other times of fasting would be in instances of crisis, and godly people were

---

79. According to Bauer et al., "οὗτος," BDAG 740, instances of οὗτος coming before a substantive with the article involving "a touch of contempt" is found here in 18:11 as well as 14:30 and 15:30. Also see: 5:21; 7:39, 49; 22:59; John 6:42, 52; Matt 13:55–56; 21:10; Mark 6:2–3. Also: Barrett, "Justification," 44; Bock, *Luke 9:51—24:53*, 1462–63; Marshall, *Gospel of Luke*, 679; Fitzmyer, *Luke X–XXIV*, 1187; Forbes, *God of Old*, 214.

80. Nolland, *Luke 9:21—18:34*, 876; Farris, "Tale," 27n11; Levine, *Short Stories*, 202, sees the prayer as gratitude and sees nothing wrong with the content but also notes that the Pharisee through this prayer negatively judges the tax collector instead of thinking about bringing him to a better position with respect to God.

81. Snodgrass, *Stories*, 467. Forbes, *God of Old*, 214, mentions possibly other days in memory of the destruction of Jerusalem (Zech 7:3, 5; 8:19); Bock, *Luke 9:51—24:53*, 1463.

expected to fast with increased frequency.[82] Pharisees fasted on Mondays and Thursdays.[83] Therefore, fasting twice a week is more than what was required for the typical Jew. As for tithing, it is normally done on agricultural products (Deut 14:22–23) although tithing beyond these products was also conducted (Luke 11:42). By tithing of all that he obtained, he goes above and beyond the law.[84]

Interpreters view the attitude behind the Pharisee's prayer in different ways. Some say that the prayer reflects a typical attitude of a Pharisee. It is an attitude that expresses a kind of righteousness or a certain piety that comes from the emphasis of following the law and the type of prayer exhibited by this mind-set is expressed in *b. Ber.* 28b *b. Suk.* 45b, 1QH 7:34; Phil 3:4–6.[85] Others say that the prayer is a deliberate caricature for enabling the hearer to sympathize or identify immediately with the tax collector.[86] The prayer may have started as a genuine prayer of thanksgiving, but in the end, it is given with the wrong spirit or attitude. It is an attitude that excludes the tax collector from God's mercy when the Pharisee specifically refers to the tax collector, compares himself to the tax collector, and restricts righteousness to his own methods.[87] Therefore, the parable does not condemn all Pharisees or a general notion of their typical piety but critiques a particular attitude or mind-set that existed within some of them. As mentioned earlier, certain attitudes of self-righteousness did exist among Pharisees and other groups.[88]

Overall, there is a sense of irony in the Pharisee's actions. In one sense, it is fitting that the Pharisee thanks God that he does not engage in the lifestyle of the others he mentioned. It is historically part of the identity of the Pharisee to note differences between people who follow the Torah and those who do not. Green notes, "Drawing distinctions—whether as 'separatists' or as those who 'specify' the correct interpretation of Torah—is endemic

---

82. 1 Sam 7:6; Ps 35:13; Zech 7:5; Matt 6:16–18; Mark 2:18–20; Luke 2:36–38; Acts 13:2–3; 2 Cor 11:27.

83. E.g., Did. 8:1; Luke 5:33.

84. Forbes, *God of Old*, 215.

85. Marshall, *Gospel of Luke*, 677–79; Bailey, *Through Peasant Eyes*, 150–52; Fitzmyer, *Luke X–XXIV*, 1184–85.

86. Downing, "Ambiguity," 80–99; Holmgren, "Pharisee," 252–61; Schottroff, *Parables*, 8–9.

87. Forbes, *God of Old*, 216.

88. Snodgrass includes b. Sota 22b in which seven types of Pharisees were described who possessed "false humility and ostentation." Snodgrass, *Stories*, 743n174.

to Pharisaic identity historically."[89] At least the majority of the Pharisees in this period focused on purity and what it symbolized for them, which are the maintenance of their Jewish identity and achievement of national liberation.[90] The emphasis on purity leads to separating themselves from those who are considered as unrighteous. The irony of separating himself from others physically and through his prayer is that the Pharisee puts himself outside of the restoration of Jesus whose central mission is to save the lost (i.e., sinners; 19:10). Their need for restoration is apparent since the Gospel's narrative portrayal of the behavior of some Pharisees is "unjust" or "unrighteous," thus describing them as sinners (11:42; 16:15).

Luke 18:13

In Luke 18:13, the tax collector is μακρόθεν ἑστὼς ("Standing far off"). The tax collector may be in the extremities of the court of Israel, which shows his low status and/or ritual impurity.[91]

His posture—οὐκ ἤθελεν οὐδὲ τοὺς ὀφθαλμοὺς ἐπᾶραι εἰς τὸν οὐρανόν—is not the normal posture for prayer (cf. Ps 123:1; 1 Esd 4:45; Mark 6:41; 7:34; John 11:41; 17:1), but an example of this alternative posture is displayed by Ezra (Ezra 9:5-6) in his prayer to God after expressing shame and embarrassment for the intermarriage of Israelites with the gentiles in the land (Ezra 9:1-2). This picture shows great remorse and grief, especially emphasized by the beating of his chest as a sign of contrition (cf. Luke 23:48; also Josephus, *Ant.* 7.10.5; Ezra 9:6; 1 En. 13:5). The chest is the seat of sin (*Eccl. Rab.* 7.2) as the heart is the seat of the emotions and will out of which sin and evil spring forth (Gen 6:5; Pss 14:1; 95:10; Isa 32:6; Mark 7:21-23; cf. Luke 6:45).[92]

---

89. Green, *Gospel of Luke*, 648.

90. Wright asserts that "all the evidence suggests that at least the majority of Pharisees, from the Hasmonean and Herodian periods through to the war of AD 66-70, had as their main aim that which purity symbolized: the political struggle to maintain Jewish identity and to realize the dream of national liberation." Wright, *Jesus*, 378. "Purity (in its very different manifestations such as food laws, handwashing, and so on) was not, in this period, an end in itself, if indeed it was ever really that. It was a symbol, all the more important for a people who perceived themselves under threat, of national identity and national liberation." Wright, *Jesus*, 379. See also Wright, *New Testament*, 187-88.

91. Forbes, *God of Old*, 217.

92. Marshall, *Gospel of Luke*, 680; Barrett, "Justification," 49.

With regards to the content of the prayer itself, the tax collector, in contrast to the Pharisee, begs for mercy as opposed to giving thanks. What makes the cry for mercy of the tax collector distinctive among the Gospels from other cries for mercy is the use of the verb ἱλάσκομαι (used only once in the Gospels) instead of the more commonly used word in the Gospels for mercy—ἐλεέω (fifteen times in the Synoptic Gospels). Due to the difference in wording, commentators translate part of the verse in a few different ways: (1) "be merciful," or "have mercy,"[93] (2) "have pity,"[94] (3) "be propitiated,"[95] (4) "make an atonement"[96] (5) "be reconciled to me."[97]

The verb ἱλάσκεσθαι belongs to a word group associated with the cultic ritual in Israel on the Day of Atonement (Exod 25:17–22; 38:5–8; Lev 16). Edwards notes that in three quarters of its occurrences in the OT, ἱλάσκομαι took the place of the Hebrew word *kipper* ("to cover") with reference to atonement for sin in the temple. The word is used only once in the NT in Heb 2:17 where it refers to Jesus as the high priest atoning for the sins of the people at the Holy of Holies. Therefore, ἱλάσθητί implies atonement.[98] David Hill argues for the prominence of the notion of propitiation, stating, "The divine wrath does not find expression in the passage (18:13), but the holy reaction of God to sin is implied. The publican's approach to God is direct; there is no idea of expiating sins."[99] Bailey, however, argues that both notions of expiation and propitiation combined with cleansing and reconciliation are behind the meaning of the Hebrew *kipper* that forms the background of the Greek ἱλάσκομαι. Therefore, Bailey rightly suggests that the full theological weight of the word is expressed if the prayer is translated as, "O Lord, make an atonement for me!" especially since the setting is in the context of a sin offering.[100] Although the prayer has been translated

---

93. Nolland, *Luke 9:21—18:34*, 873; Bock, *Luke 9:51—24:53*, 1460; Green, *Gospel of Luke*, 644; Wright, *Luke for Everyone*, 212; Ellis, *Gospel of Luke*, 215; Carroll, *Luke*, 359; Arndt, *St. Luke*, 378, 380; Edwards, *Gospel According to Luke*, 505; Jeffrey, *Luke*, 217.

94. Fitzmyer, *Luke X–XXIV*, 1183.

95. Marshall, *Gospel of Luke*, 680.

96. Bailey, *Through Peasant Eyes*, 140; Farris, "Tale," 30; Forbes, *God of Old*, 218.

97. Bovon, *Luke 2*, 541, 550.

98. Edwards, *Gospel According to Luke*, 505, 505n133; Jeffrey, *Luke*, 217.

99. Hill further says that his plea is for God to be "gracious or favorable to him, and although mercy or forgiveness is the content of the desired attitude, a trace of the ideas connected with propitiation surely lingers in the background: God is asked to be favourably-disposed or propitious towards the sinner." Hill, *Greek Words*, 36.

100. Bailey, *Jesus*, 349. Bailey, *Through Peasant Eyes*, 154, also points out that the

in quite a few different ways, the main idea of his cry for mercy implies a request for atonement and that the benefit of the atonement sacrifice may apply to him despite his moral depravity.[101] Therefore, it is more than just a generalized cry for mercy. In a broader sense, the tax collector is pleading to God for compassion, reconciliation, and restoration.

Luke 18:14a

Luke 18:14a is a pronouncement verse introduced by λέγω ὑμῖν. It turns out that the person who is righteous or justified is not the Pharisee (contrary to his assumption in 18:9) but the tax collector. This declaration would be a shock to Jesus's Jewish hearers given the low standing and reputation of the tax collector. In addition, the Pharisees are the ones normally considered as the righteous ones, especially since this Pharisee fasted and tithed in ways beyond what was normally required. The perfect passive participle δεδικαιωμένος indicates the justified state of the tax collector with God as the divine actor.[102] The term indicates a right relationship with God. Commentators note that Paul's notion of justification may have had its roots here.[103]

Why is acquittal assigned to the tax collector and not the Pharisee? What is the Pharisee's error? What about the tax collector in the story enabled Jesus to declare him justified or righteous? The tax collector, in general, has a reputation of being despised, crooked, and treasonous. But the Pharisee in the story exhibits characteristics that disqualify him from being

---

translation "make an atonement for me" is reflected in the classical Armenian and the Harclean Syriac versions of the early church texts.

101. Bailey, *Through Peasant Eyes*, 154. Snodgrass suggests that even if the translation is "be merciful to me" the sacrificial overtones remain, while Forbes considers "be merciful" as too weak. However, Snodgrass suggests that the prayer is a "poignant plea that the sacrifice will be effective enough to enable God to have mercy on him." Snodgrass, *Stories*, 473. Forbes argues that the main thought is either propitiation or expiation "depending on whether the focus is on averting God's wrath or making payment for sin, although if this prayer is made in connection with the daily sin offering, it is difficult to avoid both suggestions." Forbes, *God of Old*, 218.

102. The passive construction here as well as ταπεινωθήσεται and ὑψωθήσεται are divine passives that point to God as the one doing the action. That means only God justifies, as opposed to self-justification.

103. Snodgrass, *Stories*, 474; Fitzmyer, *Luke X–XXIV*, 1184–85; See also Bruce, "Justification by Faith," 66–69. Blomberg, *Interpreting the Parables*, 345, states that justification makes the parable's conclusion one of the most "Pauline" pieces of all of Jesus's teaching.

declared as "righteous." Luke 18:9 summarizes the characteristics displayed by those with the attitude of the Pharisee—"one who trusted in himself as righteous and disdained others." The rest of the parable demonstrates these characteristics through his physical action (i.e., standing apart from others) and through his prayer. First, the Pharisee displays an attitude of trusting in himself as "righteous." This trait has been described in several ways such as having "self-congratulation,"[104] or "self-exaltation,"[105] a sense of "religious pride."[106] This attitude shows in his thanksgiving to God that he is not like the other people he enumerated, even the tax collector (18:11). It is a righteousness that is self-confident on its own methods and own acts of piety.[107] It is also conscious of its own righteousness, specifically in this case, beyond the righteousness required in the OT as illustrated by his fasting and tithing (18:12).[108] With that state or attitude, the Pharisee becomes blind to his own sin, so he may believe that he is in right standing or right relationship with God, although he is not.[109] He is also blind to remembering that he is unable, without God's mercy, to deal fully with his sin.[110] Earlier, Jesus accuses Pharisees of neglecting justice even as they tithed in exceptional ways (11:42). He also questions their commitment to justice as he calls them people who justified in themselves (16:15), even as they were lovers of money (16:14) and breakers of the law (16:16–17). Second, the Pharisee disdains or treats with contempt people whom he considers sinners. While he fulfills aspects of the law in an exceptional way, he does not follow the command of Jesus to love by loving his neighbor.[111] By despising them, it shows that the Pharisee's love for God does not move him to have compassion with others; instead, it separates him from them.[112] The result is seeing himself as better or superior compared to others.[113] Ironically, the Pharisee does not see that he is one of the sinners whom he despises.

---

104. Snodgrass, *Stories*, 472.
105. Blomberg, *Interpreting the Parables*, 345.
106. Bock, *Luke 9:51—24:53*, 1465.
107. Green, *Gospel of Luke*, 649.
108. Marshall, *Gospel of Luke*, 677–80.
109. Kingsbury, *Conflict*, 23.
110. Barrett, "Justification," 51.
111. Snodgrass, *Stories*, 472.
112. Nolland, *Luke 9:21—18:34*, 877.
113. Marshall, *Gospel of Luke*, 677; Green, *Gospel of Luke*, 649.

On the other hand, the tax collector, through his actions and prayer, recognizes his sin and his inability to deal fully with his sin without God's mercy.[114] By his actions and prayer, he seems to recognize his sense of need and, thus, throws himself to God.[115] The tax collector is vindicated as a model of humility especially with his prayer delivered in the spirit of Ps 51.[116] His depth of feeling shows through his appeal, posture, and action as it echoes the penitential psalm.[117]

Some notice a lack of any explicit verbal reference to repentance in his prayer or any mention of restitution.[118] But due to the magnitude of the tax collectors proceeds, it would be impossible to give back what he took from the populace; thus, there could be no restitution.[119] Also, in general parables need not cover everything that is related to the topic.[120] A similar pattern is employed in the portrayal of the lost son in Luke 15:11–32 who simply returns to his father without giving restitution. Further details involving explicit repentance and restoration may not have been the most essential aspect to show in this parable,[121] but repentance is a key theme in

---

114. Barrett, "Justification," 51.

115. Snodgrass, *Stories*, 472.

116. Bock, *Luke 9:51—24:53*, 1465; Forbes, *God of Old*, 217.

117. Nolland, *Luke 9:2—18:34*, 878.

118. Hendrick, *Parables*, 226-27, mentions that the tax collector wanted mercy but with no repentance or even restitution which means that God's grace is expected to be given based on his attitude and not a requirement for any promise of restitution as Zacchaeus (19:8). Marshall, *Gospel of Luke*, 681, on the other hand, mentions that justification does not depend on works of repentance to restore the wealth. Instead, it is the attitude of the heart that matters. Justification then depends on the mercy of God to the penitent. Zacchaeus's pledge of restoration followed his acceptance of Jesus and did not come before that. In addition, recognizing repentance is Forbes who argues that Jesus was not denying the need for restitution, but that it was not the preliminary criteria for initial acceptance. The intention was to correct an attitude of self-righteousness, which tends to exclude other people from God's grace.

119. Snodgrass remarks, "Restitution of money gained by extortion required an additional fifth be added (Lev 6:1–5). The tax collector's situation would be hopeless, for he could never know everyone he had wronged." Snodgrass, *Stories*, 468.

120. Snodgrass, *Stories*, 475.

121. Another author who also sees repentance is Jones, *Studying the Parables*, 245–46. He states that the tax collector acknowledged his identity as a sinner and was aware that he has sinned. His confession does not have any qualification but a plea for mercy, but whether his life changed is not mentioned in the parable.

Luke.[122] The tax collector here, as pictured in his physical posture and the content of his prayer, represents a repentant heart.

Luke 18:14b

Luke 18:14b provides the generalizing summary at the end of the parable and sheds light on a general principle that the parable illustrates.[123] It is a wisdom saying well-known in gospel tradition as this general principle is used in multiple contexts (Matt 23:12; Luke 14:11). This saying also forms the rationale for Jesus's declaration concerning the tax collector and the Pharisee in 14a as expressed by the ὅτι that precedes 14b. The reason God accepts the tax collector's plea for mercy is that God honors and exalts the humble while the proud such as the Pharisee are brought low. The tax collector is exalted or "justified" due to the humility illustrated in his prayer and physical expression while the Pharisee is brought low because of the pride illustrated in disdaining others and in his prayer. This principle of spiritual reversal is expressed throughout Luke's narrative.[124] This motif of reversal helps bridge the parable to 18:15–17, which is a passage about receiving the kingdom of God as a child.[125] Luke 18:14b also describes the kind of faith asked for in the previous parable in 18:8. The tax collector, in effect, turns to God in faith as he humbly pleads for mercy. His overall actions and prayer, therefore, express not just repentance but both faith and repentance, as these two are linked together although distinct.[126]

---

122. In Luke 3:10–14; 5:32, the call to sinners is unto repentance; 13:3, 5 calls for national repentance; 15:11–32, 16:30, 17:3–4; 19:1–10 are examples of repentance; In 24:47 repentance is in the message of the commissioned disciples and also in Acts 2:37–39; 3:19; 5:31; 11:18; 17:30; 20:21; 26:20. Luke has a greater emphasis on repentance than do the other Gospels.

123. Snodgrass explains that this "could be either an explanatory statement originally used by Jesus with the parable or a floating logion attached to the parable by tradition or reused here by Luke as an explanatory statement." Snodgrass, *Stories,* 471. See also Jas 4:6, 10; 1 Pet 5:5–6; Prov 3:34.

124. See Luke 1:51–53; 2:24; 6:20–26; 10:29–37; 10:38–42; 11:37–41; 12:21; 14:11; 15:11–32; 16:19–31. An example in the OT of reversal is Ezek 21:26.

125. Nolland, *Luke 9:21—18:34,* 878; Forbes, *God of Old,* 219n45.

126. Barrett, "Justification," 57.

LUKE 18:9-14

The Notion of Justification/Righteousness (δικαιόω) in This Parable

The understanding of justification/righteousness in Luke 18:9-14 varies among commentators. Some unreservedly discuss how justification in this parable is not different from how Paul depicts justification in his letters. The difference perhaps is the variation in the language used or that Paul elaborated on the theme or some other assertion.[127] On the other end are those who say that the parable's notion of justification is just not comparable to Paul's doctrine. Some of the reasons include, first, no reference in the parable to the saving action of the cross, which makes it a "far cry from justification by faith." Instead in Luke, "justification" equals "forgiveness of sins."[128] Second, it does not develop the role of faith as do the Pauline epistles.[129] Third, there is just no basis in seeing the text though Paul's works.[130] Fourth, there are no soteriological issues as the term δικαιόω as used here is not a technical term for final salvation; therefore, it is not comparable. Instead, the tax collector's plea is just a generalized request for mercy.[131] Fifth, there are those who say that the notion of justification in the parable is not exactly the same as Paul's doctrine, but they are along parallel lines. Perhaps they serve as a starting point to understand righteousness through atonement,[132] or perhaps it is parallel to Paul but not in the sense that Luke is dependent upon or using Paul.[133]

True, both Luke and Paul were theologians who "though writing in different ways, in different contexts, to different audiences—share access to the traditions of the resurrected Christ (Luke by way of sources, Paul by means of personal appearance and other sources) as well as a rich understanding of the Old Testament."[134] Therefore, they would have communicated the concept of justification in their own distinct ways though relying substantially on shared sources.

---

127. Marshall, *Gospel of Luke*, 680; Bruce, "Justification by Faith," 68; Jeremias, *Parables*, 112.

128. Fitzmyer, *Luke X-XXIV*, 1184-85; Fitzmyer, "Pauline Justification," 258.

129. Forbes, *God of Old*, 218-19.

130. Nolland, *Luke 9:21—18:34*, 878.

131. Bock, *Luke 9:51—24:53*, 1465. For him, δικαιόω is "forensic but not in the decisive sense."

132. Bailey, *Through Peasant Eyes*, 156.

133. Barrett, "Justification," 54.

134. Barrett, "Justification," 54.

Overall, the sense of justification in the parable is both soteriological and eschatological. Barrett cites Richard Gaffin who claims that Paul's view of the righteousness of God has its origins in Jesus's proclamation of the kingdom of God. Gaffin claims that Paul's view is the "fruition, the doctrinally more explicit and developed delineation, of the good news of repentance for the forgiveness of sins which was announced by Jesus, and which, more importantly, was actualized in his death, resurrection, ascension, and baptism with the Holy Spirit."[135] Per Barrett, "Justification in Luke is thoroughly eschatological in that the declaration of justification is a verdict by God which is rooted in his end-times exaltation of the humble, as well as thoroughly soteriological in that God's declaration regarding the sinner effects or causes—not simply describes – a change in the status of the justified."[136] Therefore, justification as presented in this parable is both eschatological and soteriological.

The nature of justification in this parable can be highlighted in four aspects. The first is that justification is for the ungodly. Even as the tax collector is portrayed as, ironically, the positive character in the story, as the one who is justified, he is a sinner (as he himself is fully aware). His position as a tax collector was viewed historically as someone who is against God's commands and the people. He can be viewed as an unworthy recipient of God's mercy. Therefore, justification is for those characterized as sinners who are deemed as undeserving of God's grace.[137] Second, justification in this parable does relate to atonement and the benefit of restoration that atonement brings. Despite the lack of any reference to the sacrificial aspects of the cross, sacrificial overtones are present due to the setting of the narrative during temple sacrifices and the tax collector's distinctive cry for

---

135. Gaffin, "Justification," 125.

136. Barrett, "Justification," 3.

137. Barclay relates how in ancient times, "gift" (grace) was assumed to create social ties and were not generally designed as one-way, unreciprocated donations." Instead there are rules of reciprocity that impose an obligation on the recipient to reciprocate the gift. In other words, "gifts created ties and expected returns." Barclay then states, "Donors generally ensured that gifts were distributed discriminately, to fitting or worthy recipients; 'worth' could be variously defined, but even (or especially) for the gods/God, the proper distribution of significant gifts required careful selection." Barclay, *Paul and the Gift*, 184. He claims that "a perfect gift could be figured as one given without condition, that is, without regard to the worth of the recipient." Barclay, *Paul and the Gift*, 73. The type of grace that God gives as a gift is mentioned as "incongruous" as the gift's distribution does not limit giving only to worthy people.

mercy in the use of the verb ἱλάσκομαι (used only once in the Gospels).[138] The significance of the sacrificial aspects relate to its involvement in the Israelites' restoration of right relations with God.[139] Therefore, justification presented in this parable is linked with atonement, its benefit of being made right with God. In a broader sense, justification ultimately relates to the theme of salvation as the tax collector is restored, made right with God and ultimately included in God's kingdom.[140] Third, justification is to be accessed by faith and/or repentance with an overall attitude of humility not self-righteousness. The Pharisee, who is also a sinner, would have possibly obtained the same declaration from Jesus had he turned to God humbly instead of focusing more on what he has done for himself and his disdain for others. Instead, the tax collector turns to God in a decisive manner. A verbal reference to faith comes from the use of the word πείθω in 18:9, referring to ones who had "trusted" in themselves. In addition, the previous parable asks if the Son of Man will find faith on earth (18:8). It is not difficult to see the tax collector's turning to God as a response of the kind of faith that answers the question in 18:8. Another way to picture this faith is by considering the tax collector's cry for mercy (18:13) as a parallel to the beggar's cry for mercy in Luke 18:38-39 (healing of the blind beggar) that Jesus affirms as a cry of faith (18:42). Therefore, in that sense, faith is narratively pictured or played out in the story even if it does not have a more obvious direct verbal reference in the parable whereas repentance as a motif is expressed through his actions, such as "beating his breast,"[141] as well as his cry of repentance and remorse.[142] An overall attitude or stance of humility (as depicted by the tax collector) and not self-righteousness (as shown by the Pharisee) is evident for the recipient of justification. Finally, justification can be understood in this parable through the theme of eschatological exaltation. The parable temple setting represents a courtroom

---

138. Blomberg rightfully notes that it would be hard to find explicit references to the cross because at this point in the narrative, it is still before Jesus's crucifixion. These are "pre-crucifixion days." Blomberg, *Interpreting the Parables*, 345.

139. In talking about the offering of sacrifices, Green states, "In God's economy, Israelites were thus to do to their animals what they were not allowed to do to their children or themselves; animal life substitutes for human life, and this had efficacy in the restoration of right relations with God." Green, *Salvation*, 100.

140. An explicit example is the story of Zacchaeus (19:1-10) per Green, *Salvation*, 108-9.

141. Cf. *Jos. Asen.* 10:15. See also comments by Green, *Gospel of Luke*, 649.

142. Bailey, *Through Peasant Eyes*, 154.

scene where God who is the judge delivers a judicial declaration in 18:14b that gives a new status to the unrighteous. It is not a simple declaration in 18:14 about who is right or wrong in a court case, but it is about the granting of a new reality—a status of "righteousness." Connected to that declaration of a new status of righteousness is the motif of spiritual reversal—the proud are brought low, while the humble are exalted. This motif of reversal permeates the gospel tradition.[143]

Next Step

While Barrett points to a distinctive theology of justification in this parable and outlines the major features of Lukan justification, he did not develop definitive conclusions regarding the source of this understanding. The scope of his work does not involve figuring out if this theme of justification may have been plausibly derived from sources within the Jesus tradition. As mentioned in the introduction, this present study looks for the plausible fit or compatibility of this theme in the Jesus tradition through the method of the criterion of coherence as delineated by the continuum approach. Since the parable comes from unique Lukan material, this passage cannot be attested to more than once in other independent sources. Therefore, the next procedure involves looking for substantially comparable motifs and themes in the Jesus tradition. As this research focuses on comparable motifs and themes, the passages considered for source coherence do not need to be limited to texts that contain δικαιόω words and cognates. The comparable motifs considered are important aspects in the interpretation of the parable. Based on the discussion in the prior section, four aspects of the parable that highlight the soteriological and eschatological nature of justification in Luke 18:9–14 can be used to search for coherence throughout the sources of the Jesus tradition:

1. Justification is pronounced to those who are considered "sinners" or ungodly and undeserving of God's grace.
2. Justification has links with atonement and its benefits of restoration, broadly culminating in salvation as the overall theme.
3. Justification is accessed through faith and/or repentance with an overall attitude of humility not self-righteousness.

---

143. Luke 1:51–53; 14:11; Matt 18:4; 23:12.

4. Justification is marked by eschatological exaltation with the related motif of reversal.

The next chapters note the coherence across the plurality of Gospel sources and specific forms in various streams of tradition. In chapter 3, this book begins the task of looking for the coherence of justification within the unique Lukan tradition.

—— Chapter 3 ——

Coherence of Justification with the Lukan Tradition (L)

THIS STUDY NOW APPLIES the criterion of coherence by looking for comparable motifs and texts in the Jesus tradition. Essentially, the goal is to look at a variety of sources and forms that contain some invariable traits that recur and create coherence. This "coherence against the background of incoherence" may refer to specific motifs and themes expressed in different words of Jesus—the *vox ipsissima* of Jesus ("the very voice" or concepts that he expressed though not in his exact words) as reflected in various sources.[1] This chapter features specific texts that are unique only to the Lukan tradition or are uniquely shaped by Luke in such a way that it makes a substantially different point compared to the other Gospel accounts. The texts are selected because intrinsically present within each of these specific passages are most, if not all, the four aspects that are key features of the nature of justification in Luke 18:9–14.[2] Of course, the related themes and motifs for justification in 18:9–14 may be individually found in other passages beyond these specific texts. Therefore, one can argue that a reader may find one or more of these themes and motifs anyway in many or most types of texts in the Gospel, but these are chosen due to the high concentration or convergence of this particular combination of themes and motifs. The confluence of these themes and motifs makes

---

1. Theissen and Merz, "Delay," 56.

2. (1) Justification is for sinners; (2) justification is linked to restoration or the theme of salvation; (3) justification is accessed by faith and/or repentance with an overall attitude of humility and not self-righteousness, and, (4) justification is marked by eschatological exaltation and the motif of reversal.

these passages unique. Once again, as stated in the introduction, the caveat holds true with regards to source coherence: "that which we consider coherent is perhaps incoherent for others and vice versa."[3] Coherence is not a timeless standard of measurement.[4]

The specific texts examined in this chapter are as follows: (1) Luke 7:36–50; (2) some special Lukan parables and their contexts (Luke 10:25–37; 14:7–14; 15:1–32; 16:14–31; 18:1–8); (3) Luke 19:1–10; and, (4) the passion narrative.

Luke 7:36–50

In looking for the related themes and motifs that cohere with the parable of the Pharisee and tax collector, it is important to account for the context of the pericope starting from the beginning of Luke 7.[5] Prior to these passages, Jesus heals a centurion's slave and raises a widow's son (7:1–16). After that, reports of Jesus as "a great prophet" (7:16) spread and reached

---

3. Theissen and Winter, *Plausible Jesus*, 235n7.
4. Theissen and Winter, *Plausible Jesus*, 235n7.
5. Although similar anointing accounts are in Mark 14:3–9 and Matt 26:6–13, this particular account is included in this chapter because it is uniquely and substantially shaped in Luke compared with the other Gospel accounts. Bock outlines seven differences as follows: "(1) The events have different settings in terms of chronology and locale. The other event occurs in the final week of Jesus' life and takes place in the house of a leper named Simon (Matt 26:6=Mark 14:3), where Pharisees would never dine (in fact, the audience in this later meal is disciples). Luke's version occurs in the earlier Galilean portion of Jesus' ministry and takes place in a Pharisee's house, who also happens to be named Simon (Luke 7:39–40). Simon the Pharisee could not be the same as Simon the leper, since a leper could not be a Pharisee. (2) In Matthew and Mark, the woman anoints Jesus' head and not his feet as in Luke. However, John 12:3 does speak of anointing his feet. (3) The identity of the women differs. In John 12:1–3, the anointing is by the righteous Mary of Bethany, since she is placed alongside Martha and Lazarus. In Luke, the anointing is by a sinner. (4) The reaction to the event differs: in Matthew and Mark, the complaint is of the waste of the perfume; in Luke the concern is over association with a sinner, which leads to doubt about Jesus' position as a prophet. (5) The unique Lukan parable illustrates the significance of forgiving a sinner and so gives the Lukan account a different perspective. (6) The Lukan account stresses the woman's courtesy to Jesus in contrast to the Pharisee's lack of courtesy. Her act also gives Jesus an opportunity to declare that forgiveness is present. In contrast, the woman's act in Matthew, Mark, and John is seen as a preparation for Jesus' burial and thus as a cause for his commendation. (7) The conclusions differ: an act that Jesus says in Matthew and Mark will be memorialized stands in contrast to the controversy that Jesus' forgiveness in Luke cause among the Pharisees." Bock, *Luke 9:51—24:53*, 689–90.

John the Baptist (7:18). This incident leads to a discussion of the nature and identity of Jesus on whether he is "the one who is to come" (ὁ ἐρχόμενος). Not only is Jesus's identity discussed but also one's standing in God's kingdom. Ultimately, this further plays out in the narrative of the woman with the ointment who anointed Jesus's feet (7:36–50).

Luke 7:18–35 starts as a response to John's question (7:20) concerning Jesus. In his answer, Jesus describes his ministry by alluding to Isa 29:18–19; 35:5–6; 42:18; 61:1, which reflect God's salvation activity (7:22). In other words, he is doing his ministry under the leading and anointing of the Spirit (4:18–19). Afterwards, Jesus mentions a beatitude, which pronounces an eschatological blessing on those who are not offended by him. in other words, those who are approving of his mission and purpose (7:23).[6] He then discusses further with the crowds the identity of John (7:24–28). John is more than a prophet as he is also the precursor to the Messiah (7:26–27).[7] Furthermore, Jesus says John is greater than any person, although John is also no better than the least in God's kingdom (7:28). That means that what matters most is one's position in the kingdom of God. The ones counted as eschatologically blessed are those not offended by Jesus or those who have a believing response to him.[8]

The narrative suddenly focuses on the reaction of the crowd, including tax collectors, in that they declare God "just" (ἐδικαίωσαν), which means they "justify" or "vindicate" God, because they had the baptism of John (7:29). Given that John's baptism is one of repentance for the forgiveness of sins (3:3), the crowds repent and acknowledge God's judgment on

---

6. On the pronouncement of an eschatological blessing, Marshall, speaking of 7:23 notes, "The saying thus refers to the possibility of a person not accepting Jesus as 'the coming One' because he 'stumbles' at the kind of things done or left undone by Jesus, and thinks that he should have behaved differently. Stumbling is thus the opposite to believing in Jesus. The saying pronounces an eschatological verdict upon the people concerned; by their attitude to Jesus they will stand or fall at the last judgment . . . This explains its negative form: blessed is the man who retains his faith in me and does not give it up." Marshall, *Gospel of Luke*, 292.

7. Green writes, "John is the end-time prophet foretold in the Scriptures, the Elijah figure who would forerun the coming of the Lord. The primary deviation between Mal 3:1 and its reappearance in this Lukan co-text is the amendment from the first-person singular pronoun ("before me") in Malachi to the second-person ("before you") in Luke. In this divergence, Luke follows Exod 23:20, with the result that Jesus has begun speaking with greater existential urgency to those who make up his audience in this scene. John, he says, was God's agent to prepare you. It is in this way that Jesus shows how John is "more than a prophet." Green, *Gospel of Luke*, 298.

8. Barrett, "Justification," 117.

them (that they are sinners) and they accept God's forgiveness. In contrast, the Pharisees and lawyers reject God's purposes by not undergoing John's baptism.[9] Therefore, the ones who "justify" God are those who embrace the will of God (in this case, follow John's call to repent) while those who do not justify God (i.e., those who do not follow God's will by refusing John's baptism or, in other words, refusing to repent) ultimately reject God's purposes for themselves. In effect, just to be clear and for emphasis, those who respond to the ministry of John, including the tax collectors, responded to God's call to repentance legitimizes God's salvific plan, which is why in a sense, their response to God is a vindication or a verdict of approval of God's plan and purposes.

Then from 7:31–35, Jesus speaks of his ministry as well as John's. The purpose is to draw out an implication for those who do not respond positively to God's purpose. The passage shows how both John and Jesus are ultimately rejected by "the people of this generation."[10] As John preached the need for repentance (sing a dirge) and Jesus associated himself with tax collectors and sinners (for his attendance at meals with sinners), their ministries are scorned by those who reject God's purposes since John is considered as "one with a demon" and Jesus as "a glutton" (7:33–34). This passage ends with Jesus giving an aphorism that states, "Wisdom is justified by all her children." This aphorism relates to the preceding material. There is an inverted parallelism where Wisdom (7:35) is identified with God (7:29) and wisdom's children (7:35) are equated with the crowd of people (7:29), including the tax collectors who "justify God." In other words, as the crowds justified God through accepting John's baptism (7:29), Wisdom is justified by his children, meaning those who respond positively to John and Jesus's ministry and purpose.[11]

This passage leads to the episode of Jesus's encounter with Simon the Pharisee and the sinful woman (7:36–50).[12] This story gives an example

---

9. Barrett, "Justification," 118.

10. The "people of this generation" alludes to the portrayal of the people of God as stubborn, stiff-necked, and rebellious; Exod 32:9; 33:3, 5; Deut 10:16; Acts 7:51–53; cf. Ezek 2 in Green, *Gospel of Luke*, 302.

11. Green, *Gospel of Luke*, 304, charts the inverted parallelism here with verses 29 and 35 set in a chiastic structure: All the people who heard this justified God. Wisdom is justified by all her children.

12. Bock, *Luke 9:51—24:53*, 692, notes that the form of the narrative is complex as it combines pronouncement with a parable. Ultimately, he calls it a "gift" story because Jesus gives the woman a gift of a confirmation of her forgiveness.

of those who justify God (accept God's purposes) and are not offended or scandalized by Jesus, and those who have rejected God's purposes.[13] In this account, Jesus is at the home of a Pharisee as an invited guest when a woman who is known as a sinner comes in and performs actions that show humility and a high emotional devotion to Jesus. She comes to anoint Jesus's feet with expensive ointment in an alabaster jar. But before she anoints Jesus, she weeps and wipes with her hair the tears that wet Jesus's feet and then kisses them. She then finally anoints his feet with oil (7:36–38).[14] Simon the host Pharisee questions in his mind the appropriateness of Jesus's association with this sinner (7:39). Jesus responds with a parable about two people with cancelled debts (7:40–42). Afterwards he explains the significance of this parable to what the woman did (7:44–46). The woman out of a love that is borne of forgiveness loves Jesus much through her actions. Barrett rightly asserts that forgiveness has been given previously to the woman prior to her appearance in the story even if this is not explicitly stated by the narrative. The major reason for this is Jesus's statement about the motivation of her great love in 7:43 within the parable, and in 7:47.[15] She represents the first debtor in the parable. Simon the Pharisee, who represented the second debtor, did not recognize his need for forgiveness and he did not love much, especially as he did not do acts of hospitality for Jesus (e.g., no water for his feet, no kiss, no anointing). Jesus by his word then announces eschatological forgiveness for the woman's sins, even as others questioned his prerogative to forgive sins (7:48–50). Jesus drives his point home by affirming her faith (7:50).

The contrast between the woman and the Pharisee coheres with the contrast between the temple tax collector and the Pharisee in 18:9–14. In 7:36–50, the sinner justifies God (i.e., accepted God's purpose and judgment), which coheres to how the temple tax collector who is a sinner submits

---

13. Barrett, "Justification," 120, 122.

14. Per Green, *Gospel of Luke*, 313, the woman's actions are considered extravagant and humbling. She goes above what is required. Instead of providing water for Jesus's feet, she provides her tears. Instead of kissing him on the cheek or hand, she kisses his feet. Finally, she anoints not Jesus's head but his feet with costly perfume. All the actions are done on the most unclean part of the body, which makes it quite a humbling act.

15. Barrett, "Justification," 121–22. Also, Darr remarks: "Jesus's parable (vss. 41–42), his remarks to the Pharisee, and the syntax of his references to the woman's forgiveness, all imply that she was forgiven prior to her appearance in Simon's house; her ministrations to Jesus would thus seem to be a consequence rather than a cause of her pardon." Darr, *Character Building*, 19. See a list of other scholars who assert that the woman already has received forgiveness before her actions in Barrett, "Justification," 121.

COHERENCE OF JUSTIFICATION WITH THE LUKAN TRADITION (L)

himself to God's mercy and judgment (18:13). The specific actions of the humble and very devoted woman cohere with the actions of the likewise humble and devoted temple tax collector. In addition, Simon the Pharisee, who represents those who rejected God's purposes, coheres with the self-righteous temple Pharisee who was not justified by God (18:14).

To be clear, there is a distinction between justifying God and justifying oneself before God. Again, in this pericope, "justifying God" is accepting God's purpose and judgment. This notion is demonstrated by the ones who were baptized by John because they receive and vindicate his ministry as they undergo his baptism and the corresponding repentance associated with it. The same notion applies to the sinful woman who demonstrated acceptance of God by receiving God's forgiveness, which resulted in her ability to love much due to the experience of being forgiven. Likewise, this notion coheres with the temple tax collector who humbly opens himself to God and submits himself to God's mercy. All of them look to God and humbly accept God's intentions and purposes. On the other hand, "justifying oneself" represents those who do not justify God, which means they do not accept God's purposes and judgment. In this pericope that concept applies to the Pharisees and lawyers who did not accept Jesus's ministry and John's baptism and, therefore, did not repent (7:29). This idea also applies to Simon the Pharisee who considered himself above the woman (7:39) as he was unable to see himself as a sinner. He was not able to follow God's command to love not only the woman but also Jesus (7:44–46). He was blind to the possibility that he was not right with God. Simon's character coheres with the temple Pharisee who trusted in himself as righteous and disdained others (18:9–14). The temple Pharisee was also unable to see himself as a sinner and believed he was right with God even if he was not. All of them, in effect, really reject God's purposes and intentions, and instead try to make themselves right, which effectively means they justify themselves.

Also, the notions of "justifying God" and "justifying oneself" are ultimately different from "being justified by God." Being justified or being made right with God is only possible through God's declaration and action. It is God's granting the status of being "righteous" to a sinner or one in need of God's restoration who humbly looks to God and God's mercy. The woman is a recipient of God's grace despite being clearly characterized as undeserving (7:39). In this pericope, the woman who was a sinner was exalted by Jesus and given forgiveness and restoration by God.

In being justified by God, the woman is granted by God a new status of "righteousness." The granting of this new status to the woman happened prior to her being at Simon's house. Therefore, Jesus's comments in 7:48, 50 are not really necessary for the woman as she has already been forgiven and has been acting based on her new status. However, others like Simon, only recognize her as a sinner, so Jesus's declaration suggests that his main concern is the restoration of the woman to the community of God.[16] His declaration, which is meant towards the people in Simon's house, is still intended to grant restoration and reconciliation of the woman to the greater society. Thus, Jesus's comments are not just reminders of the woman's new status but are also meant to effect recognition and acceptance of the woman into full social reconciliation.

The theme of salvation, which is an aspect of 18:9–14, is depicted and characterized by the emphasis on the forgiveness of sins and the restoration it brings (7:47–48).[17] Salvation is also highlighted in Jesus's statement that the woman's faith has saved her (σέσωκέν). She stands accepted before God. This announcement is usually reserved for the conclusion of miracles for healing (8:48; 18:42; 17:19). The language of salvation used here is not limited to "spiritual" well-being or physical well-being only, but it speaks of a restoration to wholeness.[18]

Repentance and faith also figure prominently in this passage. In 7:18–35, repentance is featured in the sense that those who accept John's baptism accept a baptism of repentance (3:3). Refusal to be baptized is refusal to repent and accept God's purpose (7:30). Faith is demonstrated here by the woman as she embraces Jesus's ministry. She and the crowd, including tax collectors (7:29), are examples of those who are blessed as they are not offended by Jesus but are instead drawn to him. The woman's faith is made evident by her works. Her response of faith came before her presence in the meal. It is a faith expressing itself in extraordinary love, which motivates her response. As a result, Jesus makes the confirming statement by noting that her faith has saved her (7:50). She is truly an example of Wisdom's child who vindicates God through her faith and repentance (7:35).

---

16. Green, *Gospel of Luke*, 314.

17. Salvation is tied to the forgiveness of sins (Acts 3:19, 26; 5:31; 10:43; 13:38; 22:16; 26:18).

18. Green, *Gospel of Luke*, 314.

Eschatological forgiveness is expressed by Jesus's words for the woman in 7:48.[19] Her forgiven status confirms the fact that she is greater than John as one who is "in the kingdom" (7:28–29). The forgiveness given her coheres with the eschatological forgiveness granted to the temple tax collector who is declared "justified" (18:14). Their eschatological fate is the same although expressed in different words. The motif of reversal, present in 18:9–14, is also evident here. Explicit in this regard is the specific comment by Jesus regarding how the least in the kingdom of God is greater than even John who is deemed "more than a prophet" and is greater than any human being (7:28). It is the "least" who have been the focus of Jesus's saving activity (the blind, lame, leprous, deaf, dead, poor—7:22). In effect, the greatest are those who are not offended by Jesus (7:23) or are responsive to Jesus's and John's ministry (7:35), or accept God's purposes (7:28–29), who will experience eschatological blessing (7:23), such as the woman who demonstrated her extraordinary actions in front of a scandalized meal host.

Special Lukan Parables

Luke 10:25–37

Before looking at the parable's key features and themes, it is important to address briefly the issue of the passage's overall unity. In terms of the major components of the passage, the story of the good Samaritan itself (10:30–35) is preceded by a dialogue between Jesus and the lawyer concerning eternal life and the love command. This dialogue continues in 10:36–37 after the story. The preceding conversation between Jesus and the lawyer has parallels with Matt 22:34–40 and Mark 12:28–34. Therefore, Luke may have joined two originally separate narratives. However, for a few reasons, this study takes the position that 10:25–37 is a unity in its present form. The dialogue does not have much in common with its alleged parallels in Matthew and Mark other than the use of the love commands. If the love command is central to Jesus's teaching, it makes sense for Jesus to teach it more than once in different settings. In addition, if the

---

19. Regarding Jesus's words of eschatological forgiveness, Nolland comments, "In the pericope already the connection is drawn between the woman's forgiveness and Jesus and his coming. Now this connection becomes explicit by means of Jesus' authoritative word: it is Jesus who brings the eschatological forgiveness of God." Nolland, *Luke 1–9:20*, 359.

Lukan evangelist is dependent on Mark, he would not likely have a lawyer speak Jesus's words in the story.[20]

This parable has been in the past compared with the parable of the Pharisee and tax collector. Mikeal C. Parsons, who assumes that Luke's travel narrative is chiastic, assigns the two parables as counterparts to one another. He noted the following similarities: (1) the negative depiction of the religious establishment; (2) the explicit identification of the religious leaders (Priest/Levite; Pharisee), which is "unparalleled" in other parables in Luke; (3) the unlikely hero as the protagonist; (4) the verbal connection between them due to the use of δικαιόω (10:29 concerning the lawyer's desire to justify himself; 18:14—being justified by God); and, (5) the conceptual link of mercy (the good Samaritan's actions and the tax collector's prayer).[21] Other comparisons have been made also with the rich young ruler (18:18–30) and the healing of Bartimaeus (18:35–43).[22]

Luke 10:25–37 is located at the end of a larger narrative that starts with the mission of the seventy-two (10:1–20) and its significance (10:21–24).[23] As the parable is part of an overall narrative structure, it is again important to consider the significance of the wider context to identify the relevant themes and motifs of the parable appropriately. There are several themes and motifs that bring these passages together as a coherent pericope. Within these themes and motifs are also the themes and motifs that cohere with the notion of justification in the Pharisee and tax collector.

The first notable theme is eschatological salvation/judgment in the kingdom. This theme is evident from the preparation and sending of the seventy-two in various towns with their mission of healing and proclaiming the nearness of the kingdom of God (10:1–9) and the resulting reception or rejection of the missionaries and their message (10:8–12). Eschatological salvation is granted to those who receive them and judgment to those

---

20. Young, *Parables*, 104. In addition, Snodgrass notes that 10:25–37 "fit set phrases of Jewish scholarly debate, and both the narrative setting and the parable allude to Lev 18:5 (Luke 10:28, 37), a crucial verse in Jewish views of the Law, and may well reflect prior debates about the passage." Snodgrass, *Stories*, 349. See his notes in Snodgrass, *Stories*, 699n95. See also Blomberg, *Interpreting the Parables*, 230–31, for another argument that supports regarding the context and the parable as a unity.

21. Parsons, "Landmarks," 40.

22. Bailey, *Poet and Peasant*, 80–82; Talbert, *Reading Luke*, 111–12; Van Elderen, "Another Look," 109–19.

23. Green, *Gospel of Luke*, 425. The lawyer suddenly comes up to test Jesus while he was addressing the disciples privately. Therefore, this passage appears as a narrative interruption.

who do not. Receiving the disciples corresponds to receiving Jesus and ultimately God who sent Jesus (10:16). Eschatological salvation is also the concern during the introduction of the parable as expressed by the lawyer's question about gaining eternal life (10:25). This topic is the main concern that the parable of the good Samaritan answers. This concern for salvation coheres with the Pharisee and tax collector in which salvation is reflected in Jesus's declaration of who is justified (and eschatologically exalted) and judgment for the one who is not (18:14). It coheres also with the parable of the wedding feast with its declaration of the salvation of those who accept the invitation to the banquet and into the resurrection of the just (14:14) and judgment for those that did not (14:11).

A second theme is eschatological contest. Behind the mission of proclaiming the kingdom of God and eliciting responses to its coming is a cosmic contest between the seventy-two missionaries and the forces of evil (Satan, the demons, the enemy, the spirits). The actual battle is not depicted in the story, but the result of the encounters prompts joyous remarks from the disciples with how the demons submit to them in Jesus's name (10:17). Under Jesus's authority they are victorious against the evil forces that will ultimately fail (10:18–19). This conflict between the dark spirits and the seventy-two speaks to the parable's own eschatological contest between the lawyer and Jesus. This contest is initiated by the lawyer who challenges Jesus with a question to test him. This conflict with the motif of testing is also memorably expressed in Jesus's time of testing (against Satan) in the wilderness (4:1–13), and in Jesus's trials later in the passion narrative. This theme of contest also coheres with the contest between the unjust judge and the widow (18:1–8), and between the Pharisee and tax collector (18:9–14). For the good Samaritan, this theme of contest is not only between the lawyer and Jesus but also between the Samaritan and the priest/Levite.

With regards to characterization, the lawyer's desire to justify himself coheres with the Pharisees who justify themselves before men (16:15), and the temple Pharisee who trusted in his own righteousness (18:9, 11–12). Specifically, in this pericope, what it means for the lawyer to justify himself is his initial refusal of the standard of God's purpose in the law. While he acknowledges Lev 19:18 as a summary of the law, his love for his neighbor is limited or qualified.[24] His love for neighbor does not include

---

24. Green, *Gospel of Luke*, 428–29 states that there was an ambiguity attached to Lev 19:18 in the Second Temple Judaism context. Originally this law means love for fellow Israelites and resident aliens (19:33–34). He mentions that the entry of the Roman occupation and Hellenistic imperialism muddied the perspective of who can be considered

those considered as outcasts or even enemies such as the Samaritans, but for Jesus, a neighbor is anyone, even a supposed enemy, who requires his love.[25] In other words, this love is extended even towards those who are undeserving of God's grace. Likewise, the temple Pharisee's love, in his self-righteousness, is also limited. His disdaining of others he considers as unrighteous and his blindness of his own sin coheres with the lawyer's inadequate treatment of the love command.

Also, within this parable is the motif of reversal that can be seen in several levels. First, the reversal of the expected actions by the Samaritan helped the unfortunate man and the neglect of the priest/Levite who both passed him by. Although no motivation is indicated as to why both the priest and Levite did not help the man in need, they do not have any reasonable cause to pass him by.[26] The expectation is that they would have helped him.[27] Instead, the Samaritan, motivated by compassion, decides to help in a comprehensive manner.[28] Therefore, the unworthy social outcast helps the needy man and exhibits what is needed to gain eternal life while the priest/Levite did not.[29] There is also the motif of reversal between the self-justifying lawyer and the Samaritan whose actions portray someone who follows God's law of love and inherits eternal life. Finally, there is the reversal between Jesus and the lawyer. The content of the lawyer's question about the identity of the neighbor assumes a certain qualification when it

---

as a "neighbor."

25. Kingsbury, *Conflict*, 92.

26. No real motivation to let him die; ritual purity does not excuse helping (Luke 6:1–5; 6:6–11).

27. Snodgrass mentions two beliefs: First, "Jews were required on religious grounds to bury a neglected corpse. Even though a high priest or a Nazarite was not to contract uncleanness from the body of a dead relative, they could do so—or were expected to do so—from a neglected corpse. In fact, texts debate which of them should contract defilement first to bury a neglected corpse. Second, at least for most Jews, nothing—not even purity laws—legitimately stood in the way of saving a life. Laws were suspended when life was endangered." Snodgrass, *Stories*, 355. For other sources that support these beliefs see Snodgrass, *Stories*, 703n130, 131.

28. Green notes the risky nature of the Samaritan's compassion whose actions include stopping on the road to Jericho, not knowing the person who was robbed, executing generosity from his own money and making arrangements at an inn, which is a place where he could be potentially exposed to extortion from the innkeeper. Green, *Gospel of Luke*, 432. Also see Bock, *Luke 9:51—24:53*, 1032–34.

29. Green states that not only is the Samaritan an outcast (similar to a "sinner") he is also not presented as a holy man (but most likely a traveling merchant) in contrast with the priest and Levite who were on their way back from Jerusalem. Green, *Gospel of Luke*, 431.

comes to the recipient of the commandment of love, but Jesus's parable and ending comment makes a "focal shift" from the identity of the neighbor to the actions of the true neighbor. From someone who is trying to justify himself, the lawyer becomes the one who is suddenly put to the test, which is contrary to his initial intention. In other words, he goes from justifying himself, which in this case means asserting his own status on his erroneous interpretation of the law for the broader purpose of making himself right in the eyes of others to needing justification from God, which means needing to be made right by God, which is something only God can do. The parable does not resolve whether the lawyer's response is to continue to justify himself or if he follows the actions of neighborly love.

The motif of faith is not an emphasis in this parable. Doing God's word is the more predominant issue, especially with the numerous references to ποιέω (10:25, 28, 37—twice). "Doing God's word" is a response for which Jesus asks that coheres with other responses in other passages, such as giving full allegiance to Jesus (18:28) and eschatological perseverance and persistence (18:4–5, 8).

Overall, the themes and motifs of the good Samaritan display most of the related themes of justification as expressed in the parable of the Pharisee and tax collector with the exception of faith and repentance. Within the major themes in the good Samaritan of eschatological salvation, eschatological contest, and the hearing and doing God's word, there are related themes and motifs of reversal, and justification to the undeserving outcast. The combination of these related themes coheres with the notion of justification as presented in the parable of the Pharisee and tax collector.

Luke 14:7–14

The setting for the larger narrative of Luke 14:1–24 is a meal at the house of the ruler of the Pharisees during the Sabbath (14:1). There are three distinct events presented in this table fellowship setting in Luke 14:1–24, of which the second set of verses (14:7–14) is an L parable and the third event (14:15–24) is considered by this report as part of "Q." The whole narrative is taken up to aid in identifying the parable's relevant themes and motifs. The first story is the Sabbath healing of a man who had dropsy (14:1–6). This narrative displays the theme of confrontation/contest between Jesus and his opponents and demonstrates the power of restoration that Jesus brings. Under the watchful eyes of the Pharisees, Jesus heals a man who had dropsy who was somehow present in the house (14:1–4).[30] Jesus then confronts the Pharisees' apparent lack of approval of his action with a rationale that appeals to their own sense of how they would practice the Sabbath if their own domestic animals or children were in danger (14:5–6). In the end, the Pharisees remained silent with regards to Jesus's questions and his healing.[31] As none of them objects to his rationale, their silence shows the impact of Jesus's authority. He then uses this authority to teach beyond the issue of healing on a Sabbath.[32]

The account then moves on to the second event in the banquet. The theme of invitation is prominent in this event whether it speaks of what to do as someone who is invited or who to invite in someone's capacity as a host. Jesus notices how the guests looked to take the seats of honor around the table (14:7).[33] Jesus then uses a parable to address this behavior of those invited, advising them specifically to go against the common practice by

---

30. The rationale for the Pharisees being watchful of Jesus: to catch Jesus doing something wrong (see 6:7; 11:54). Per Green, Jesus may have been invited for various reasons, which include the following: (1) Jesus as a pilgrim was afforded hospitality on the Sabbath; (2) Jesus was a known and recognized teacher who had the status to be invited by the Pharisees; and, (3) Jesus was invited to be trapped, especially given the presence of the man with dropsy, who seemed out of place in the setting of the house of one of the leaders. Green, *Gospel of Luke*, 546. Green also notes that the metaphorical use of "dropsy" in ancient times was as a description for "money-lovers, the greedy, the rapacious—that is, for the persons who share the very condition for which the Pharisees are indicted in the Gospel of Luke (11:37–44; cf. 16:14)." Green, *Gospel of Luke*, 547. For him it means that the man with dropsy also represented the spiritual condition of the people around the table in this meal.

31. According to Bock, *Luke 9:51—24:53*, 1257, in 14:3–4, the scribes and the Pharisees were in a bind. If they approve of the healing, they believe that it brings into question their traditions and view of the Law with regards to the Sabbath. If they do not approve of the healing, it will show that they are against doing good and being compassionate even on the Sabbath. A third option for the silence would be that they could not object or they were astonished (20:26; Acts 11:18).

32. Green, *Gospel of Luke*, 549.

33. Regarding the ancient practices on table fellowship, Green writes, "This was a world in which social status and social stratification were vital considerations in the structuring of life, with one's status based on the social estimation of one's relative honor—that is, on the perception of those around a person regarding his prestige. For example, where one sat (was assigned or allowed to sit) at a meal vis-à-vis the host was a public advertisement of one's status; as a consequence, the matter of seating arrangements was carefully attended, and in this agonistic society, one might presume to claim a more honorable seat with the hope that it (and the honor that went with it) might be granted." Green, *Gospel of Luke*, 550.

seeking the lowest honored seats.³⁴ The objective of Jesus's advice is for them not to take the initiative in claiming honor and possibly encounter humiliation by being asked to move to a lower seat. Instead, they are to have their position be given to them by the host (14:8–10). The rationale for this logic is given in 14:11 in the form of a wisdom saying that highlights the theme of humility, which coheres with the saying in 18:14b. Jesus then turns to the host and gives him counsel regarding whom to invite when hosting a dinner or banquet. Instead of inviting people who can reciprocate, such as friends, family, or rich neighbors, he is to invite those who cannot pay him back, such as the poor, the maimed, the lame, and the blind (14:12–13).³⁵ In other words, he is supposed to give grace to people who are considered undeserving, especially as they are unable to reciprocate.

In telling the guests and the host this parable, Jesus is not simply giving them advice on how to prevent shame and embarrassment or how to be a more gracious host. How one responds to the aspect of invitation (either as a guest or host) coheres with the response and example shown by the temple Pharisee and tax collector (18:9–14). Those who are invited and pursue seats of honor will have a tendency towards self-exaltation, which coheres with the confidence shown by the example of the Pharisee in the temple (18:9). The motif of faith and repentance are not overtly present here. What is more emphasized is a stance of humility, illustrated in this narrative of Jesus's advice for invited people to seek the lowest place of honor at the table. The same posture of humility is also present in a host who invites people who cannot reciprocate. The ones who tend to choose places of honor will also tend not to invite as guests those rejected by society, such as the poor, the maimed, the lame, and the blind, but the ones who have humbled themselves can also invite the outcasts of society to

---

34. A "parable" here is a collection of sayings that contains admonition and proverbial counsel per Bock, *Luke 9:51—24:53*, 1261.

35. This admonition to invite those who cannot pay back contradicts the ethics of reciprocity or patronage. Per Green, "Because invitations served as currency in the marketplace of prestige and power, there is nothing extraordinary or particularly objectionable to the inclusion of one's social peers and family, persons from whom one could expect reciprocation." Green, *Gospel of Luke*, 552. Therefore, the powerful and privileged would not normally invite the poor or those of lower status to their meals as they could not reciprocate. Jesus's proposal calls for extending hospitality without any concern for reciprocity. Therefore, the hospitality he desires is motivated by generosity. See also, Bock, *Luke 9:51—24:53*, 1266. The payback for generosity instead will occur in the "resurrection of the righteous" (14:14).

their feast or banquet.[36] Ultimately, they will be exalted by God while those who exalt themselves will be left out of the meal altogether (in this case, the eschatological banquet).[37] The eschatological kingdom is in mind here given the setting of a marriage feast and the notion in 14:14 that the humble will be repaid through the "resurrection of the righteous" (ἀναστάσει τῶν δικαίων).[38] The guests (the invited) and hosts (the inviter) who humble themselves cohere with the humble tax collector who is declared "righteous" or "justified" (δεδικαιωμένος) in 18:14. In other words, God grants them restoration and salvation through entry into the kingdom. Therefore, the theme of salvation is likewise here as well.

Luke 15:1–32

Luke 15 is comprised of three parables linked together by a common context provided in 15:1–2. As the tax collectors and sinners were drawing closer to listen to him, the Pharisees and scribes were grumbling (διεγόγγυζον) that Jesus welcomed and dined with tax collectors and sinners.[39] In response to the Pharisees and scribes who challenged him in line with the theme of contest, Jesus presents three parables as a defense of his ministry towards these "sinners" (15:3).

The first two parables—the lost sheep (15:4–7) and the lost coin (15:8–10)—are similar in structure. However, the third parable is certainly linked with the other two as it shares with them certain themes and motifs, such as rejoicing, and a common general narrative progression from the loss of something (a sheep, coin, son) to its recovery, restoration, and the ensuing celebration and rejoicing. The motif of celebrating and rejoicing is further enhanced with the mention of the joy of the angels of God in one

---

36. Noel notes, "Choosing the lowest place at table, demeaning yourself, is like inviting the poor, the maimed, the lame, and the blind to your feast. These people, rejected by society, are precisely the ones ultimately invited to the feast in the parable of the Great Banquet. Those who choose places of honor tend also to ignore the poor and the outcasts. Those who humble themselves can also invite the poor to their tables." Noel, "Wedding Guest," 21.

37. Barrett, "Justification," 136.

38. Marriage feast represents the image of the kingdom feast, that is the heavenly feast provided and hosted by God (e.g., Isa 25:6; Rev 19:9).

39. Those who witnessed Jesus being welcomed by Zacchaeus in 19:7 likewise grumbled or complained (διεγόγγυζον).

COHERENCE OF JUSTIFICATION WITH THE LUKAN TRADITION (L)

sinner who repents (15:10), a repentance that is graphically displayed by the behavior of the prodigal son.

Like the tax collector in 18:14–15, it is the "tax collectors and sinners" in 15:1–2 who are the objects of God's mercy and salvation. There is symbolic identification of the lost sheep/coin with the sinner in 15:11–31.[40] All of them altogether point to the "tax collectors and sinners" who are coming near to listen to Jesus (15:1). The Pharisees and scribes who are grumbling (15:2), the elder brother who got angry at his brother's restoration (15:28), and the ninety-nine "righteous" persons who do not need repentance (15:7) cohere with the temple Pharisee who was an example of someone who trusts in himself as "righteous" and looks with contempt at others (18:9). Not realizing that they are lost, they do not consider themselves as such.

Also, in this parable, alongside the motif of celebration is the theme of salvation. At stake in the narrative is ultimately not the norms concerning table fellowship and how Jesus seriously deviates from them. It deals more with Jesus's mission to seek and save the lost (15:32; 19:10). Each pronouncement of recovering what was lost (15:7, 10, 32—especially as it refers to the son who is pronounced dead but came back to life) coheres with the declaration of righteousness to the temple tax collector (18:14). Salvation and restoration are pictured in detail with the parable of the prodigal son. The father, upon seeing him from a distance does not wait for him to come nearer but instead accepts his son out of compassion and welcomes him by running towards him, embracing him, and kissing him (15:20). Even before the son carries out his original intentions of telling his prepared speech, the father announces a celebration banquet for him (using a fatted calf) and restores him to the family through his words ("this son of mine was dead and is alive again"), and his orders to clothe him with the best robe, a ring, and sandals (15:21–24). Similar to what the shepherd and the woman did after finding the lost sheep and the lost coin, the father illustrates restoring and saving what is lost and announces a celebration because of his great joy (15:6, 9, 23, 24).

Another clear theme seen in these parables centers on repentance as explicitly mentioned in 15:7 and 15:10 and depicted by the prodigal son. The positive response of the prodigal son and the tax collectors and sinners as they gathered around Jesus (15:1) represent the restoration or

---

40. See Bock, *Luke 9:51—24:53*, 1301–05; Green, *Gospel of Luke*, 573.

recovery of what was lost.⁴¹ These are the ones who gain access to God's kingdom, which coheres with the temple tax collector's justification on account of his repentance. The notion of faith is not as prominent in these parables. However, the attitude of humility is on display by the prodigal son as he illustrates it through his openness in being at the mercy of his father. He shows this humility most especially in pleading and expressing his desire to come back and not be treated as a son by the father but instead be treated as a mere hired hand.⁴² This depiction coheres with the temple tax collector's posture of humility through his plea of mercy and physical actions of beating on his chest.

Finally, eschatological themes are predominant in this passage. The motif of eating, inviting people to share in joy, the banquet motif (as exhibited by a full-blown banquet with the best meat and numerous guests) point to the occasion of being accepted in God's eschatological kingdom (14:15–24). The notion of Jesus welcoming (inviting) those who are not normally invited to the table, in other words, those who are undeserving or unworthy (15:1–2), coheres well with Luke 14 when Jesus exhorts people to welcome "the poor, the crippled, the lame and the blind" (14:13, 21). It also coheres with Jesus's stance in dining with the tax collector Zacchaeus (19:6–7). The parable has the motif of reversal—the lost younger brother who is thought to be the outsider is now in the kingdom while the older brother who stayed and does his duty faithfully but disdains his younger brother and is too angry to join the family is literally out of the joyful celebration by his own doing.⁴³ Again, the one who deems himself righteous and disdains the other is actually the one who is considered the outsider although in this case the parable is left open-ended in terms of whether the older brother will repent and join the father in celebration or not.

Luke 16:14–31

The parable of the rich man and Lazarus (16:19–31) comes at the end of a unit of text that begins with the Pharisees issuing an initial challenge to Jesus's authority (16:14). The Pharisees, who are referred to in this chapter as "lovers of money," interrupt Jesus in reaction to Jesus's teachings from the

---

41. See Bock, *Luke 9:51—24:53*, 1320-21; Green, *Gospel of Luke*, 569.

42. Bock, *Luke 9:51—24:53*, 1313; the younger son wants to be the lowest of the low in his request.

43. Bock, *Luke 9:51—24:53*, 1313.

COHERENCE OF JUSTIFICATION WITH THE LUKAN TRADITION (L)

previous parable (16:1–9) and some subsequent instructions on wealth and allegiance to God (16:10–13). This parable comes as part of Jesus's response to the Pharisees' challenge. Since the parable is just part of a broader narrative context, the themes and motifs depicted in the first part (i.e., 16:14–18) help highlight the parable's relevant themes and motifs.

Numerous diverse themes have been historically associated with this parable. For Bock, the themes are "(1) the treatment of people in this life, (2) the consequences of being callous to the needs of the poor, (3) the permanence of judgment, and (4) the inability of a person not hearing the Scripture to respond to God's action in the world—even miraculous action." He states that the major point is "once one dies, one's fate is sealed." Those "who seem poor now will experience the riches of heaven later. It is not necessarily the case that the rich are blessed, and the poor are not."[44] Blomberg writes that the themes here are "(1) Like Lazarus, those whom God helps will be borne after their death into God's presence, (2) Like the rich man, the unrepentant will experience irreversible punishment, (3) Through Abraham, Moses and the prophets, God reveals himself and his will so that none who neglect it can legitimately protest their subsequent fate."[45] Snodgrass states that the themes include a warning to the wealthy with respect to the neglect of the poor, the need for repentance especially in the presence of the kingdom, which means using wealth appropriately and promoting justice: in short, the judgment for the use of wealth and the sufficiency of Scriptures.[46] Green states that the parable concerns (1) wealth and its use, and (2) the relevance of the law. He further states that the parable is an indictment or denunciation of the rich who disregarded the Scriptures concerning the will of God for the poor.[47] Johnson states that the theme for 16:19–26 is the reversal of fortunes as an expression of the Beatitudes and woes in 6:20, 24. The second theme in the polemical appendix of the parable (16:27–31) tells us that it is a parable of rejection to those who do not follow the law with regards to taking care of the poor.[48] Outi Lehtipuu considers the theme of focus of the story as "the reversal of fate of the rich man and poor man and on the call to repentance according to Moses and

---

44. Bock, *Luke 9:51—24:53*, 1361–62.
45. Blomberg, *Interpreting the Parables*, 206.
46. Snodgrass, *Stories*, 429, 432–33.
47. Green, *Gospel of Luke*, 599–610.
48. Johnson, *Gospel of Luke*, 254–56.

the prophets."⁴⁹ Stephen I. Wright asserts that the parable has a prophetic message of denunciation and warning to those who allow injustice and a wisdom message about obeying and listening to the law and the prophets. The rich are called to obey, and the poor are called to be encouraged and put their hope in God.⁵⁰ For Hultgren the most relevant theme and point is that the parable is a warning to those who still have time to repent and do the will of God as revealed by the law and the prophets.⁵¹

For both the parable and its surrounding context, the motif of contest is evident.⁵² The contest or conflict between the Pharisees and Jesus is initiated by the Pharisees when they reacted to Jesus's teaching by ridiculing or sneering at him (ἐξεμυκτήριζον αὐτόν).⁵³ The narrative aside, which mentions the Pharisees as "lovers of money," does not point to the Pharisees as necessarily wealthy. In Greco-Roman and Hellenistic Jewish culture, a phrase such as "lovers of money" is used in association with self-glorification that is polemically applied to false teachers and prophets.⁵⁴ In a culture where one's amount of wealth measures one's ability to use it to acquire status or honor, those who excessively put their interest in their honor and status tend to disregard using wealth for the poor or for God's purposes.⁵⁵ Therefore, they are deemed to be "justifying" themselves before others (16:15) in the sense that they have the characteristic or attitude of self-glorification or self-exaltation and they strive to make themselves right in the sight of or before men and rejecting God's purpose for themselves. These general characteristics cohere with the attitude of self-righteousness of the temple Pharisee (18:9–14). In response, Jesus gives them a warning on the use of wealth, the importance and appropriate treatment of the law, and the eschatological consequences involved in the response to these exhortations. The parable itself also displays the motif of contest but it is now between the rich man and Lazarus. The rich man as portrayed

---

49. Lehtipuu, *Afterlife Imagery*, 6, 41.

50. Wright, "Poverty and Riches," 232.

51. Hultgren, *Parables*, 115.

52. Green, *Gospel of Luke*, 601. Bock calls the context of 16:14–18 "abbreviated controversy account." Bock, *Luke 9:51—24:53*, 1348.

53. The only other time ἐκμυκτηρίζω appears is when the rulers "scoffed" at Jesus during the crucifixion (Luke 23:35).

54. See Green, *Gospel of Luke*, 601; Johnson, *Sharing Possessions*, 249–50; Moxnes, *Economy*, 6–9. Also cf. Acts 20:33–34; 1 Thess 2:5–6; 1 Tim 6:5; 2 Tim 3:2; Tit 1:11; Philo *Praem.* 127; Dio Chrysostom, *Disc.* 32:9–11; 35:1; 54:1–3; Lucian *Tim.* 56.

55. Green, *Gospel of Luke*, 601. Also see Luke 11:39–43 and 14:7–14.

in both the opening scene of the parable and in the ensuing dialogue with Abraham "justifies" himself in the role as the "lover of money" (as an illustration of 16:14–15) specifically in his use of wealth and his lack of love for his neighbor, resulting in neglect for the poor in opposition to God's purposes. This notion is illustrated in the first scene, which depicts the rich man in pure opulence but is somehow able to live alongside Lazarus who was in deep need at his gate.[56] This lack of love is opposite the response God calls for in the parable of the good Samaritan in how one should treat one's neighbor. Also, many OT passages urge the care of the most vulnerable members of society such as the poor, the widows, the orphans, and aliens.[57] The rich man in the parable not only justifies himself by not following the OT laws of caring for the poor (in effect, not following God's purposes), but he also continues to justify himself in the afterlife in his discussion with Abraham (16:24–31). In his question and answer exchange with Abraham, he continues to display self-justification for his conduct during his earthly life through his series of appeals where he even asks for the help of both Abraham and Lazarus despite ignoring him before they died (16:24, 27–28, 30). Self-justification in this sense is exhibited in the sense of still seeing himself as above Lazarus whom the rich man presumes can do an errand on his part.[58] In terms of characterization, the presence of Abraham also serves as a foil in the story with reference to the rich man. That is the case because Abraham was a rich man who was a prime example of hospitality, unlike the man in the parable. Abraham is not just a pertinent figure that traditions portray in afterlife stories.[59] Abraham was a rich man who owned plenty of livestock, silver, and gold (Gen 13:2), as well as many horses and the services of trained men (Gen 14:13–24). He is an example of a rich man who was righteous and known for hospitality as he welcomed everyone rich or poor, the crippled, the helpless, his

---

56. The presence of a "gate" in Luke 16:20, is an echo of Amos 5:11–15, especially Amos 5:12, 15 where the poor is "turned aside at the gate." In these verses, the prophet Amos accuses the wealthy and powerful members of the community that are taking advantage of the poor (5:11) and needy (5:12). The gate is normally the location where the legal process takes place and justice is served. But in this case, Amos refers to a time of judgment in 5:13. He exhorts the wealthy and powerful to seek the Lord and establish justice at the gate (5:15). The parable, likewise, displays the image of an injustice happening at the rich man's gate.

57. Cf. Exod 22:21–22; 23:9; Lev 19:9–10; 19:33; 23:22; Deut 10:17–19; 15:7; 24:15, 17–18; 19–21; Isa 58:7, 10; Zech 7:9–10.

58. Green, *Gospel of Luke*, 608.

59. Such as Abraham's heavenly journeys in T. Ab. 10–15 and Apoc. Ab. 9–32.

friends, or strangers.⁶⁰ The characterization of Lazarus in the story is not as detailed as the rich man. Clearly, Lazarus is not a sinner. However, his lowly and humble character counts him among those who are not perceived to be righteous, such as those of low socio-religious status including characters such as the crippled, lame, and blind, and who need forgiveness and restoration. In other words, he belongs to the category of those who are unworthy or undeserving of grace. His character coheres with others in Luke who are recipients of God's justification, salvation, or restoration such as the temple tax collector (18:9–14), the widow (18:1–8), the blind beggar (18:35–43), and the prodigal son (15:11–32). Lazarus's name means "God has helped" and is derived from the Hebrew name El-azar. The poor man has an identity as someone whom God helps given that he is dependent on God and is eventually elevated from his position of destitute poverty to an intimate position near Abraham.⁶¹

The motif of reversal prominent in this parable is aided by the illustrative depiction of the stark contrast of the rich man and Lazarus on earth and their reversal of fortunes after their deaths. The contrast is done in a very comprehensive sense through spatial, social, architectural, afterlife destination, temporal, clothing, and other aspects. It is contrast in a spatial sense as the rich man is on one side of the gate and Lazarus at the other, as well as the rich man on the far and bad side of Hades and Lazarus at Abraham's bosom. It is a contrast in a social sense as the rich man lived

---

60. T. Ab. A 1:1–25; 2:2; 4:6; 17:7; 20:15; B 4:10; 13:5. Abraham receives three men, washes their feet, provides food and clothing and then sends them on their way (Gen 18:4–8). According to Sandmel, *Philo's Place*, 84, citing 'Abot R. Nat. 13, there is also a tradition that mentions Abraham's hospitality exceeding that of Job's. While Job only welcomed strangers when they passed by, Abraham, just recently circumcised, looked for strangers as he put himself next to his tent.

61. According to Stegemann and Stegemann, *Jesus Movement*, 89–92, there is a distinction between those who are relatively poor and those who are absolutely impoverished such as the character of Lazarus in this parable. Those who are relatively poor could still meet the basic needs of life, while the ones who are absolutely poor include those who do not even have enough to live, meaning, those who are hungry and thirsty, with rags for clothes, homeless and hopeless. In addition to beggars, the impoverished people also include ones who were chronically ill or physically disabled like the blind, the lame and the lepers. Rohrbaugh, *Biblical Interpreter*, 77, argues that Lazarus did not belong to the urban poor who make up the majority of the city population (e.g., merchants, artisans, craftsmen), nor did he belong with those he classified as rural poor (e.g., peasants), but he belonged to a small group of outcasts that inhabit gutters of every ancient city. He also states that there are those who see the absolutely poor people as an outcast class and were in their specific condition because God was punishing them for their sins.

COHERENCE OF JUSTIFICATION WITH THE LUKAN TRADITION (L)

joyously in splendor (16:19), celebrating and eating (cf. 12:19; 15:23). This indicates his status of being in the wealthy class. On the other hand, Lazarus is not invited to the meals, and longs to be fed by what falls from the rich man's table (16:21), a description of someone from a totally different social class.[62] In terms of architecture, the presence of a gate indicates that the rich man possessed an estate as opposed to Lazarus who was ἐβέβλητο ("thrown") at the gate, which possibly makes him a cripple (Matt 8:6; 9:2). In terms of their location in Hades, the rich man is far away and in torment from a flame (16:23–24), while Lazarus being at Abraham's bosom is in a position of honor (16:23).[63] At a temporal level, in the duration of the rich man's life he received good things (16:25), which means he was always materially blessed. On the other hand, in the duration of the poor man's life, he received bad things (16:25). In Hades, the rich man lives in agony from the fire for the duration of time there, while the poor man is comfortable (16:23). In terms of clothing, the rich man wore purple and fine linen (16:19).[64] In contrast, Lazarus's clothes were not mentioned and instead he was covered with sores (16:20), which the dogs licked (16:21).[65] Definitely, the whole parable's picture presentation coheres with the notion of reversal that portrays the humble being exalted and those who exalted themselves being humbled (14:11; 18:14).

The afterlife scene, which is an integral part of the motif of reversal, also highlights the eschatological underpinnings present in this parable. The coming kingdom is marked by a divine reversal between the rich and the poor. Jesus inaugurated the kingdom of God in his announcement that he will preach the gospel to the poor (4:18). The beatitudes and woes (6:20–26) portray blessings that come to the poor and discomfort to those who are rich (6:24) and well fed (6:25). In the Song of Mary (1:46–55), the humble are exalted (1:52), and God filled the hungry with good things and

---

62. Not to mention that he had sores (16:21), which is indicative of his status of being unclean.

63. Resseguie, *Spiritual Landscape*, 107.

64. Per Hamel, *Poverty and Charity*, 65–65, Tyrian purple, made from mollusks, and fine linen called *byssus*, were very expensive. Those who were dressed in splendid clothing and lived in luxury were from the royal palaces (7:25). In addition, according to Resseguie, *Narrative Criticism*, 108, the rich garb also represents spiritual deficiency as it characterizes his preoccupation with material excess.

65. Per Green, *Gospel of Luke*, 606, dogs hunt around for refuse in the city. Also, in Isa 56:10–12, dogs are equated to unjust rulers who are not satisfied and possess unjust gains.

sent away the rich empty-handed (1:53). The poor are invited to the eschatological banquet (14:21). Therefore, the scene's eschatological tones bring together the notion of the promised rewards of salvation and restoration for the poor and the humbling of the rich.[66]

The afterlife scene not only provides an eschatological backdrop to the parable. The primary purpose of it in the parable is as a paraenetic tool.[67] The afterlife scene's primary purpose is not to explain life after death or the intermediate state.[68] Instead it intends to give a sense of urgency and exhortation to the rich and a sense of peace and perseverance to the lowly. That brings up the importance of the motif of hearing Moses and the prophets, which is explicitly mentioned in the parable twice (16:29, 31), making it also a motif of emphasis.[69] This motif of hearing is supported narratively in Luke-Acts. For example, Jesus considers as blessed those who hear the word of God and observe it (11:28). In the parable of the sower (8:4–15), the seed in the good soil are said to be the ones that have heard the word in an honest and good heart and hold fast to it and bear fruit with perseverance. Jesus also says that everyone who hears his words and acts on them is like someone who built a house on a good foundation (6:46–49). Jesus also mentions in the immediate context of this parable the law and the prophets and affirms their continuing validity (16:16–17).

The motif of hearing in this parable is also a call for a response of repentance. In addition, there is a specific verbal reference for repentance in 16:30. For this parable, repenting is about taking seriously injustices, especially in this case, the impoverished living alongside the wealthy. This kind of repentance coheres with other instances where the repentance requires a radical renunciation of one's possessions (e.g., 5:11, 28; 12:32–34; 18:22). Therefore, the important motif of hearing the word of God highlights the motif of repentance as well in this parable. Finally, for this parable, the

---

66. Lehtipuu, *Afterlife Imagery*, 165–66.

67. Lehtipuu, *Afterlife Imagery*, 163–70.

68. Per Bock, *Luke 9:51—24:54*, 1363. In addition, Blomberg, *Interpreting the Parables*, 206–7, comments that there are scholars who try to read too much out of this parable because there are not a lot of passages that speak about the afterlife. See also Lehtipuu, *Afterlife Imagery*, 4; Hultgren, *Parables*, 113; Snodgrass, *Stories*, 427; Green, *Gospel of Luke*, 607.

69. The heightening of the appeals the rich man made is met with heightening negative answers from Abraham until Abraham gives him the answer of hearing Moses and the prophets. This also supports Jesus's emphasis on the authority of the law in the overall context of the passage that the parable supports (16:16–18).

COHERENCE OF JUSTIFICATION WITH THE LUKAN TRADITION (L)

motif of faith is not at the forefront as the notion of repentance seems to have the greater emphasis.

Overall, the parable of the rich man and Lazarus presents most of the related themes and motifs of justification in Luke 18:9–14. Its rich portrayal of eschatological reversal, salvation for the lowly, the importance of hearing and doing God's word as a response of repentance, these cohere with the related themes and motifs of justification in the parable of the Pharisee and tax collector.

Luke 18:1–8

Luke 18:1–8, on the surface, coheres with the parable of the Pharisee and tax collector with regards to the theme of prayer and the prominence of righteousness language consisting of the δικαιόω word group.[70] Also notable is the eschatological context preceding the parable. As Jesus is going on his way to Jerusalem (17:11), he heals ten lepers (17:12–19) and then responds to a question of the Pharisees concerning the arrival of the kingdom of God (17:20–21). He responds to them by saying that they should not expect any telltale signs or warning messages. Afterwards, Jesus then describes and instructs his disciples as to what to expect by mentioning the kingdom's sudden arrival by way of the Son of Man's coming (17:22). His response is an implicit call for the disciples to persevere in anticipation of its obvious coming (17:24) and the crisis that comes due to the Son of Man's suffering and rejection by his generation (17:25). In other words, it is an inherent call for perseverance and endurance for the eschatological coming kingdom.

The parable of the unjust judge reinforces this call for perseverance and endurance through the character of the persistent widow. This call is the eschatological background behind the need to pray and not lose heart (18:1).[71] This instruction plays a part in preparing the disciples to remain

---

70. ἀντίδικος ("opponent," v.3), ἀδικία ("unjust," v. 6), ἐκδικέω ("vindicate," vv. 3, 5), and ἐκδίκησις ("vindication," vv. 7, 8).

71. Infinitival use of Dei; Snodgrass writes, "Luke's introductory comment is not an encouragement to persistent prayer in general, an assumption often made because of the influence of 11:5–8, though the Unjust Judge must not be forced to conform to the earlier parable. Luke's concern in 18:1 is not prayer in general but praying and not becoming weary... with respect to the eschaton, the time when deliverance comes. This injunction to pray and not give up derives its significance from the context of the whole eschatological discourse, which began in 17:20." Snodgrass, *Stories*, 467.

steadfast despite the coming eschatological crisis. The widow is shown as someone who needs justice or vindication after being taken advantaged of (possibly financially) by an adversary or opponent.[72] She successfully persists in bringing her case before the judge, who seems more interested in his own convenience than providing justice as he does not fear God nor respect other people (18:4). Jesus calls the disciples to endurance by comparing the willingness of the judge to give justice with God's willingness to help his elect people (18:7). If an unjust judge is willing to give justice to a widow he does not care for out of a sense of his own convenience, how much more will God respond to his elect people who persist and remain steadfast?[73] The justice that God will grant the elect implies eschatological vindication.[74] Furthermore, God will grant this vindication quickly compared to the way the judge delayed for a while in giving it to the widow (18:4a).[75]

Significant coherences can be drawn from the characterization present in Luke 18:1–8 and in Luke 18:9–14. The motif of contest between "righteous" and "sinners" present between the Pharisee and the tax collector is also present here between the unjust judge (who may be considered an additional adversary) and the widow. The widow is not a sinner, but she is an outcast among society's weak and thus similar in a way to a sinner in the sense that she is in need of restoration. The judge exhibits contempt toward the widow whom he considers a mere nuisance (18:2, 4, 5). This attitude coheres well with the contempt the Pharisee shows toward the tax collector (18:9, 11, 13). Faith is present in the widow's perseverance and persistence

---

72. See Jeremias, *Parables*, 153; Snodgrass, *Stories*, 453; Marshall, *Gospel of Luke*, 672; Green notes, "Inasmuch as the ancient court system belonged to the world of men, the fact that this woman finds herself before the magistrate indicates that she has no kinsman to bring her case to court; the fact that she must do so continuously suggests that she lacks the economic resources to offer the appropriate bribe necessary for a swift settlement." Green, *Gospel of Luke*, 640. Bailey cites b. Sanh 4b: "An authorized scholar may decide money cases sitting alone." Bailey, *Through Peasant Eyes*, 150–52. Other kinds of cases need three judges.

73. From lesser to greater logic.

74. Marshall states that eschatological vindication is the intent here and not just "a purely this-worldly answer to prayer." Marshall, *Gospel of Luke*, 674.

75. Barrett notes, "Just as the judge was unable to endure the widow's persistence, God will not behave like the judge who endured the widow for a season (Luke 18:4a), rather he will act to vindicate his people quickly since he loves his elect. Their cries will be answered by God quickly and gladly. Though it seems God is delaying, his elect will soon experience vindication." Barrett, "Justification," 68. Bock outlines twelve possible interpretations of the second question "and will he delay over them" due to the use of the word μακροθυμεῖ. Bock, *Luke 9:51—24:53*, 1451–54.

in coming to the judge (18:4–5, 8). This faith coheres with the tax collector's implied faith in his humble cry for mercy (18:13).[76] The widow's faith is the kind that answers the Son of Man's search for faith on earth (18:8).[77] Both the widow and the tax collector receive "justification" when the widow was finally granted justice from the judge (18:5) and the tax collector went home justified by God (18:14a). Finally, eschatological elements in both parables cohere with one another. The humble widow is given vindication (in an eschatological sense), which coheres with the eschatological exaltation given to the tax collector who presents himself in humility.

Luke 19:1–10

This story comes near the end of the travel narrative and can be classified as a "pronouncement-story" due to the climax in 19:9.[78] It is about Jesus's encounter with a chief tax collector named Zacchaeus in the town of Jericho. The motif of "seeking" is present here, notably because of the verb "to seek" (ζητέω) which underscores his quest to see Jesus. This motif of quest coheres with comparable quest stories of characters who encountered difficulty such as the widow (18:3–4), the children (18:15), and the blind beggar (18:39).[79] Zacchaeus strives to see Jesus after becoming aware of his presence, but he could not because his short stature did not allow him to see through the crowd (19:1–3). To see him, he climbs up a tree (19:4). As Jesus passes by the tree, he calls Zacchaeus down and tells him that, by necessity, he will dine at his house (19:5). As Zacchaeus joyfully accepts this invitation (19:6), the crowds grumble over Jesus's choice to have fellowship with a "sinner" (19:7). After Zacchaeus pledges to give the poor and make restitution to those whom

---

76. Barrett, "Justification," 57.

77. Son of Man's search for faith is an allusion to the OT story of Noah then Lot (17:26–32). In the story of Noah, the Flood is preceded by a second fall in which humanity went in its own way and became wholly corrupt (Gen 6:9–13). People were doing routine things in their daily lives when destruction just suddenly came. However, because of their faith in God, Noah and his family were the only ones who did something and were spared (Gen 6:22). In the story of Lot, unrighteousness was ubiquitous in Sodom and Gomorrah (Gen 13:13). The cities were destroyed even as Abraham appealed to God on their behalf if there are any righteous people in them. Since the righteous could not be found, Sodom and Gomorrah were judged. Barrett, "Justification," 68.

78. See Fitzmyer, *Luke X–XXIV*, 1219.

79. Green, *Gospel of Luke*, 666. The tax collector in the temple is also in a quest as he seeks for God's mercy.

he defrauded, Jesus pronounces or declares that salvation has come to Zacchaeus and his home "today" (19:8–10).

Zacchaeus, being a tax collector (more than that, a "chief" tax collector—ἀρχιτελώνης), falls under the category of a "sinner" (19:2, 7) like the tax collector in the temple.[80] Both tax collectors have been referred to as "sinners" by those who think of themselves as "righteous" (18:9, 19:7). In addition, Zacchaeus is wealthy like the rich ruler (18:23). Either way, as a sinner and as a rich person, he would not be counted as someone who has access to God's kingdom.[81] In other words, he would be undeserving and unworthy of God's grace. Supporting this notion are Jesus's comments on the difficulty (and impossibility) of those with wealth to enter the kingdom of God (18:23–25). In addition, his physical limitation (i.e., being short) restricts his access to Jesus as he is literally unable to see and approach him due to his height and the crowds (19:3).[82] But despite his characteristics and status, he is the recipient of salvation, which coheres with how the tax collector (sinner) in the temple is the unlikely beneficiary of God's justification.

After Jesus states the necessity to stay with him, Zacchaeus goes down hurriedly from the tree and receives the news with joy (19:6). The presence of the motif of joy is all over the Gospel of Luke (1:14–17; 2:10; 6:23; 10:20; 15:5–7, 10; 15:32), and it is associated with those who are responding from the news of salvation. Therefore, his joy indicates that Zacchaeus already made a response of faith after hearing the news

---

80. ἀρχιτελώνης or chief tax collector is a kind of "district manager" who has other toll collectors working as his subordinates. He is a person of high status, and being a type of ruler, he has some power and privilege. See Green, *Gospel of Luke*, 668. He was an administrator who "bid for and organized the collection and took a cut from the labor of his underlings. His wealth is probably related from his job and comes from commission that such officials took from the taxes." Bock, *Luke 9:51—24:53*, 1516.

81. Being "rich" is portrayed negatively in many parts of Luke (1:53; 6:24; 12:13–21; 14:12–14; 16:19–31; 18:18–30; 20:45—21:4).

82. Parsons finds interesting significance in Zacchaeus's key physical limitation. He states that in the ancient world, "Smallness in physical stature was generally seen in physiognomic terms as reflective of 'smallness in spirit.'" Parsons, "Short in Stature," 53. Furthermore, he states, "This unflattering characterization joins with the other two descriptors of Zacchaeus, in relation to socio-economic status and occupation, to paint a thoroughly negative picture of the man." Parsons, "Short in Stature," 56. He cites that birth defects and infant mortality were associated with sinfulness with the Jews (2 Sam 12:15b–23; Ruth Rab. 6.4), Christians (John 9:2), and Greeks (Hesiod, *Op*. 1.235; Herodotus, *Hist*. 1.105; 4.67). Parsons, "Short in Stature," 55.

COHERENCE OF JUSTIFICATION WITH THE LUKAN TRADITION (L)

from Jesus.[83] In addition, Zacchaeus expresses fruits of repentance in his commitment to help the poor and his restitution (19:8).[84] This picture expresses a turning away from sin to follow Jesus. This action brings into mind what John the Baptist taught to the crowds that came to him to be baptized (3:8–14) and also the example of the woman with the alabaster jar (7:36–50).[85] Zacchaeus's implicit movement of faith in his turning away from sin and towards Jesus coheres with the implicit demonstrations of faith of the tax collector in the temple.[86] On the other hand, the account of the crowd grumbling coheres with the negative responses that others have against those who are thought of as "ungodly" and unworthy to receive Jesus's acceptance and grace (5:30; 15:2; 18:11).

Salvation is a key theme in this story as Jesus declares that salvation has come to Zacchaeus's house (19:9). Jesus's mission and purpose is to come and save the lost (19:10; 15:32). The whole story illustrates certain aspects of this salvation, including the presence of joy in those who receive it (19:6). Also, there is the aspect of urgency associated with it in Jesus's statement that salvation has come into Zacchaeus' house "today."[87] Jesus's positive declaration of salvation for Zacchaeus coheres with Jesus's declaration of righteousness to the temple tax collector (18:14a).

---

83. Zacchaeus's immediate response calls into mind the shepherd's response to the announcement of Jesus's birth (2:10, 16), and the call of Levi (5:29). Bock states that the response "does not explicitly mention faith, but his actions show that Jesus has made a deep impression upon him." Bock, *Luke 9:51—24:53*, 1518. Green notes, "Because of the association of "joy" with news of divine intervention and salvation, that Zacchaeus welcomes Jesus with joy signifies genuine receptivity on the part of Zacchaeus." Green, *Gospel of Luke*, 670.

84. An alternative view suggests that Zacchaeus was expressing his ongoing habit and not his future intention of providing for the poor and making restitution. Therefore, Zacchaeus was vindicated in the sense that he was not an outsider to God's kingdom but his current practices with his wealth indicate that he was. This takes the tense of the verbs δίδωμι and ἀποδίδωμι as present progressive tenses. Therefore, Zacchaeus says, "I always give to the poor . . . I always pay back." Green, *Gospel of Luke*, 672. Thus, it views Zacchaeus's experience not of conversion, which is the traditional view, but of restoration. The traditional view takes the verbs as iterative ("I will begin to give to the poor . . . "). As a result, this makes it a resolution for the future because of his conversion or transformation. This book takes the traditional view.

85. Bock, *Luke 9:51—24:53*, 1520.

86. Barrett, "Justification," 104, also notes that Zacchaeus's repentance goes beyond the requirement of the Law (19:8) while noting that the temple Pharisee's obedience also goes beyond the Law as well (18:12).

87. σήμερον communicates the immediacy and urgency of salvation in 2:11; 4:21.

The eschatological aspect of the story is reflected in several ways. Zacchaeus, the rich, chief tax collector ("sinner") experiences salvation although the crowds believe he is the least likely candidate to experience that from Jesus and grumble about him as someone not even worthy to be a host to Jesus (19:7). Therefore, Zacchaeus, the "sinner," the one who expresses humble repentance, restitution, and a joyful response is also the one exalted. Also, the statement of Jesus that the Son of Man came to seek and save the lost possibly brings into mind several possibilities. It may bring into focus Jesus's prior teachings in Luke 15:1–32 when he was criticized for having table fellowship with tax collectors and sinners who responded to him and his message. Therefore, the statement in 19:10 clarifies how his fellowship with sinners is part of God's purposes in saving the lost. Luke 19:10 may also bring into mind the picture of the coming Son of Man in Dan 7:13 and in Luke 7:34.[88] Finally, 19:10 may also allude to Ezek 34 where Yahweh and David seek out the lost to shepherd them.[89] This scriptural background is part of Jesus defining his eschatological purpose to save the lost, and, specifically, in this case, the salvation of a Son of Abraham.

The Passion Narrative

The theme of justification is likewise prominent as demonstrated in the life of Jesus throughout the Gospel of Luke, especially in the passion narrative. Specifically, this notion is shown in Luke through its understanding of Jesus as the Righteous One of Israel (Luke 23:47; cf. Isa 53:11).[90] Related themes and motifs that illustrate the notion of justification in Luke 18:9–14

---

88. Beale notes that Daniel 7 depicts the Son of Man surrounded by an angelic royal host as he is given the kingdom, while in Luke 7, the Son of Man fulfills the Daniel prophesy in an "incipient" way, surrounded instead by tax collectors and sinners. Beale, *Biblical Theology*, 197.

89. Green, *Gospel of Luke*, 673.

90. Within the Gospels, it is asserted that portions of Isaiah's "Servant Songs" (Isa 42:1–4; 49:1–6; 50:4–9; 52:13—53:12 and parts of Isa 61) are used to illuminate the mission of Jesus. For example, Isa 53 seems to portray the vicarious and redemptive suffering of Jesus. France, "Servant of Yahweh," *DJG*, 745. Luke records the title "Servant of God" for Jesus in Acts 3:13, 26. Isa 61:1–2 is prominent in Jesus's sermon in Luke 4:16–27, which depicts the themes about the ministry of the servant in delivering his people. France, "Servant of Yahweh," *DJG*, 746; also, Seccombe, "Luke and Isaiah," 255. The notion of the "Righteous One" is mentioned in Isa 53:11 and is in apposition with my "servant" who "make many to be accounted righteous, and he shall bear their iniquities." Seccombe, "Luke and Isaiah," 257.

COHERENCE OF JUSTIFICATION WITH THE LUKAN TRADITION (L)

are also reflected broadly in the events portrayed in Jesus's ministry and trials as the Righteous One and reach their highest point in his passion and culminate in his vindication and exaltation through the resurrection. Jesus's resurrection reflects his vindication of all the charges and accusations laid against him, his arrest, his trial, and subsequent crucifixion. The resurrection functions as the reversal from his previously acquired guilty verdict rendered at the cross. The themes and motifs that come from portraying this aspect of Lukan Christology come from passages not just from the passion narrative but also throughout his life and ministry.

An aspect that shows the motif of reversal is the theme of contest in Luke with respect to Jesus and his antagonists. This aspect of contest is seen throughout Jesus's ministry not just against the Pharisees, scribes, the crowds and other groups. This theme of contest is also prominent in Jesus's conflict with Satan. Contest is demonstrated in the wilderness testing (4:1–13), his encounters with Satan and his evil spiritual beings in his ministry (4:33–37; 6:18; 8:2, 26–39; 9:37–43; 11:14; 13:11, 16, 32; 10:17–18), the event of Satan's direct attack through entering into Judas so that he betrays Jesus (22:3–4), and Satan's demand that the disciples surrender (22:31–32). This conflict intensifies and becomes even more prominent during Jesus's betrayal and arrest at the specific "opportune time" (22:53; cf. 4:13). Another significant depiction in the passion account of Jesus's testing against Satan includes his time in Gethsemane (22:40–45; cf. 4:2).

The attitude and behavior of Jesus's antagonists cohere with those of the proud or self-justifying characters throughout the Gospel of Luke such as the temple Pharisee who justify themselves and treat the people against whom they are in contest with contempt (18:9, 11). This picture is particularly evident in the passion narrative. The rulers scoffed as he was being crucified (23:35),[91] the soldiers mocked him (23:36–37), and a criminal crucified with him railed against him (23:39). In many instances, Jesus's identity is being questioned. The ones who held Jesus in custody mock him and ask him sarcastically to prophesy and blaspheme him, indicating their lack of belief in him as a prophet (22:63–65). The chief priests and scribes ask if he is "the Christ" (22:67) and the Son of God (22:70). While he was being crucified, the rulers, the soldiers, and the criminal next to him question his ability to save himself and ask if he is the "Chosen One"

---

91. The verb ἐκμυκτηρίζω, which describes the action of the rulers, appears also when the Pharisees "scoffed" at Jesus while he was teaching his disciples about wealth and allegiances (Luke 16:14).

(23:35) or the "King of the Jews" (23:37), or simply "the Christ" (23:39). The presence of these accusations and behavior within the contest or trial motif coheres to the "righteous" (self-righteous) making accusations against sinners (e.g., 7:39; 18:11—"unjust"; 19:7).

Within this overall conflict, Jesus is not a sinner such as the temple tax collector (18:9–14) or the woman with the alabaster jar (7:36–50). But he is comparable in the sense that he needs God's vindication (like the widow in 18:1–8), especially since he is accused and pronounced guilty despite being righteous, and experiences crucifixion despite being innocent.

The theme of Jesus's innocence is an important feature in the aspect of Jesus's righteousness. This theme is featured in several different ways in the passion narrative. Pilate finds no guilt in him and declares him innocent three times (23:4, 14, 22; cf. Mark 15:14). Likewise, Herod declares Jesus innocent as well, unable to find him guilty of any kind of capital offense (23:15). His innocence is evident due to the contrast between him and Barrabas who was thrown in prison for insurrection and murder (23:25). Even as he is being crucified, the repentant thief next to him also declares him innocent (23:39–43) as well as the centurion (23:47). Finally, the people who witnessed these matters return home, beating their breasts (cf. 18:13). Perhaps these actions reflect the people's deep sorrow from witnessing the crucifixion of an innocent man.

Through the resurrection God justifies Jesus and declares him righteous. The resurrection serves as the vehicle for the motif of reversal, showing how Jesus who suffers and dies as the "Righteous One" is risen and thus vindicated through the reversal of the verdict declared by his accusers. Not only does the resurrection declare Jesus righteous, but it also condemns those who accused Jesus. Luke's passion narrative also portrays Jesus in terms of Isaiah's Suffering Servant (22:37; cf. Isa 53:12) as he endures humiliation, indignity, and death.[92] Jesus displays great humility while in the presence of his proud and self-justifying accusers. His vindication and resulting exaltation and the condemnation of his accusers cohere with the generalizing principle that those who exalt themselves will be humbled, and those who humble themselves will be exalted (14:11; 18:14). Jesus's faith in God and his faithfulness is on display through all the trials he endured from the wilderness testing, his ministry, his passion, and crucifixion.

---

92. General allusions to the Servant in Isa 52:12—53:12 include Jesus silent before Herod (Luke 23:9; cf. Isa 53:7); innocent (Luke 23:4, 14–15, 22; Isa 53:9); crucified with the wicked (Luke 23:33, 39; cf. Isa 53:9); with a rich man in his death (Luke 23:50–51; cf. Isa 53:9).

COHERENCE OF JUSTIFICATION WITH THE LUKAN TRADITION (L)

As the "Righteous One" who suffers and dies and is vindicated, he will also justify many (cf. Isa 53:11). This notion is explicitly shown in the story where he offers justification to the repentant thief hanging on the cross next to him (Luke 23:39–43). This story within itself also portrays themes that cohere with the Pharisee and tax collector (Luke 18:9–14). Although the repentant thief believes that his punishment is just, being undeserving of grace, he adopts a stance of humility and faith in Jesus. His verdict is likewise reversed as Jesus declares his acceptance (and salvation) into paradise and the kingdom of God. Therefore, the themes and motifs of faith, reversal, justification of the ungodly, and salvation are reflected in this short episode. Although justification is not stated explicitly, the concept of justification is narratively depicted and illustrated in the short story within the passion narrative.

Conclusion

Within the unique Lukan tradition are pericopae that cohere with Luke 18:9–14 via related themes and motifs. These texts come in different forms with the themes and motifs expressed in words that may be different from Luke 18:9–14, but their coherence indicates the *vox ipsissima* of Jesus. Justification is for the "sinner," the ungodly, or those in need of forgiveness and restoration, and considered as undeserving of God's grace. This aspect is portrayed by the chief tax collector Zacchaeus (19:1–10); the poor, crippled, lame, blind, and those who cannot pay back but are in need of restoration (14:7–14); the younger son (15:1–32); the woman with the ointment (7:36–50); the good Samaritan (10:25–37); and, Lazarus who is not a "sinner" but is not perceived as righteous and as a destitute person in need of restoration (16:19–31).[93] Justification is linked ultimately to salvation, which in this chapter is expressed in terms of being granted justice (18:5), being sought and found by Jesus in line with his mission (19:5), being invited to the eschatological banquet and given seats of honor (14:10) and participating in the resurrection of the just (14:14), being restored or recovered (15:7, 10, 32), having one's sins forgiven (7:47–48),

---

93. Per Green, "sinners" in Luke represent those who "cannot be included among the righteous and are therefore, persons of low socio-religious status counted among the excluded, even damned... presented by the Third Evangelist as persons in need of forgiveness, as recipients of good news, and as those who comport themselves as willing to repent and are thus numbered among the people of God." Green, *Gospel of Luke*, 570 (cf. 5:29–32; 7:35, 36–50); See Neale, *None*, 148–54.

and having eternal comfort (16:22). Access of justification is through faith and/or repentance as expressed and worked out through love (7:50) with a faith that perseveres (18:8) as evidenced by a response of joy and fruits of repentance (19:6, 8), and a repentance that needs to happen in response to God's Word (16:31). The overall stance of humility (by those who are considered "sinners") in contrast to that of self-righteousness (by those who deem themselves righteous) is on display in various passages. Finally, each individual pericope highlights an eschatological perspective. A sense of eschatological exaltation for the "sinner" with the motif of reversal is prevalent in every passage.

The texts come in various forms within the Lukan tradition as follows:

1. Parable (15:1–32; 16:14–31; 18:1–8),
2. Pronouncement story (19:1–10),
3. Admonition or proverbial counsel (14:1–14),
4. Combination pronouncement story and parable (7:36–50; 10:25–37), and
5. The passion narrative.

Recurrence of the related themes and motifs in different forms bolsters the case of the theme of justification's (in Luke 18:9–14) presence as a theme that may possibly come from Jesus tradition.

— Chapter 4 —

Coherence of Justification with Mark and Q

THIS STUDY NOW APPLIES the criterion of coherence by looking for comparable motifs and texts in the Jesus tradition that come from Mark and Q. This report assumes the two-source hypothesis, and it is important to see if these comparable themes are present not just in Luke's unique material but also in the two major early sources of the Gospels. This chapter highlights specific texts or passages that are all used by Luke but come from Mark and Q. Once again, like the previous chapter, the texts here are selected due to the intrinsic presence of practically all the four aspects and key themes and motifs that that are features of the nature of justification in Luke 18:9–14.[1] Of course, the related themes and motifs for justification in 18:9–14 are in other passages beyond these selected material, but the ones chosen have most, if not all, of the key themes and motifs. However, these are chosen due to the high concentration or convergence of this particular combination of themes and motifs. It is the confluence of these themes and motifs that makes these passages unique. Once again, as stated in the introduction and in the last chapter, the caveat still holds true here regarding source coherence: "That which we consider coherent is perhaps incoherent for others and vice versa."[2] Coherence is not a timeless standard of measurement.

---

1. (1) Justification is for those deemed as "sinners" undeserving of God's grace; (2) justification is linked to restoration or the theme of salvation; (3) justification is accessed by faith and/or repentance, with an overall attitude of humility and not self-righteousness, and, (4) justification is marked by eschatological exaltation and the related motif of reversal.

2. Theissen and Winter, *Plausible Jesus,* 235n7.

The specific texts considered here from Mark are (1) Mark 10:13–16//Luke 18:15–17//Matt 19:13–25 (Jesus blesses the children); (2) Mark 10:17–31//Luke 18:18–30//Matt 19:16–30 (the rich man); and, (3) Mark 10:46–52//Luke 18:35–43//Matt 20:29–34; 9:27–31 (healing of the blind man). The materials from Q are (1) Luke 13:22–30//Matt 7:13–14, 22–23; 8:11–12; 19:30 (the narrow door); (2) Luke 14:15–24//Matt 22:1–14 (parable of the banquet); and, (3) Luke 7:1–10//Matt 8:5–13 (the faith of a centurion).

Mark

Mark 10:13–16//Luke 18:15–17//Matt 19:13–15 (Jesus Blesses the Children)

Mark 10:13–16; Luke 18:15–17; and Matt 19:13–25 record the interaction of Jesus with his disciples concerning the people who were bringing children to him so that he may bless them.[3] In Mark, this material is part of a block of tradition concerning Christian discipleship (10:1–31). More specifically, this section speaks of family issues such as marriage and divorce (10:2–12), children (10:13–16), property (10:17–31), and what discipleship means within these matters. Jesus discusses the cost of discipleship and living by the principles of the kingdom but ends this section speaking about the high reward that will be granted in the age to come (10:30). The setting of the teaching is the region of Judea and across the Jordan where crowds of people came to him as he taught them (10:1). Some people, presumably parents or family members, were bringing children to him, eliciting rebuke from his disciples (10:13). This rebuke may reflect how people viewed children in those times: Children were less important than adults and were not important enough to be brought to a teacher such as Jesus.[4] The role of children in Greco-Roman society was defined through social and economic systems: "Children were seen as part of the kinship tradition who carried on the family name and business and who provided care for elderly parents. In religious contexts, children were regarded as innocent, chaste, and naïve."[5] Children were considered as "unformed adults who lacked reason

---

3. See Gen 48:14.
4. Witherington, *Gospel of Mark*, 279.
5. Stamps, "Children in Late Antiquity," *DNTB*, 197.

and thereby required training."⁶ "Weak, handicapped, unwanted girls, or another unwanted mouth to feed, would be left on the ground with the implication that the child should be exposed. Exposure was the practice of leaving an unwanted child at a site, usually a garbage dump or dung heap, where the child either died or was taken by a stranger to be raised, usually as a slave."⁷ This is not to generalize that Greco-Roman society did not value children at all as grave epitaphs show parental love and affection. In Jewish society in general children were perceived as a blessing (Ps 127:3–5) and means of guaranteeing Jewish descendants through procreation (Gen 1:28; 12:3). Children were likewise considered a blessing because a childless woman is shamed (1 Sam 1:10–11; Luke 1:25). It was the parents' duty to teach and pass on the faith. Practices of infanticide, abortion (Exod 21:22–25) and birth control (Gen 38:8–10) were often condemned (Philo *Spec.* 3.1110–19; Tacitus *Hist* 5.5).⁸ Jesus becomes indignant at his disciples and gives his own rebuke.⁹ Unfortunately, his disciples do not receive the children in Jesus's name as he taught them previously (9:36–37).

In Luke this account is located immediately after the parable of the tax collector and the Pharisee. There are several ways in which this pericope displays thematic cohesiveness with the previous parable. The children and tax collector can both be considered as the "humble" who are exalted.¹⁰ As the rationale or generalizing principle in 18:14b is applied to the tax collector, the principle is likewise applied to the children (and those who brought them) who function as examples of the humble who are exalted.¹¹

Also cohering with the Luke 18 parable in this account with the children is the motif of the "righteous" having contempt for the "unrighteous." The people who were rebuked by the disciples cohere with the tax collector

---

6. Stamps, "Children in Late Antiquity," *DNTB*, 197.
7. Stamps, "Children in Late Antiquity," *DNTB*, 197–99.
8. Stamps, "Children in Late Antiquity," *DNTB*, 197–99.
9. Luke's account does not include being "indignant."
10. Barrett, "Justification," 71.
11. In the Gospel of Mark, greatness as defined by Jesus is shown in being a servant of all, even to the point of being able to welcome and serve a child who, like a slave, is a subordinate member of the household (9:36–37) per Witherington, *Gospel of Mark*, 270. In Luke, there is emphasis on gracious mercy of God toward the poor, the weak, and the marginal. Examples include the "children of wisdom" identified as including tax collectors and sinners (7:34–35), the healing of a man's only son (9:37–43), and mercy over the younger son in 15:11–32. Barton, "Child, Children," *DJG*, 103.

being treated with disdain by the temple Pharisee.[12] While the children and those who brought them are not categorically "sinners," they analogously function in the sense as outcasts, which also fits the description of the temple tax collector.[13] They were not welcome to approach Jesus, and instead they were initially rejected by the "righteous." They were considered as unworthy of God's grace. Granted, that their initial rejection would have been culturally acceptable and justifiable given the low regard of children in those times. However, this way of regarding people, which may be valid in that context, no longer serves God's purposes and also disregards the notion of hospitality to the outcast and disadvantaged.[14] Fortunately, in the end they were given access to Jesus (10:16).

The exaltation present in this story is eschatological in nature as it is described in terms of the children being admitted into the kingdom of God. The motif of reversal is present as the children and those who brought them (the humble) are exalted while those who do not receive the kingdom like a child will not enter the kingdom (10:15).[15] As the tax collector in Luke's parable went home justified, likewise, the children gaining access to God's kingdom also portray this "justification." The theme of salvation is certainly depicted here as "entering the kingdom of God" (Mark 10:15).[16]

One way to look at "receiving" the kingdom like a child within the Gospel of Mark is as a metaphor for faith although, admittedly, that is just one way of construing this phrase out of a few possibilities.[17] Therefore, faith is not obviously emphasized in this passage; nor is repentance. But if "receiving" the kingdom like a child is highlighted as faith, a child ends up as the example or model to be emulated in terms of what faith needs to

---

12. Technically it was those who brought the children who really received the rebuke, but the end goal was to prevent the children from having personal access to Jesus.

13. Barrett, "Justification," 75.

14. Green, *Gospel of Luke*, 650–51.

15. In 10:14, "to such" (τοιούτων) can be interpreted as "to these children (and not just adults)" belongs the kingdom of God. But it can also be interpreted as "to people like these children," which means to such a class or group of people like this; Stein, *Mark*, 463; Witherington, *Gospel of Mark*, 279; Best, *Following Jesus*, 107.

16. Stein, *Mark*, 464, notes that "receiving the kingdom" happens in the present time, as in one can receive the kingdom brought by the ministry of Jesus; but "entering the kingdom" lies in the future realm. Thus, the theme of salvation presented is both present and future.

17. The meaning of "childlike receiving" is not necessarily made explicit so there are many suggestions for what it means to necessarily follow an example of a child; Best, *Disciples and Discipleship*, 94–97. Legasse, *Jesus et L'Enfant*, 189.

look like.[18] Given the status of children in antiquity, it was counterintuitive to present children's behavior as an example of what adults should do. Children were ranked low in ancient society compared to adults. Thus, 10:15 begins with ἀμὴν λέγω ὑμῖν to highlight the importance of the authority of Jesus in this statement, but the meaning of receiving the kingdom is not explicit in the text. The various ways children receive things include "in simple obedience," "in humility and faith/trust," "in lack of self-reliance," or through "helplessness."[19] Most of these only relate indirectly to faith. Therefore, the posture of "receiving" the kingdom pertains to qualities that one is to take up before God. This notion of "receiving" coheres with the stance of the tax collector in his humble posture away from himself and what he has done and instead towards God and God's mercy.

Mark 10:17–31//Luke 18:18–30//Matt 19:16–30 (Rich Young Man)

The account of the rich young man immediately follows the pericope about Jesus and the children (Mark 10:13–17).[20] This narrative expresses themes and motifs that cohere with the adjacent story and the parable of the Pharisee and tax collector such as eternal life, salvation, faith, humility, and reversal.[21] The subunits within the account are (1) Mark 10:17–22—Jesus's encounter with the rich man, (2) Mark 10:23–27—Jesus

---

18. In the Gospel of Mark, the main teaching concerning children is in the central section of 8:27—10:45 of which the focus is on the nature of discipleship of Christ (i.e., 9:33-37; 10:13-16). In this section, the child is also a metaphor of discipleship (cf. 10:24b). Barton, "Child, Children," *DJG*, 102.

19. See Best, *Following Jesus*, 107–8; France, *Gospel of Mark*, 397–98; Evans, *Mark 8:27–16:20*, 94; Hooker, *Saint Mark*, 239; Gundry, *Mark*, 550–51; Edwards, *Gospel According to Mark*, 307; Witherington, *Gospel of Mark*, 279–80; Barrett, "Justification," 77.

20. Matthew and, likewise, Luke put it adjacent to the same story of Jesus blessing the children. This account is commonly called the rich young ruler because, while all the Synoptic Gospels refer to the man as rich, Matthew indicates that this person was a young man (Matt 19:22), and Luke states that the man is a ruler (18:18).

21. The story of the rich man who could not follow Jesus because of his riches is a contrast to the previous example of childlike faith that is needed to receive/enter the kingdom of God according to Stein, *Mark*, 466. Green, *Gospel of Luke*, 653, notes that the position of this narrative in Luke 18:18–30 right after Jesus's encounter with the children in Luke 18:15–17 has a purpose or significance in that it illustrates "the principle of status transposition" (reversal) Jesus articulates in Luke 18:14 about the humble being exalted as opposed to the proud.

teaching his disciples about and entering the kingdom of God, and (3) Mark 10:28–31—Jesus's concluding teaching on rewards in God's kingdom plus a closing proverbial statement.²²

The story begins with Jesus continuing his journey to Jerusalem. A man approaches him and kneels before him and asks a question about what he must do to inherit or enter eternal life (Mark 10:17; Luke 18:18; Matt 19:16). That the man addresses Jesus as διδάσκαλε ἀγαθέ ("good teacher") may be taken as a sincere greeting instead of flattery.²³ Before answering his question, Jesus first states his objection to the man's address, by referring to God as the only one who is good (10:18). Various interpretations to what that means include (1) It is a way of saying that only God is ultimately good without saying Jesus is not good; (2) It is a statement to probe the sincerity of the man's initial address; (3) It is a way for Jesus to ask the man to reevaluate his idea of goodness; (4) It is a statement meant to jar the ruler and prepare him to respond positively to Jesus.²⁴ Then Jesus answers the man's question by referring to some of the commandments of the law, quoting five of the Ten Commandments plus "do not defraud."²⁵ The rich man affirms that he

---

22. Note the concentric structure:

    A Question about eternal life (v. 17)

        B Rich man cannot leave possessions and follow

            C Jesus's explanation, disciples' reaction (twice)

        B' Disciples have left possessions and followed

    A' Answer to eternal life question (v. 30)

See Witherington, *Gospel of Mark*, 281; Myers, *Binding*, 272.

23. Per Witherington, "This form of address seems basically without parallel either in Hebrew Scriptures or early Jewish literature." Witherington, *Gospel of Mark*, 281. Mark nowhere else associates "good" with "teacher." The unusual greeting combined with his running up to Jesus and kneeling before him overall shows the man's respect for Jesus as well as his sincerity. This is supported also by how Jesus responded with an answer in 10:19 and his attitude towards him in 10:21; France, *Gospel of Mark*, 401; Stein, *Mark*, 468; Witherington notes further that the address "may be that an Oriental custom is at the root of this interchange, for if the remark is flattery, then the man is setting up a reciprocity exchange in which he expects a flattering remark in return." Witherington, *Gospel of Mark*, 282. Instead of the reciprocity exchange, Jesus replies with a reproof.

24. Bock, *Luke 9:51—24:53*, 1477-78; Stein, *Mark*, 468-69; France, *Gospel of Mark*, 401-2.

25. Do not defraud may be the equivalent of "do not covet," Gundry, *Mark*, 553; or just an attempt to express "covet" in terms of what the practical result is of coveting, France, *Gospel of Mark*, 402; but it could just be a variant of do not steal, Stein, *Mark*, 469. Also, in terms of Jesus's reply to the rich man as to what he must do to inherit

has observed all of them ever since he was young (10:20). Jesus responds by focusing on one issue only, which is the man's great possessions and his attachment to them. Jesus asks him to get rid of these things by selling them as these were keeping him from gaining eternal life (10:21). After hearing this instruction, the rich man was upset and left because he could not do what Jesus asked of him (10:22).[26]

Next, Jesus looks around and addresses his disciples, teaching them the difficulty for the wealthy to inherit the kingdom (10:23). The disciples were amazed.[27] Then Jesus restates and intensifies his teaching by adding a hyperbole to make the point even sharper (10:25).[28] The astonishment of his disciples also correspondingly increased περισσῶς due to their concern over anyone's ability to be saved. There was an aspect of their culture that believes God blesses the rich and wealthy due to the fact that they have possessions.[29] In response, Jesus indicates that what is impossible for humans to do is possible for God.[30] His response holds out hope that sal-

---

eternal life, Jesus gave him some of the commandments not in order for the rich man to earn salvation, but actually to trust in God's grace. Jesus believed that keeping the Law in the way God intended would result in eternal life as it would involve trusting in God's grace in the process of loving God with all of one's heart, soul, mind, and strength. "It involves trusting in the sacrificial death of Jesus (10:45; 14:24), even as OT believers trusted in the grace of God provided through the Day of Atonement and the OT sacrifices." Stein, *Mark*, 469.

26. The allegiance that wealth demands was in direct competition with allegiance to Jesus and his commands (Luke 18:22; Mark 10:21; Matt 19:21). See Barrett, "Justification," 85. The rich man seemed to believe that living a good life and obeying God's commandments will allow him to enter God's kingdom. But, per Witherington, "the demands of discipleship to Jesus go beyond the demands of the Law. The ultimate test of obedience, then, is seen as the willingness to assume the yoke of discipleship to Jesus." Witherington, *Gospel of Mark*, 283.

27. According to France, *Gospel of Mark*, 404, perhaps the disciples were already dismayed by the rich man leaving as he could have been a desirable follower.

28. This statement is to be taken as a hyperbole and not literally. It serves as "an empathic warning" about the obstacle that riches pose to entering the kingdom of God. See Stein, *Mark*, 472. See also how others may take this point literally or rationalized per Witherington, *Gospel of Mark*, 283–84.

29. Wealth is a sign of blessing. Rich people have the means to perform charitable acts and the wealth they possess indicate God's blessing and favor; France, *Gospel of Mark*, 405; Stein, *Mark*, 472. Per Bailey, *Through Peasant Eyes*, 167, rich men were able to contribute in significant ways such as building synagogues, funding orphanages, providing alms to the poor, refurbishing the temple. The notion was that salvation is more open to them because of their capability to perform good deeds.

30. Salvation is not by human effort but is a gift from God per Witherington, *Gospel*

vation can be attained even if humans, both rich and poor, are ultimately incapable of doing it by themselves.[31]

Finally, after that exchange, the focus turns to Jesus's disciples who have sacrificed and left their wealth to follow him (Mark 10:28–31). Speaking on behalf of the disciples, Peter expresses to Jesus the sacrifice they made to be his disciples (10:28).[32] Jesus's next pronouncement reassures them and teaches them of the hundredfold rewards that come to those who follow Jesus (Mark 10:29–30). There are both present rewards (and persecutions) and future rewards in the age to come. The concluding proverbial statement expresses the reversal of status and human expectations when it comes to the kingdom of God (Mark 10:31).

This narrative certainly expresses themes and motifs that cohere with the adjacent story of Jesus with the children and the parable of the Pharisee and tax collector in Luke 18:9–14. The theme of salvation is prominent through various expressions of σῴζω (10:26): the rich man's desire to "inherit eternal life" (10:17), Jesus's comment about what to do to obtain the "treasure in heaven" (10:21), and the difficulty of those with riches "to enter the kingdom of God" (10:23). Like the previous pericope, the image of eternal life and that of salvation pertain to the same reality.[33] Therefore, this theme coheres with the preceding passage (Mark 10:13–16), which has the notion of entering, belonging, or receiving the kingdom of God. This notion coheres as well with the state of being "justified" in the parable of the tax collector and the Pharisee (Luke 18:14). The motif of reversal is certainly present as illustrated by the rich man not attaining the kingdom due to his competing allegiance toward his wealth in contrast with the disciples who left "everything" to follow Jesus (Mark 10:25). Part of their culture assumed that the rich was in a better position to receive the kingdom since the presence of wealth and prosperity was taken as an indication of God's favor and blessing.[34] However, it is not about the amount of wealth one has

---

of Mark, 284. The way to figure out who is saved cannot be determined from a human perspective but from God's perspective according to France, Gospel of Mark, 406.

31. Barrett, "Justification," 88.

32. The question indicates concern for the disciples to know their standing after hearing the teaching from Jesus. In other words, they would like a word of assurance for what they did fulfill what the rich young man could not do which is give full allegiance to Jesus. Barrett, "Justification," 89.

33. Barrett, "Justification," 88; Stein, Mark, 468.

34. Stein, Mark, 471; Rabbis such as Hillel and Akiba rose from poverty to wealth and influence are commended; France, Gospel of Mark, 399.

but about allegiance to Jesus that determines whether you are given both present and future blessings in the eschaton (Mark 10:30). Furthermore, the generalizing statement in 10:31 makes explicit the motif of reversal that coheres with the summary statement of the humble being exalted as opposed to the proud (Luke 18:14).

In the same manner that justification is for the "ungodly" but humble tax collector (Luke 18:9–14), the rich man's entrance to eternal life is determined not by his effort or riches but by God (Mark 10:27). In this case, the riches of the man were not a blessing but a curse. It did not matter that the rich man carefully followed the law from his youth (10:20) such as the way the Pharisee in Luke 18:11–12 carefully observed the statutes. Salvation is an undeserved gift/grace from God received by those who have humbly given total allegiance to Jesus Christ. Total allegiance is demonstrated by the disciples who left "everything" to follow him (10:28). The theme of faith is presumed here as the action of "following" Jesus as a disciple (10:21, 28). Following Jesus is a response that comes from faith, part of which involves leaving whatever is in the way of the commitment or allegiance to Christ and then also making a radical orientation of life towards God.[35] For the disciples who did leave "everything," Jesus exalts them by pronouncing the "hundredfold" rewards of the kingdom both for now and in the future, which includes gaining a new family of faith (10:29–30). The self-righteous attitude of the Pharisee in Luke 18:9–14 has no exact parallel in this narrative, especially as there is no explicitly expressed indication that neither the rich man's inquiry nor Peter's comment comes from a sense of self-pride.[36] However, the rich man ultimately giving allegiance to riches over following Jesus means that he does not accept God's purposes (as indicated in his refusal to follow Jesus's direct command), which coheres with what it means to justify oneself.[37] Therefore, the rich man, who was seemingly a

---

35. The actions described here reflect a fulfillment of the programmatic call to "believe" as well as to "repent" in Mark 1:15.

36. The rich man's ultimate choice of his riches does reflect his choice of separating from God although this is done with much grief. France assumes there is perhaps a "touch of smugness" in Peter's comment, but it is not explicit in the text. France, *Gospel of Mark*, 407. Another way to look at Peter's comment is that it is a product of a lack of spiritual understanding, according to Witherington, *Gospel of Mark*, 284. If that is the sense of the comment, an empathic word of assurance was needed, which Jesus provided according to Stein, *Mark*, 473.

37. Please see pages 49–51 in the analysis of Luke 7:36–50.

good example in his own mind and with the blessing of wealth and obedience to the Law fell short like the Lukan Pharisee.

Mark 10:46–52//Luke 18:35–43//Matthew 20:29–34; 9:27–31 (Healing of the Blind Man)

In the Mark 10:46–52 narrative, Jesus encounters and heals a blind man.[38] It is the second of two healings of blind men in Mark, the first of which is in 8:22–26. This story reflects themes and motifs that cohere with stories that are in close proximity in the Gospel of Mark such as the rich young man (Mark 10:17–31) and Jesus blessing the children (Mark 10:13–16). In addition to its coherence with other stories in Mark, this portrayal of Jesus's healing/salvation of a social outcast and his acceptance into God's reign also coheres with themes and motifs present in the parable of the Pharisee and tax collector (Luke 18:9–14). In some sense, this story, which shows someone who experiences God's saving reign, presents in an analogous way a broad picture of the notion of justification without necessarily expressing this idea in an explicit way.[39]

This pericope is comprised of the introductory setting (10:46), the blind man's cry for help (10:47–48), Jesus's call (10:49–50), and the miracle and response (10:51–52). In 10:46, Jesus, his disciples, and a great multitude were leaving Jericho when they encounter a blind man named Bartimaeus (son of Timaeus) on the side of the road.[40] When he hears people mention that Jesus of Nazareth was passing by within his vicinity, he cries out to Jesus, "υἱὲ Δαυὶδ Ἰησοῦ, ἐλέησόν με" (10:47). It is notable how he refers to Jesus as the "Son of David" as opposed to how the crowd refers to him as "Jesus of Nazareth." This passage is the only instance in the Gospel of Mark that Jesus is called the "Son of David." This description pertains to the promised royal descendant of King David—the Messiah or the Christ in Mark 8:29. As a result of his cry for Jesus, many (πολλοί) rebuke him and tell him to be quiet (10:48). There are various speculative reasons why the

---

38. It is the last healing miracle in Mark. It is a story that highlights a christological point but given how it ends, it is also a call narrative and serves as an example of what discipleship in Christ looks like. Stein, *Mark*, 491–92.

39. Barrett, "Justification," 94–95.

40. It may have been a good location for collecting alms as pilgrims pass by as they head towards Jerusalem; Stein, *Mark*, 494. Being on the side of the road also illustrates the blind man's status as someone who is marginalized per Edwards, *Gospel According to Mark*, 329.

blind man was rebuked, but regardless, Bartimaeus continues to cry out to the Son of David for mercy (10:48).[41] Jesus stops as he hears his cries and asks those around him to call Bartimaeus so that he can engage with him (10:49). Then they (the passage does not specify who) encourage Bartimaeus and ask him to rise in order that he can face Jesus (10:50). He jumps up while getting rid of his ἱμάτιον (outer clothing), which may have served to collect alms when he spread it on the ground or on his lap.[42] Jesus asks Bartimaeus what he wants. He responds that he wants his eyesight restored (10:51). Jesus then miraculously heals Bartimaeus who then begins to follow Jesus afterwards ἐν τῇ ὁδῷ ("in the way"; 10:52).

In the Gospel of Mark, the theme of blindness and sight is prominent. Blindness in the Gospels, as well as deafness, is frequently used not just to express the physical deficiency of the eyes and ears but also figuratively communicate a lack of spiritual sensitivity or understanding. Salvation is associated with sight in many examples of Jewish and Christian literature.[43] Along with the theme of blindness and sight is the aspect of salvation in this passage, which coheres with the salvation theme in the parable of the Pharisee and tax collector (Luke 18:9–14), although it is illustrated in a different sense.[44] Furthermore, the word σῴζω, which is the word used for "healed" (10:52), shows a holistic understanding of salvation as in this case it shows both physical and spiritual dimensions of healing.[45] Although Jesus is never

---

41. Some ideas as to why the blind man was rebuked include (1) the crowd being annoyed at him; (2) Bartimaeus lacking status and not deserving Jesus's time, as they did not want to delay Jesus's mission of setting up his kingdom in Jerusalem; (3) he being rebuked for the same reason bringing children to Jesus was discouraged; (4) if Pharisees were in the group, the title "Son of David" being considered blasphemous and unwise to be said in the crowd. See Stein, *Mark*, 495; France, *Gospel of Mark*, 424; Witherington, *Gospel of Mark*, 291; Barrett, "Justification," 96–98.

42. Stein, *Mark*, 496.

43. Exod 14:13; 2 Chr 20:17; Pss 50:23; 91:16; 119:123; Isa 40:5; 42:16–17; 59:11; 1QS 112–13; CD 20:34; *T. Gad* 5:7; 2 Clem. 1:6–7; 9:2.

44. "Being saved" in this passage is expressed in terms of "healing," while in Luke 18:9–14 it is in terms of "justification." Communicating what salvation means especially in terms of the salvation brought about by the cross can be expressed in different terms and images (e.g., the term "justification" is used for a court of law; "redemption" is for the world of commerce; "sacrifice" in the realm of worship). See Green, *Salvation*, 110–11.

45. The term "saved" can refer to both physical healing (3:4; 5:23, 28, 34; 6:56; cf. also 13:20; 15:30–31) and spiritual healing (8:35; 10:26; 13:13) per Stein, *Mark*, 497. Spiritual and physical are not two different realms that have nothing to do with one another. Salvation being holistic in nature, having to do with one's relationship with God, also issues forth in physical wholeness; see Barrett, "Justification," 99.

pictured as calling the disciples blind, his disciples are presented as spiritually dull, especially in two stories of healings of the blind (Mark 8:22–26; 10:46–52).[46] Ironically, blind Bartimaeus is presented as more spiritually responsive to Jesus than his disciples, and his healing results in his salvation both in the physical and spiritual sense.[47]

In Jesus's ("Son of David") healing of blind Bartimaeus, this picture brings about eschatological overtones as the title points to the Davidic descendant promised in 2 Sam 7:11–14. This descendant is the Messiah who is coming, deemed as a warrior king who will punish in Pss. Sol. 17:21.[48] But here this Messiah is one who gives mercy, the one who brings healing and wholeness.[49] In the rest of the Synoptic Gospels, Jesus healing the blind is also part of messianic expectation (Matt 11:1–5; Luke 7:18–23; 4:16–21). Adding to the eschatological underpinning is the motif of reversal. The blind man is an example of someone who is marginalized, a social outcast, someone who is by the roadside initially (in contrast at the end of the story where he was able to get "on the way"). He stands in contrast in terms of status with the rich man from 10:17–22 who ended up not becoming a disciple of Jesus due to his allegiance to his possessions (10:22). But here he is comparable to the children (Mark 10:13–16), the disciples who left everything (Mark 10:28), and, most importantly, the Lukan tax collector (Luke 18:9–14) as an example of an outcast who is undeserving of God's grace but who has been brought closer to the kingdom against expectations (as reflected by the crowd that initially rebuked him).[50]

An aspect that especially coheres with the tax collector is the blind man's cry for mercy (Mark 10:47–48), which indicates or testifies to his faith (Mark 10:52). This cry coheres with the tax collector's cry for mercy to God

---

46. These two stories frame Mark's central section (Mark 8:22—10:52) as Jesus moves from north to south up to his arrival in Jerusalem. The content of the section focuses on discipleship. Jesus predicts his suffering and relates it to the nature of true discipleship; Howard, "Blindness and Deafness," *DJG*, 501.

47. He is deemed as the prototypical disciple. His response of faith has healed/saved him; see Howard, *DJG*, 81. "The actions of Bartimaeus is a paradigmatic example of what it means to be a Christian." Stein, *Mark*, 498.

48. Some Messianic texts include Isa 11:1, 10; Jer 23:5; 33:15; Ps 89:4–5; Pss. Sol. 17:21–40; 4 Ezra 12:32; 4QFlor 1:11–13.

49. Lohse, "*huios David*," *TDNT* 8:482–92; Edwards, *Gospel According to Mark*, 330; Witherington, *Gospel of Mark*, 291.

50. Barrett, "Justification," 102. Also, the crowd coheres with those disciples who tried to impede the children's access to Jesus (Mark 10:13).

although his faith is not explicitly mentioned (Luke 18:13).[51] The blind man's faith is further reflected by his persistence in calling out to Jesus. His healing depends on God and not on his own merit, and he knows that Jesus, as the Son of David, can bring him salvation.[52] He shows humility as he asks only for his sight and not some other things such as power or wealth.[53] His actions after receiving healing, which consist of following Jesus and abandoning everything else, including his cloak on the ground for collection of his alms, are responses borne of faith in contrast to the rich man who left and did not follow Jesus on account of his great possessions (Mark 10:22). Also, as the tax collector goes home pronounced by Jesus as "justified" (Luke 18:14), the blind man is declared by Jesus to be "healed" as he is given sight and salvation (in terms of his standing before God).

"Q Source"

Luke 13:22–30//Matt 7:13–14, 22–23; 8:11–12; 19:30 (The Narrow Door)[54]

This pericope comes after the stories of Jesus teaching in the synagogue where he also heals a demonized woman (13:10–17) and describes the kingdom in terms of a mustard seed (13:18–19) and yeast (13:20–21) but not before Jesus issues warnings about the coming time of judgment, his coming to divide families, and the need for repentance (12:49—13:9).

---

51. The blind man's persistent cries for mercy also brings into mind the persistent widow (Luke 18:1–8). Both stories display "strong thematic and lexical ties." Barrett, "Justification," 98–99.

52. As opposed to the crowd who misses Jesus's significance as he is referred to as Jesus of Nazareth (Mark 10:47).

53. Edwards, *Gospel According to Mark*, 331.

54. This report assumes that this passage is part of Q while acknowledging the diverse viewpoints of scholars about this passage's source as a whole and in individual verses. Bock argues that Luke 13:22–30 "is an independent tradition that Luke alone has or that represents the combining of various materials from Jesus' ministry." Bock, *Luke 9:51—24:53*, 1230. Fitzmyer considers Luke 13:24–29 as Q material and the rest as coming from Luke himself. However, he does share his uncertainty about the cause of the divergences with the Matthean parallel either as Matthean redaction, Lukan redaction, or even from L or M. Fitzmyer, *Luke X–XXIV*, 1021–22. Marshall attributes the door imagery in Luke to an independent source but sees the rest of the passage as Q Because of its differences with Matthew, he asserts that "Luke has thus probably taken over a set of sayings from Q which were available to Matthew in a variant form." Marshall, *Gospel of Luke*, 564. See also Hoffman, "Redaktion und Tradition," 188–214.

From these warnings and talks about the kingdom, someone asks Jesus if only a few will be saved (13:23).[55] Jesus does not give an answer to the question directly but instead gives a warning by telling the person to "strive" or "contend" to enter the narrow door now because a future time will come when many will seek to enter it and fail (13:24).[56] A time will come when the master of the house will close that door and not open it even if people will come to seek entry.[57] The people will miss out on coming through this door that leads into the banquet of the kingdom of God (13:29). The master will not even recognize who they are as they failed to respond within the right timeframe (13:25). It does not matter that those knocking on the door associated with the master (Jesus) during his ministry, signified in terms of eating with him and hearing his teaching (13:26).[58] In addition to not being able to come into the banquet, those unable to enter will be sent away to the place marked by "weeping and gnashing of teeth (13:28)." They will see themselves separated from the patriarchs outside the kingdom of God (13:28). In the end-times feast, all kinds of people from everywhere get together to eat at God's table (13:29).[59] The passage concludes with the generalizing statement that expresses eschatological reversal: Some of the last will be first, and some of the first will be last (13:30). The last refers to the inclusion of those from near and far who "strive" with their faith (faith is just indirectly implied here), as opposed

---

55. According to Barrett, "Eschatological salvation is clearly in view given the apocalyptic imagery Jesus employs." Barrett, "Justification," 73. This apocalyptic imagery pertains to 13:28-29.

56. ἀγωνίζεσθε εἰσελθεῖν "strain every nerve to enter"; see Bauer et al., "ἀγωνίζομαι," BDAG 17. In 1 Tim 4:10; 6:11-12; 2 Tim 4:7-8, ἀγωνίζεσθε is connected with exhorting believers to have faith in God in light of the eschatological salvation that God brings; see Nolland, *Luke 9:21—18:34*, 733. Bock states that "make every effort" is not about working to get to God but "labor hard at listening and responding to his message." Bock, *Luke 9:51—24:53*, 123. Green, *Gospel of Luke*, 530, cites that the metaphorical use of word is with respect to the practice of virtue and obedience to the law of God.

57. Matt 7:13-14 also uses the imagery of a narrow door or gate but contrasts this with the wide gate and road that leads to destruction.

58. The parable reveals Jesus as the owner and judge. Bock, *Luke 9:51—24:53*, 1236; Green, *Gospel of Luke*, 531.

59. "The gathering of God's elect is common in the OT, where it usually referred to the dispersed, defeated Gentiles who come to worship God in Zion, as Israel also reclaims its authority in ultimate victory." Bock, *Luke 9:51—24:53*, 1239. Per Green, the eschaton is "an appropriation and celebration of divine blessing in the form of a feast, is well rooted in the literature of the OT and Second Temple Judaism." Green, *Gospel of Luke*, 532. See Isa 25:6-8; 55:1-2; 65:13-14; Zeph 1:7; 1QSa 2:15-22.

to those who presume to be included (by relying on their ancestry, especially as descendants of the patriarchs) but fails to strive or respond to Jesus until it was too late (13:30).

The eschatological background is clear in terms of the apocalyptic imagery as well as the motif of reversal that is referred to by 13:30. The ones who are expecting to participate in God's eschatological kingdom in the end will not qualify unless they truly have faith in Jesus. It does not matter whether they are Jew or gentile as they come from every place. The "ungodly" and unworthy gentiles who respond will be able to sit at the table with Abraham, Isaac, Jacob, and the prophets. This exaltation of the "ungodly" coheres with Jesus exalting the humble. The presence of the theme of salvation is also obvious given the initial question of someone in the beginning about the number of those who will gain salvation in the end. Gaining entry in God's banquet coheres with acquiring the justification that the tax collector received in Luke 18:9–14. In addition, this pericope also graphically presents how those who show a lack of response to the ministry of Jesus will be brought low. They exalt themselves and expect entry into the banquet by even claiming association with Jesus. However, they cohere to those who are humbled, such as the Pharisee in Luke 18:9–14 who did not receive justification from Jesus.

Luke 14:15–24//Matt 22:1–14 (Parable of the Banquet)

In Luke 14:15–24, Jesus is speaking of eschatological matters in the parable of the banquet (14:15–24) during a Sabbath meal at a Pharisee's house in Luke 14:1–24.[60] Jesus silences his antagonists over his healing of a person

---

60. This report assumes that the source of Luke 14:15–24 and Matt 22:1–10 is Q (Matt 22:11–14 is Matthew's special source M) although there are diverse assessments of how closely related they and their source are. Fitzmyer, *Luke X–XXIV*, 1052, for example, believes that Luke 14:16–21 and Matt 2:2–10 is derived from Q. Luke then composed 14:15 as a transitional verse. Nolland, *Luke 9:21—18:34*, 754, also sees Luke 14:15–24 as parallel with 13:22–30 as well as with Matt 22:1–10 although mentioning certain disputes about whether Luke and Matthew received the parable in the same form. The difficulty is accounting for the differences between the passages. Then there are those such as Bock, *Luke 9:51—24:53* 1268–70, who argue for a separate source tradition for the two versions, which means Luke 14:15–24 is from L because of the distinct vocabulary and differences in the story. Hagner, *Matthew 14–28*, 627–28, asserts that Matthew and Luke agree substantially enough to attribute them to Q despite the small agreement in wording and important differences between them. Notable also is the mention of a form of the parable in the *Gospel of Thomas* 64.

on the Sabbath (14:1–6). Then he addresses those guests who were seeking honor at the banquet and addresses the host concerning humility (14:7–14). After one of the guests mentions the blessedness of those who will dine in the eschatological kingdom (14:15), Jesus replies with a parable of a man who gave a great banquet at his house.[61] In this parable, the people whom Jesus characterizes as blessed are those who were not originally invited to the banquet. The original invitees had inexcusable reasons for not taking up the invitation.[62] So the ones whom the host invites next are those who are normally considered marginalized (i.e., the poor, maimed, blind, and lame), and those who can be found in highways and hedges (14:16–23).[63] This man in this parable illustrates the advice Jesus gave the host about inviting those who cannot reciprocate (14:12–14). In the end, the outcasts of society who are considered weak and undeserving of God's grace (like a "sinner") get to be in the banquet and are considered to be the blessed ones who will

---

61. Table of differences of the parable between Matthew and Luke per Bock, *Luke 9:51—24:53*, 1269.

Element	Matthew	Luke
Giver of the banquet	King	Master of the house
Banquet	Wedding feast	Dinner banquet
Structure of the first invitation	Two invitations by many servants	One invitation by one servant
Reaction to the invitation	Invitees return to the field and business with laughter while others beat the servants	Three excuses given, no beatings
Host's response	King sends troops to destroy invitees and invites other guests	Host invites new guests

62. These are excuses that deal either with finances, possessions, or family issues. In 14:18 the first person bought a field and must see it. In 14:19 the person bought five yoke of oxen and needed to try them out. In 14:20 the person just got married. In all these cases, the invitation to the eschatological banquet of the kingdom should understandably take precedence. See: Luke 8:19–21; 9:59–62; 14:26.

63. Per Bock, *Luke 9:51—24:53*, 1276, the highways refer to roads outside of the city and the hedges around highways are those outside of the town located around vineyards, which contain beggars. This means that the host will admit anyone who will accept the invitation.

eat bread in the kingdom of God (14:15) and end up in the seats of honor (14:10). But the ones who were originally invited will be absent (14:24). This picture coheres with the motif of reversal in the parable of the Pharisee and the tax collector where the one person assumed to be acceptable before God was not justified and the other person unexpectedly finds vindication (18:14). The theme of salvation is expressed here in terms of whom the master allows inside the banquet, of who are, ultimately, the ones blessed in dining in the eschatological kingdom. Faith, or the lack of it, is expressed in the conflicted allegiance that the original invitees have, which coheres with the rich man's lack of allegiance in Mark 10:17-31//Luke 18:18-30//Matt 19:16-30. Instead, it is the humble ones, even those begging along the highways outside the city, who have accepted the invitation. They will receive the restoration that the banquet brings. Matthew additionally adds the theme of judgment in the passage with the king instantly destroying the original invitees as well as burning their city (Matt 22:8).

Luke 7:1-10//Matt 8:5-13 (The Faith of a Centurion)

The story of the healing of the centurion's slave comes after a significant block of Jesus's teaching (the great sermon) for both Luke and Matthew.[64] This story and the raising of the widow's son at Nain (7:11-17) is meant to be an illustration of part of the expectations of John with regards to the coming Messiah (7:18-23), specifically the expectation in 7:22 where "the dead are raised up" (with the centurion's servant being at the point of death; 7:2). Therefore, the healing of the centurion's slave represents part of the eschatological visitation from God, revealing Jesus as the one whom God entrusted with full authority.[65] Also, this account can be considered as the playing out of Jesus's missionary program as expressed in Luke 4:16-30. The three stories in 7:1-10, 11-17, and 36-50 reveal the character of the salvation of the ministry of Jesus. His healings in these accounts certainly bring into mind his prophetic ministry where his healing of the servant of a gentile soldier (7:1-10) coheres to what Elisha had done (4:27); his

---

64. Note John 4:46-54 is mostly considered to be based on the same tradition. Per Nolland, "but it is certainly from a quite different line of transmission and could have its basis in a separate episode." Nolland, *Luke 9:1—18:34*, 314. Contra Bock who would consider the differences problematic enough and see John basing the account on a totally different situation. See Bock, *Luke 1:1—9:50*, 630-31 for the differences between John and the synoptic accounts.

65. Nolland, *Luke 1:1—9:20*, 313-15.

ministry for a woman and her son (7:11–17) brings into mind Elijah (4:25–26); and, his forgiveness of a sinful woman (7:36–50) displays release of the oppressed (4:18–19).[66] Matthew's insertion of additional Q material in 8:11–12 further makes a point concerning the eschatological age.[67] The occasion where many from the east and west will come and be at the table with the patriarchs refers to the eschatological banquet anticipated in both the OT and the NT.[68] But instead of the expectation that the covenant people of Israel will gather and feast with the patriarchs, it is the gentiles here who are being called to participate in the banquet. The insertion of these verses seems to suggest that the gentile centurion is an example of one of those gentiles who will come from the east and west to join the eschatological banquet, especially as evidenced by his response of tremendous faith that Jesus claims he cannot find in all of Israel.[69]

The account is as follows. After a brief transition from the sermon and Jesus's entrance to Capernaum (Luke 7:1//Matt 8:5), the centurion's need is made known (Luke 7:2–3//Matt 8:5–6). The delegation delivers their message and Jesus agrees and moves towards the centurion's home (Luke 7:4–6). In Matthew, the response of Jesus is out of the centurion's direct request as opposed to the delegation doing the task in Luke (Matt 8:7). In Luke, a second delegation meets him on the way and gives another message, which results in Jesus's comment regarding the centurion's outstanding faith (Luke 7:6–9). In Matthew, the centurion himself expressed his unworthiness, which elicits Jesus's comment (Matt 8:8–10). Those who were sent to deliver the message then go back home and discover that the slave is healed (Luke 7:10). In Matthew, after additional Q material is presented concerning the banquet in the kingdom of heaven (Matt 8:11–12), Jesus heals the servant (Matt 8:13).

A theme of eschatological visitation fulfills what was inaugurated through the ministry of John and expresses God's intentions as declared by Jesus in Luke 4:16–30. In this pericope, the gentile centurion is featured

---

66. Green, *Gospel of Luke*, 281–82.

67. Luke uses this additional material for the account in Luke 13:22–30 without the part where the sons of the kingdom will be judged.

68. Such as Isa 25:6; Matt 22:1—4; 25:10; Rev 19:9; Luke 14:15–16. It is an expectation that the people of Israel will be blessed in this banquet and that the gentiles will also be blessed but not as direct participants. The people coming from the east and west were deemed to be the Jewish diaspora returning to Israel. See Hagner, *Matthew 1–13*, 205–6.

69. See Hagner, *Matthew 1–13*, 205–6.

with a response of exemplary faith and humility.[70] He is an example of an "outcast" who is brought closer to God's kingdom, cohering with the tax collector who is a sinner (Luke 18:9-14; 19:1-10), the widow (Luke 18:1-8), and the children (Luke 18:15-17). He is not rebuked for his need for Jesus unlike the rebuke that others give to the "outcasts" who seek Jesus (e.g., Luke 18:11, 39). Instead, friends who are emissaries lobby on his behalf due to his affection for the nation and his generosity in building a house of Jewish worship. In other words, he is a friend who is actually deemed worthy because he has the means and desire to contribute. So even if they are not necessarily rebuking him, they are facilitating access to Jesus (although perhaps for the wrong reasons).[71] But in the end, Jesus did not exalt him due to those things. The theme of humility is displayed in the centurion's actions, especially his word to Jesus that he is not worthy to receive Jesus at his house. He did not want Jesus to defile himself by coming to his home.[72] Therefore, he counts himself as one undeserving of God's grace, even if his friends do not have the same perception of him. He also trusts that it will take just the word of Jesus to heal because he recognizes Jesus's authority. The motif of reversal unfolds when Jesus declares to the multitude that the centurion's faith

---

70. A centurion is a Roman commander in charge of about a hundred men per Bauer et al., "ἑκατοντάρχης," BDAG 298-99. They are either mercenary soldiers, tax soldiers, or policemen coming from a variety of nationalities. Per Bock, "Centurions earned significant amounts of money: in a period where the lowest-paid soldier earned 75 denarii, a centurion earned between 3,750 denarii and 7,500 denarii." Bock, *Luke 1-9:50*, 635. The centurion in this account is not Jewish, given Jesus's comment in Luke 7:9 and the comments of the Jewish elders testifying to his love for the nation and his contribution of building a synagogue (Luke 7:5).

71. This is similar in how the judge in Luke 18:5 gave access for the wrong reason. In other cases, they hinder access of "outcasts" also for the wrong reasons (Luke 18:15, 39). Green notes that the Jewish elders "portray him as a broker and benefactor of the people. As Rome's representative in an outpost like Capernaum, the centurion would have found himself in the role of intermediary between the local population and the demands of the Empire. It would not be unusual for such a person to adopt the religion of the local population, nor would it be unusual for him to have underwritten the building of the synagogue as a calculated maneuver to win favor among the local Jewish leadership." Green, *Gospel of Luke*, 286. The Jewish elders in lobbying for him "discharge something of their ongoing obligation to acknowledge and advertise their benefactor's generosity and eminence." In other words, they act not based on Jesus's teaching in Luke 6:27-38 but they assume "the insider-outsider categories of honor and obligation prevalent throughout the Empire." Green, *Gospel of Luke*, 287. In other words, they grant him access for the wrong reasons.

72. See Acts 10:28; 11:3; See also the literature survey in Feldman, *Jew and Gentile*, 160-70; Esler, *Community and Gospel*, 78-86.

sets him apart from Israel's people (Luke 7:9). Implicit in this comment is that it is God's people who are supposed to be the ones to exhibit this kind of humility and faith towards Jesus. In this way, the centurion, although a gentile, is exalted as the one who recognizes the eschatological visitation of God. Although not explicitly stated, the theme of salvation is present as this account demonstrates the healing that Jesus God brings even to those who are dead (or, in this case, near death). In addition, this story presents the theme of faith in that the centurion displays the kind of faith and humility that Jesus expects. Once again, the last (the humble gentile) will be first, and the first (Jewish people) will be last.

Conclusion

Like the unique Lukan tradition, the Mark and Q sources have passages that cohere with Luke 18:9–14 via related themes and motifs. All these sources have a certain eschatological backdrop that includes the motif or reversal. As the humble are exalted such as the centurion (Luke 7:1–10), the blind man (Luke 18:35–43), and the children (Luke 18:15–17), the proud are brought low such as the rich ruler (Luke 18:18–30). The undeserving "sinner" or outcast is restored. The theme of salvation is expressed in terms of entering the kingdom of God (Luke 18:17), gaining eternal life (Luke 18:18), being made right in a wholistic sense (Luke 18:35–43), and attending the eschatological banquet (Luke 14:15–24). Access of this restoration is through faith as evidenced also by humility and not self-righteousness.

The following is a summary classification of the forms of the specific texts within the L tradition, Mark, and Q. Luke is included for the purpose of comparison.

The following are forms with the passages from Luke:

1. Parable (15:1–32; 16:14–31; 18:1–8),
2. Pronouncement story (19:1–10);
3. Admonition or proverbial counsel with a parable (14:1–14),
4. Combination pronouncement story and parable (7:36–50; 10:1–37), and
5. Passion narrative.

The following are forms with the passages from Mark:

1. Pronouncement story (Mark 10:13-16//Luke 18:15-17//Matt 19:13-25—Jesus blesses the children),
2. Pronouncement story/apophthegm/isolated sayings (Mark 10:17-31//Luke 18:18-30//Matt 19:16-30—the rich man), and
3. Miracle story or healing narrative (Mark 10:46-52//Luke 18:35-43//Matt 20:29-34; 9:27-31—Healing of the blind man).

The following are forms with the passages from Q:

1. Minatory sayings (Luke 13:22-30//Matt 7:13-14, 22-23; 8:11-12; 19:3—the narrow door),
2. Parable (Luke 14:15-24//Matt 22:1-14—parable of the banquet), and
3. Pronouncement story with healing miracle (Luke 7:1-10//Matt 8:5-13—the faith of a centurion).

This recurrence of the related themes and motifs in different forms and in diverse traditions strengthens the case that the theme of justification in Luke 18:9-14 may be sourced from Jesus material.

— Chapter 5 —

Jewish Palestinian Background of Luke 18:9–14

This chapter seeks to establish the contextual plausibility of Luke 18:9–14 by underscoring its Jewish Palestinian background. The more elements this passage has that makes it comprehensible for the early first-century Palestinian audience, the greater the plausible fit of this parable in the Jewish Palestinian context. Reviewing the parable's "local color" involves bringing to light some ancient sources that illuminate the background of this parable to bring further understanding on how the first-century audience would have heard the parable. Therefore, Jewish and Christian sources are examined, as well as general Mediterranean ones given its impact in the first-century culture. Rabbinic sources later than Luke are also included although objections can be raised about their applicability in analyzing the early first century Jewish context. However, these sources may also reflect early Jewish culture in writings that had been closely transmitted and preserved for long periods of time through oral tradition.[1]

The first verse of the parable is the introduction. Then what follows is the beginning of the parable narrative where two men are portrayed as going up towards the temple. In terms of the two, the parable portrays these characters with each of their qualities, mind-set, physical posture, and status set in contrast with one another.[2] The contrast would have been very evident to its

---

1. Keener, "Ancient Context," 155. Keener, states, "Even the earliest rabbinic sources are much later than Luke, but (in contrast to modern Western culture's emphasis on novelty and innovation) they reflect a culture that valued the preservation of tradition and skills in oral memory." Keener, "Ancient Context," 155n3.

2. Compare this to other parables that also have contrasting figures such as the

first-century audience given the general cultural and societal characteristics of the two people groups represented by these characters.

The Pharisee

According to Josephus, the Pharisees were a highly influential group especially among the people.[3] Among the Jews they had a reputation of excellence compared to all other Jewish people in terms of how they observed the religious practices and laws.[4] They were considered "the most accurate interpreters of the laws."[5] The Pharisees were known as righteous and tried to please God in everything.[6] They gave the people regulations and directions for worship, prayer, and the practice of "the highest ideals in their way of living and in their discourse."[7]

Beyond Josephus, other limited ancient sources that describe the Pharisees are comprised of the NT, rabbinic literature, and Qumran literature. Anthony J. Saldarini's synthesis of his findings from these sources reveal that the Pharisaic association functioned like a social movement organization that espoused changes in society. They sought a "a new, communal commitment to a strict way Jewish way of life based on adherence to the covenant."[8] As a type of sect, they are "reformist" in the sense that they seek gradual, divinely ordered changes in their world. They had a program of reform for Jewish life, aided by a particular interpretation of Scripture and also a "definable and sometimes controversial outlook on fundamental matters crucial to Judaism."[9] The rabbinic sources that can be dated to the

---

prodigal and his brother (Luke 15:11–32), Simon and the woman (Luke 7:36–50), and the Samaritan and the priest/Levite (Luke 10:25–37). At this point, the narrative audience already has two images of both the Pharisees and the tax collectors given how Jesus interacts with both groups. But without any sense of prior impact of Jesus's teaching, the audience can be assumed to have a positive image for the Pharisee and a negative one for the tax collector; see Nolland, *Luke 9:21—18:34*, 875.

3. Josephus, *Ant.* 18.15.
4. Josephus, *J.W.* 1.110–12.
5. Josephus, *J.W.* 2.162.
6. Josephus, *Ant.* 13.289.
7. Josephus, *Ant.* 297–98; 18.15.
8. Saldarini, "Pharisees," *ABD* 5:302.
9. Saldarini, "Pharisees," *ABD* 5:302.

first century portray the Pharisees' strong interest in tithing, ritual purity, and Sabbath observance.[10]

But even as Pharisees strived to inculcate a higher standard of religious faith for the people in terms of their teaching and life, it is not unknown for sincere Pharisees occasionally to think highly of themselves over other people.[11] Some thought they were, at times, guilty of false humility. The two Talmuds record seven varieties of Pharisees of which only one is favorable. According to the Palestinian Talmud, the "shoulder" Pharisee shoulders good works to be seen by people; the "wait-a-bit" Pharisee excuses himself to do good works if asked to do other things; the "reckoning" Pharisee does a good work to compensate for being at fault for something else; the "economizing" Pharisee tries to do a good work in the most economical way possible; the "show me my fault" Pharisee asks to show him his fault and he will do an equivalent good work; the Pharisee of fear; and, the Pharisee of love, like Abraham.[12] Some were guilty of "the evils of exaggerated self-esteem, or self-righteousness."[13] Johanan ben Zakkai gave a warning to those who think of themselves more highly than they should: "If you have learned a great deal of Torah, do not claim credit for yourself, for that is what you were made for."[14]

Overall, the people viewed the Pharisees as a significant group whom people revered during the time of Jesus. They were known for their rigor and zeal for excellence in all aspects of the Jewish religion. But at times some among them were also known to have a certain attitude (even by some of their sincere followers) that comes from perceiving themselves as better than everyone else, resulting in a faulty sense of self-esteem and self-righteousness.

The Tax Collector

The Pharisee is set in contrast to the tax collector, whom the parable hearers would have distinguished as significantly unlike him in many ways. Tax collectors describe those who bid for and purchased the right to collect taxes and were contracted by civic officials. They pay, in advance, the

---

10. Saldarini, "Pharisees," *ABD* 5:302.
11. Moore, *Judaism*, 2: 192–94; see also Saldarini, "Pharisees," *ABD* 5:289–303.
12. Moore, *Judaism*, 2:193, cites y. Ber. 14b, y. Soṭah 20c.
13. Moore, *Judaism*, 2:194.
14. Moore, *Judaism*, 2:245.

sum for the year for tax collecting in a specific region. What these tax or toll collectors receive beyond their contracts was profit. Various taxes were levied, such as direct taxes, poll taxes (determined by census), land taxes, toll charges on travel and transportation of goods from one region to another, sales taxes, and inheritance taxes.[15] When Judea was under Roman prefects starting in 6 CE, the tax collectors collected the direct taxes, the poll tax, and land tax. Indirect taxes were subcontracted. Jewish tax collectors were regarded as traitors because they did business with or worked for the rulers to collect taxes and tolls.[16] The man portrayed in the parable was possibly a lower level toll collector as are other collectors that Jesus encountered (except Zaccheaus).[17]

The people had a negative general impression of tax or toll collectors. This attitude towards tax collectors is reflected in ancient sources, both in the Jewish and Greco-Roman world. For instance, Roman and Hellenistic literature associates tax collectors with beggars, thieves, and robbers.[18] They were paired with sinners in the NT.[19] They were also paired with immoral people.[20] They were deemed to be like the gentiles.[21] In Rabbinic writings, tax and toll collectors are linked together with robbers, murderers, and sinners.[22] Tax collector appears in a list of "despised trades" that no observant Jew should follow.[23] The qualities of the tax collectors serve as a sharp contrast to the qualities of the Pharisees. Since the tax collectors had a reputation of dishonesty, as they reputedly took more than they ought from the people (Luke 3:11–12; 19:8), they were thought of as sinners for whom repentance was difficult: "For herdsmen, tax collectors and publicans, repentance is hard."[24] Also because of their general dishonesty, they are linked in the Mishnah with murderers and robbers who are people to whom one does

---

15. This is all in addition to religious taxes like the temple tax and tithes on produce for Jerusalem priests.

16. Donahue, "Tax Collector," *ABD* 6:337–38; Snodgrass, *Stories*, 467.

17. Donahue, "Tax Collectors and Sinners," 39–61; For taxation in Galilee, see Josephus, *Ant.* 12.154–59, 175–86; *Select Papyri* 2, selections 286, 358, 382, and 420.

18. Cicero, *Off.* 15–51; Dio Chrysostom, *Or.* 14.14.

19. Mark 2:15; Matt 9:10; 11:19; Luke 7:34; 15:2.

20. Matt 21:31.

21. Matt 5:46; 18:17.

22. m. Ṭehar. 7.6; m. B. Qam. 10.2; m. Ned. 3.4.

23. b. Sanh. 25b; Jeremias, *Jerusalem*, 302–12.

24. b. B. Qam. 94b.

not have to tell the truth. Tax collectors were later deprived of civic rights and were not allowed to be judges or witnesses in court.[25]

The Temple Setting

Both men are depicted as going up to the temple at the beginning of the story and then going down from temple near the end of the narrative due to the elevation of the temple mount (Luke 18:10, 14).[26] Bailey correctly points out that the concept of going to the temple to pray may, for those who are brought up in more western traditions, give them the impression that the Pharisee and tax collector went to the temple for private devotions.[27] But there is good evidence to suggest that the text really reflects the context of public corporate worship. In the OT and NT, to "pray" can signify either private devotions or corporate worship. As Zechariah burned incense as part of participating in the daily atonement sacrifice, the multitude of people were praying outside (Luke 1:9–10). The temple is called the "house of prayer" (Luke 19:46; Isa 56:7). A reference to the ninth hour as the "hour of prayer" is indicated in Acts 3:1, which points to the afternoon service of the daily liturgy.[28] One of the activities that the early Christians did as a community, in addition to being taught by the apostles, having fellowship, and breaking bread, was to pray (Acts 2:42). A place designated for prayer is pictured also in Acts at a location where people come to gather (Acts 16:13, 16). Of course, there are many passages that show prayer as an individual activity or as private devotions (Luke 5:16; 6:12; Matt 14:23; 26:36; Mark 6:46), but overall prayer can either be private or corporate, depending on the context.

Many came to the temple to do certain tasks such as give offerings and sacrifices, worship and pray during the liturgy or outside of it, study the Torah, and participate in the worship. Israelites came to be ritually cleansed. Many Jews went daily to the temple to be at the worship, receive the benediction, pray during the burning of incense, and prostrate themselves before God as the Levites sang songs.[29] A good argument can be

---

25. m. Ned. 3.4; b. Sanh. 25b. Cf. m. 'Abot 3.17.
26. Pss 122; 134; 135; Josephus, *Ant.* 12.164f.; Marshall, *Gospel of Luke*, 679.
27. Bailey, *Through Peasant Eyes*, 145.
28. Hamm, "Tamid Service," 223.
29. "The Temple," in Safrai and Stern, *People in the First Century*, 2:877.

made that the parable portrays the Pharisee and tax collector participating in the daily temple worship.

Bailey describes this scenario. The Pharisee and the tax collector both went up to the temple at the same time perhaps for public worship, as that is one of the main purposes for people to make that trip. The Pharisee stood by himself, meaning apart from other worshippers. Likewise, the tax collector stood far off not just from the Pharisee but also from other worshippers. They both pray, but one evidence that may indicate that their prayer was in the context of the daily worship is the tax collector saying ἱλάσθητί (Luke 18:13) from ἱλάσκομαι, which is a word with cultic overtones unlike the more commonly used word ἐλέησόν (Luke 16:24; 17:13; 18:38–39). The use of the less common cultic word means it is possible that the prayers were taking place while the incense was being burned during the liturgy.[30] During the offering of the incense, people prayed in the court and outside the temple as well (Luke 1:10; Jdt 9:1).[31] This was accepted as the right time for private prayers especially for people with their own special petitions at that time, particularly during the afternoon sacrifice.[32] The sacrifices prepare the people for prayer as these make possible the meeting between God and Israel through the priest's action in bringing Israel near to God. The burning incense represented the prayer that followed the sacrifice. Ps 141:2 comes into mind: "Let my prayer be counted as incense before you, and the lifting up of my hands as an evening sacrifice." Then after the service, both the Pharisee and the tax collector went down at the same time from the temple.[33] Overall, the manner indicated gives the picture of private prayers being offered as part of corporate worship during the atonement sacrifice ritual done twice everyday (the morning at dawn and at three in the afternoon).[34] Of course, prayers can be offered outside the context of corporate worship, as any Israelite could offer private prayers in front of the altar with the burning sacrifice anytime between the two services.[35] However, given that there are other notable passages in Luke-Acts that possibly allude to this daily temple

---

30. m. Tamid; see also Sir 50:1–21, where the atonement ritual in the temple is described, specifically 50:19 where the people offered their prayers until the service was done even as the singers are singing hymns of praise.

31. "The Temple," in Safrai and Stern, *People in the First Century,* 2:888.

32. m. Tamid 5.1; cf. Sir 50:5–18; Jdt 9:1; "The Temple," in Safrai and Stern, *People in the First Century,* 2:885–90.

33. Bailey, *Through Peasant Eyes,* 145.

34. cf. Acts 2:15; 3:1.

35. Bailey, *Through Peasant Eyes,* 147.

service, it seems more likely that the prayers of the Pharisee and tax collector were made in the context of corporate worship.[36] This setting suggested by this parable would have been very intelligible for the first-century Jewish Palestinian hearers of this passage.

The Pharisee Stands Apart

The Pharisee stood by himself (Luke 18:11). Standing was the common posture for prayer.[37] A few reasons may have been behind the Pharisee's position of being apart from the others. One possibility concerns ritual purity. Rabbinic texts talk about the need for Pharisees to avoid *midras*—uncleanness. They can get this kind of ritual uncleanness if they were somehow in contact with the "people of the land" or the *am-haaretz*. These were Jews who did not follow ritual purity rules and improperly set apart their tithes from their produce. The tax collector would fit perfectly as one of the *am-haaretz*. The people who faithfully kept the law such as the Pharisees were called "associates" or *haberim*. A Pharisee who even accidentally touches an *am-haaretz* would incur *midras* because even the clothes of the *am-haaretz* can cause this kind of ritual uncleanness.[38] If a tax collector enters someone's house, that house and all that is in it is considered unclean. If an associate's wife let the wife of an *am-haaretz* grind flour within her house and the wife stops grinding, the house becomes unclean. These topics and more in connection with avoiding types of contact with the *am-haaretz* are known in the culture.[39] The *haberim* who were mindful of these ritual laws had every incentive to separate themselves physically even at the daily temple service. In addition, further separation was done when the delegation of Israel, as part of their responsibility, made the unclean stand at the eastern gate.[40] The Assumption of Moses, in referring to impious leaders, states, "And though their hands and minds touch unclean things, yet their mouth

---

36. E.g., Luke 24:50–53; Luke 1:5–25 shows Zechariah doing the offering in the afternoon sacrifice; Acts 3:1 speaks about Peter and John going to the temple in the ninth hour which is the time for the afternoon sacrifice; Acts 10; Luke 23:45–47; Arguments that these passages allude to the daily "Tamid" service are in Hamm, "Tamid Service," 217–27.

37. 1 Sam 1:26; 1 Kgs 8:14, 22; Matt 6:5; Mark 11:25.

38. m. Ḥag. 2:7, Danby 214.

39. m. Demai 2.3; m. Ṭehar. 7.4–6; 8.3.

40. m. Tamid 5.6.

shall speak great things, and they shall say furthermore: "Do not touch me lest thou shouldst pollute me in the place (where I stand)."[41] However, so as not to overstate or mischaracterize Pharisees, even if some of them had the incentive or tendency to be separate, Pharisees did not disconnect from the people as they were looked upon as highly respected teachers of the people. In other words, they were not necessarily obsessive about separation to the extent that they joined the community at Qumran.[42]

Connected also to the tendency to separate was the attitude of being set apart. Hillel said, "Keep not aloof from the congregation and trust not in thyself until the day of thy death, and judge not thy fellow until thou art thyself come to this place."[43] This advice reveals inclinations by religious leaders to have a certain aloofness from the people. Technically, there is no indication in the parable that the Pharisee is regarded as a leader in the temple. Normally, the Pharisees' sphere of influence is based in the village and not in the temple. However, Josephus reportedly describes how Pharisees strived to influence Temple practice in terms of what is done in worship, prayers, and sacrifices.[44] In that sense, they take initiative as leaders do. It is still not hard to imagine the relevance of this portrait for the first-century Jewish Palestinian perspective. This possible attitude of the Pharisee makes Luke's introduction even more intelligible because it states that this parable is for those who trusted in themselves that they were righteous and viewed others with contempt (Luke 18:9).[45]

A third option would be that the Pharisee simply stood in the inner court of the temple as far as an Israelite who was not a priest would have been permitted in the court of Israel in a contrast to the tax collector who was standing far off.[46]

---

41. As. Mos. 7:9–10, cited by Snodgrass, *Stories*, 464.

42. In agreement with Levine, *Short Stories*, 199. But Levine, disagrees that ritual purity laws have anything to do with his conduct inside the temple. Levine, *Short Stories*, 204. But in this case, the ancient texts do speak of the tendency to separate. This was brought in part from observing the purity rules outside the temple.

43. m. Pirke Aboth 2.5.

44. Levine, *Short Stories*, 193.

45. Not that the introductory verse is meant to stereotype the Pharisees. Jesus is addressing his own disciples with this parable (Luke 17:22) perhaps within earshot of some Pharisees (Luke 17:20). Therefore, the parable is meant generally for anyone who thinks of himself or herself as "righteous."

46. Bock, *Luke 9:51—24:53*, 1462; Fitzmyer, *Luke X–XXIV*, 1186, Barrett, "Justification," 42.

The standing posture of the Pharisee for prayer was normal.[47] The reverent attitude of the person praying as prescribed by the rabbis required standing with his body facing the Holy Place. Also, prayer in this context was normally done aloud.[48] Bailey suggests, for added color, that the Luke 18:9–14 Pharisee's stature and practice of praying aloud may have given him the opportunity to preach to those around him, especially to the unclean within his visual vicinity (such as the tax collector as reflected in Luke 18:11). It was a chance to provide the people with a closer experience of a Pharisee's teaching in living righteously.[49]

Overall, given these reasons discussed, the Pharisee's posture and attitude would have been comprehensible in the Jewish Palestinian first-century environment. The next important aspect to consider is the Pharisee's prayer.

The Prayer of the Pharisee

The prayer that is most commonly compared to the Pharisee's prayer is from the Babylonian Talmud:

> I give thanks to Thee, O Lord, my God, that Thou hast set my portion with those who sit in the Beth ha-Midrash and Thou hast not set my portion with those who sit in street-corners; for I rise early and they rise early, but I rise early for words of Torah and they rise early for frivolous talk; I labour and they labour, but I labour and receive a reward and they labour and do not receive a reward; I run and they run, but I run to the life of the future world and they run to the pit of destruction.[50]

Some commentators have either cited this prayer as a comparable example of the attitude of self-righteousness of the Pharisee in the story.[51]

---

47. b. Ber. 31a.

48. 1 Sam 1:13; Marshall, *Gospel of Luke*, 679.

49. Bailey, *Through Peasant Eyes*, 149. Perhaps it is with regards to tithing and fasting (Luke 18:12). Levine also notes that Pharisees were mostly based in the village and not at the temple, which is the bastion of the priests. Therefore, it would make sense to picture Pharisees as wanting to exert influence on the people in the temple regarding worship, prayers and sacrifices. See also Levine, *Short Stories*, 193; Josephus, *Ant*. 297–98.

50. b. Ber. 28b; parallel in y. Ber. 4.2.

51. Bailey comments that this is a "striking illustration of a similar prayer from the period" after describing the Pharisee's prayer as "self-advertisement," and "self-congratulatory." Bailey, *Through Peasant Eyes*, 150.

Others would say that this kind of prayer is neither derogatory nor self-congratulatory but is more about gratitude, comparable to Deut 26:1–15, especially vv. 12–14.[52] Another prayer to consider is 1QH 7.34: "I praise thee, O Lord, that thou hast not allowed my lot to fall among the worthless community, nor assigned me a part in the circle of the secret ones." In addition, here is 1QH 15.34–35: "[I give you thanks], Lord, because you did not make my lot fall in the congregation of falsehood, nor have you placed my regulation in the counsel of hypocrites, [but you have led me] to your favour and your forgiveness."

Whether self-congratulatory or pure gratitude, the Pharisee's word to God is a real type of prayer of which the audience would have been aware, which, therefore, reflects a fit in the Jewish Palestinian environment. Guided by the introductory verse in Luke 18:9 and the generalizing comment in Luke 18:14b, the prayer of the Pharisee is meant to be perceived as having the attitude of self-righteousness and pride without necessarily eliminating the gratitude to God behind the prayer. The key reason is that the Pharisee singles out the tax collector (ἢ καὶ ὡς οὗτος ὁ τελώνης) among the other people. The word οὗτος possibly carries a derogatory impression associated with the tax collector and, in a sense, turns him into a concrete example of who the Pharisee is not like instead of the more general references to robbers, adulterers, and the unjust.[53] It is possible that the Pharisee is merely putting the tax collector in the same category as the rest of the unrighteous group, but a similar pejorative use of οὗτος can also be found in 15:2 and Acts 17:18. Therefore, this particular disparaging use seems to be in mind here. The overall expression then differentiates the tax collector from the individuals in the list of "other people."[54]

As for the content, the Pharisee states that he fasts twice a week and give tithes of all that he possesses (Luke 18:12). Moses prescribed fasting on the day of atonement (Lev 16:29, 31; 23:27, 29, 32; Num 29:7), which is the only day it is required. In addition, people facing crises would fast and particularly pious people would do it more frequently (e.g., 1 Sam 7:6; Ps 35:13; Zech 7:5; Matt 6:16–18; Mark 2:18–20; Luke 2:36–38; Acts

---

52. Levine, *Short Stories*, 200; Holmgren, "Pharisee," 257.

53. Barrett, "Justification," 44; Bock, *Luke 9:51—24:53*, 1462–63; Marshall, *Gospel of Luke*, 679; Fitzmyer, *Luke X–XXIV*, 1187; Forbes, *God of Old*, 214.

54. Nolland, *Luke 9:21—18:34*, 876; Farris, "Tale," 27n11; Levine, *Short Stories*, 202, sees the prayer as gratitude and sees nothing wrong with the content but also notes that the Pharisee through this prayer negatively judges the tax collector instead of thinking about bringing him to a better position with respect to God.

13:2–3; 2 Cor 11:27). Fasting was also perceived as a means of overcoming temptation, especially in the *Testament of the Twelve Patriarchs*.[55] Therefore, the Pharisee goes beyond what is needed in fasting twice a week, although this practice was done in certain groups among the Pharisees and their disciples.[56] Fasting twice a week would have been on Monday and Thursday.[57] The Pharisee may have seen himself as making atonement for all of Israel through his practice of fasting.[58]

The OT is clear on the requirement for tithing. Tithes are levied on grain, wine, and oil (Lev 27:30; Num 18:27; Deut 12:17; 14:13). Safrai states, "In tannaitic times the law was extended to take in anything used as food."[59] There were exceptions: rue, purslane, celery, and other agricultural products.[60] At this point, the practice of tithing nonagricultural products was just beginning to appear, and "the custom was never really widespread, and was confined to those who were particularly strict."[61] Even tax collectors tithed.[62] What distinguished the Pharisee was that he tithed everything. Some say that his exemplary tithing was also an act performed on behalf of the rest of the community, meaning, it was not just for his benefit but for the benefit of Israel, in a vicarious sense, especially for those who were not able to tithe as they should have.[63] However, even if that was the case, it does not mean that an attitude derived from seeing oneself as righteous and disdaining of others was mutually exclusive from the actions he may have done on behalf of the community. The OT and the NT present certain Israelites as people who can more than excel in some aspects of the Law but neglect its weightier matters.[64]

Therefore, the prayer and the exceptional actions mentioned by the Pharisee are culturally intelligible in the Jewish Palestinian environment. The next step is to assess the actions and prayer of the tax collector.

55. Snodgrass, *Stories*, 740n139.

56. Safrai, *Jewish People in the First Century* 2:186.

57. See m. Ta'an. 1.6; b. Ta'an. 12a; Did. 8:1; also Safrai, "Religion in Everyday Life," *Jewish People in the First Century* 2:814–16.

58. Snodgrass, *Stories*, 467.

59. Safrai, *Jewish People in the First Century* 2:825; cf. m. Ma'aś. 1:1.

60. m. Šeb. 9:1.

61. Safrai, *Jewish People in the First Century* 2:825.

62. Safrai, *Jewish People in the First Century* 2:819.

63. Levine, *Short Stories*, 204; Hultgren, *Parables*, 123; Snodgrass, *Stories*, 467; Friedrichsen, "Temple," 111; Farris, "Tale," 28.

64. E.g., Matt 23:23; Hos 6:6; Mic 6:7–8.

JEWISH PALESTINIAN BACKGROUND OF LUKE 18:9-14

The Tax Collector Stands Far Off, Downcast

A distance away from the other worshippers is the tax collector. He may have felt unworthy to stand with the worshippers before the altar, or since the Pharisee recognized him as a tax collector (so perhaps others can as well), he may have feared any untoward reactions from the other worshippers given his manner of life. In terms of precise location, he may have been in the extremities of the court of Israel, which portrays his low status and ritual impurity.[65]

With regards to his body language, he beats his chest in extreme sorrow and aguish. Similarly, after Jesus's death, the crowd returns to their homes, beating their chest (Luke 23:48). In a commentary on Ecclesiastes 7:2, "R. Mana said, "And the Living will lay it to his heart: these are the righteous who set their death over against their heart; and why do they beat upon their heart? As though to say, 'All is there,'" (note . . . the righteous beat their heart as the source of evil longing.).”[66] "Out of the heart come evil thoughts, murder, . . . theft, false witness, slander" (Matt 15:19). Again, standing is common in prayer.[67] Lifting one's eyes is common in prayer,[68] but being unable to raise eyes to heaven describes fallen angels because of their shame of their sins.[69] Aseneth is described as striking her breast, bowing her head, and having no confidence in approaching God when she sought forgiveness for her sins.[70] Ezra was ashamed to look up at heaven because of the sins committed by the people (Ezra 9:6).[71]

These striking descriptions portray a person who is sorrowful and in extreme anguish and shame. This image clearly communicates to the audience in the first-century Palestinian context.

---

65. Forbes, *God of Old*, 217.

66. Bailey, *Through Peasant Eyes*, 153, cites *Midrash Rabbah*, Eccl. VII, 2, 5, Sonc., 177.

67. 1 Sam 1:26; 1 Kgs 8:14, 22; Matt 6:5; Mark 11:25.

68. Matt 14:19//Mark 6:41//Luke 9:16; Mark 7:34; John 11:41; 17:1.

69. 1 En. 13:5.

70. *Jos. Asen.* 10.2—13.15.

71. Josephus, *Ant.* 11.143.

The Tax Collector's Prayer

The tax collector's prayer uses ὁ θεός, ἱλάσθητί μοι τῷ ἁμαρτωλῷ with ἱλάσθητί as the key term. This word is used only four other times in the NT in the context of atonement (Rom 3:25; Heb 9:5; 1 John 2:2; 4:10). One can easily imagine the tax collector, who was highly aware that he was a sinner and was in extreme anguish about it, expressing a desperate desire for the benefit of atonement. The tax collector may have made this prayer in combination with his emotions and actions of extreme anguish after he witnesses what was involved in public worship, which includes hearing the announcement through the silver trumpets that the sacrifice was about to be offered, the priest slaying the sacrificial lamb, with some blood sprinkled on the altar and the rest poured at the base, the cleansing of the altar of incense and dressing the golden candlestick in the Holy Place, the preparing and burning of the incense, the offering of prayers by the priest and the people, the blessing, and hearing the temple music from the choir of Levites accompanied by instrumental music. These and other details were involved in the Tamid service and would have been an appropriate setting for the tax collector to deliver his plea to God as depicted in the parable.[72] His prayer may bring into mind the *Prayer of Manasseh:*

> Therefore you, O Lord, God of the righteous, have not appointed repentance for the righteous, for Abraham and Isaac and Jacob, who did not sin against you, but you have appointed repentance for me, who am a sinner. For the sins I have committed are more in number than the sand of the sea; my transgressions are multiplied, O Lord, they are multiplied! I am not worthy to look up and see the height of heaven because of the multitude of my iniquities.[73]

Exacerbating the issue for the tax collector is his inability to provide restitution as money gained by extortion required an additional fifth to be added (Lev 6:1–5). Plus, it would be difficult to identify everyone whom he may have defrauded. These complications severely limit the repentant tax collector's ability to make full restitution.[74] His helplessness about his situation and plea to God is in the spirit of Ps 51:1–4:

> Have mercy on me, O God, according to your unfailing love; according to your great compassion blot out my transgressions.

---

72. Bailey, *Through Peasant Eyes*, 154.
73. Pr Man 1:8–9, cited by Snodgrass, *Stories*, 464.
74. See b. B. Qam. 94b for the difficulty of tax collectors in making restitution.

> Wash away all my iniquity and cleanse me from my sin. For I know my transgressions, and my sin is always before me. Against you, you only, have I sinned and done what is evil in your sight; so you are right in your verdict and justified when you judge.

Even if the prayer took place not in the context of the corporate worship but through private prayer at a different time, the setting of being at the temple, which is a special place for God's presence and forgiveness, would be important to consider in picturing the circumstances surrounding the intention of the tax collector's prayer and stance.[75]

In the end, the tax collector went down declared as righteous as opposed to the Pharisee (18:14a). This mercy and forgiveness that God extends to the lowly and those in need of mercy is known in the NT (e.g., Matt 5:3–7; 18:21–35; Luke 6:20–21; 7:36–50) as an emphasis of Jesus in various texts, but the rationale in Luke 18:14b sheds light on the reversal that took place.[76] This logion, which states how the humble are exalted while the proud are brought low, is also the explanatory statement in other places in the NT and the OT.[77] This specific type of reversal is also familiar in later Jewish writings as expressed in the Babylonian Talmud: "This teaches you that him who humbles himself, the Holy one, blessed be He, raises up, and him who exalts himself, the Holy One, blessed be He, humbles; from him who seeks greatness, greatness flees, but him who flees from greatness, greatness follows."[78]

Humility is also the condition of true learning as expressed by a saying from the rabbis in Jamnia:

> I am a creature and my fellow is a creature; my work is in town and his work is in the field; I rise early to my work, and he to his. As he does not esteem his occupation superior to mine, so I do not esteem mine superior to his. Perhaps you may say, I accomplish much and he little, but we are taught, it matters not whether much or little, if only a man directs his mind to heaven.[79]

---

75. Snodgrass, *Stories*, 473. The parable is not a critique the temple as oppressive due to the temple taxes as depicted in Herzog, *Subversive Speech*, 173–93. Farris, "Tale," 23–33.

76. cf. Matt 18:4; 23:12; Luke 14:11.

77. Jas 4:6–10; 1 Pet 5:5–6, quoting Prov 3:34.

78. b. ʿErub. 13b. See also 4 Ezra 8:47–50.

79. Moore, *Judaism*, 2: 245–46; b. Ber. 17a.

Therefore, the prayer of the tax collector and the depiction of God as merciful to the humble would have been understandable to the first-century Jewish Palestinian audience.

The Notion of Justification

Fitzmyer comments, "The notion of justification does not transcend that of the OT; it is rooted in the spirit of justification which pervades such psalms as 51 or 24:3–5 or 2 Esd 12:7. In other words, one should beware of reading this parable with all the connotations of Pauline justification or thinking that it has a 'Pauline ring' to it."[80] Likewise, Marshall asserts that as for the righteousness language in the parable, "this is the only occurrence in the Gospels of this characteristically Pauline use, . . . but the language is not based on Paul (cf. Ps. 51:19; 1 QSb 4:22; 4 Ezra 12:7)."[81]

Some of the other scriptures that reflect the notion of justification (or its spirit) and its related themes are already mentioned in this chapter, including the ones from Rabbinic sources. In addition, other authors such as Mark A. Seifrid trace the development of Paul's notion of justification in intertestamental literature, such as the Psalms of Solomon and The Community Rule.[82] In addition, the source material provided by Snodgrass takes up some of the material in this chapter and more, such as Ps 79:9; Ezra 9:6; Prov 3:34; 27:2; 29:23, and the "Psalms of Innocence" 5, 7, 17, and 26.[83] These and other sources may possibly have some background that both Paul and Luke had in common.

Conclusion

Overall, from the contrast of the characters to their prayers and disposition, the setting of the pre-70 CE temple, the Tamid service and the implications of atonement, everything about this parable gives a picture that is contextually plausible with the first-century Jewish Palestinian audience. Therefore, this chapter further supports the notion that Luke 18:9–14 and its theme of justification originated from Jesus material.

---

80. Fitzmyer, *Luke X–XXIV*, 1185.
81. Marshall, *Gospel of Luke*, 680.
82. Seifrid, *Justification by Faith*. See also Seifrid, *Christ Our Righteousness*, 38–45.
83. Snodgrass, *Stories*, 463–65.

—— Chapter 6 ——

The "Inauthenticity" of Luke 18:9–14, Other Unique Lukan Parables

FROM THE PREVIOUS CHAPTERS, this book uses the criterion of coherence to determine the possible effect made by the historical Jesus. Coherence of the themes and motifs of justification in independent sources (i.e., Mark, Q, L) and forms (e.g., pronouncement stories, miracle stories, parable) suggests the possibility that the theme of justification as portrayed in the parable of the Pharisee and Tax Collector (Luke 18:9–14) comes from Jesus tradition and is not necessarily a theme imported from Paul's writings and thought.

In 2016, John Meier published his fifth volume of *A Marginal Jew* in which he specifically focuses on the authenticity of the parables.[1] Meier presents what he calls his "Seven Unfashionable Theses" for which thesis seven is the most controversial. In thesis seven, Meier states, "Relatively few of the synoptic parables can be attributed to the historical Jesus with a good degree of probability. In other words, relatively few of the parables can meet the test of the criteria of authenticity that other sayings and deeds of Jesus

---

1. Meier, *Marginal Jew*. Meier's previous volumes involve the following: (1) vol. 1—The basic principles of the quest of the historical Jesus, which includes observations about the social, cultural, economic, and other background to give historical context for the quest; (2) vol. 2—John the Baptist as a mentor for Jesus; Jesus's eschatological message, his mighty deeds and signs that reveals the arrival of the kingdom; the sayings and narratives from sources and the use of the criteria of historicity; (3) vol. 3—Focus on the major Jewish groups and other generalizations of the people portrayed in the Gospels such as the crowds, the Pharisees, Sadducees, Samaritans; and, (4) vol. 4—Jesus and the Law.

are supposed to meet."[2] He claims that this proposition goes against modern research on synoptic parables, which currently presumes or assumes (instead of proves) that most of these parables come from the historical Jesus.[3] Through employing what he regards as a rigorous application of the standard criteria of authenticity, he posits a contrary view: Most of these parables should not be presumed as authentic but instead need to be designated as "*non liquet*" (i.e., not clear). This expression means that there is not enough evidence either to render each parable as authentic or to consider it inauthentic.[4] He repeatedly stresses that he is declaring neither that most of the parables are necessarily inauthentic nor that Jesus did not teach in parables. He rightly states that the notion that Jesus taught in parables has multiple attestations and the use of parables in his teaching coheres with the use of parables by the OT prophets and rabbinic teachers.[5] However, in several other places in his book, Meier does indicate a firm belief that most individual L parables are "inauthentic." For example, concerning the L parables he writes, "Stripped of their unearned presumption of historicity, most of the parables cannot mount convincing arguments in favor of their authenticity. Creation by the early church or by the evangelists seems a likely explanation . . . in my view, for most if not all of the L parables."[6] Instead of coming from Jesus, he claims that the L parables, which include Luke 18:9–14, strongly show the redactional theology of Luke and are "reinforced by vocabulary, grammar, literary form, and style that are typical of Luke."[7] He also implies that Pauline themes of justification apart from the Law and the inclusion of the gentiles who seem to be present in the prodigal son, the Pharisee and the tax collector, and the good Samaritan are actually Lukan imports from Paul's thought. Therefore, he asks, rhetorically: "By what criterion or argument can we attribute any L parable back to the historical Jesus?"[8] To bolster the answer to this question, he performs an analysis of the good Samaritan as a test case. He concludes that this

---

2. Meier, *Marginal Jew*, 5:48. Thesis one through six are his arguments that build up to thesis seven.

3. Meier, *Marginal Jew*, 5:xiii.

4. Meier, *Marginal Jew*, 5:5, 8, 49, 56, 190, 210, 367.

5. Meier, *Marginal Jew*, 5:48.

6. Meier, *Marginal Jew*, 5:210.

7. Meier, *Marginal Jew*, 5:198.

8. Meier, *Marginal Jew*, 5:198.

THE "INAUTHENTICITY" OF LUKE 18:9-14

parable, together with its introduction, is a thoroughly Lukan creation and does not come from the historical Jesus.⁹

To scholars and advocates of the criteria of authenticity and its traditional use in historical Jesus studies, Meier's theses and conclusions bring into question justification in Luke 18:9-14 as a probable theme in the Jesus tradition. In their minds, most, if not all, of the L parables, including that of the Pharisee and tax collector, are not "authentic," then the distinct notion of justification found in Luke 18:9-14 is also not "authentic." For them, the plausibility of the hypothesis that Luke may have just copied this notion of justification from Paul greatly increases. Therefore, tracing its related themes back to other independent sources such as Mark, Q, and L passages is nothing but a needless exercise if Luke 18:9-14 is not considered to be truly "authentic" Jesus tradition.

Because of his book's potential influence, it is important to understand and respond to Meier's work by looking carefully and commenting on his arguments, claims, and assumptions. Meier is not the only scholar who believes that Luke 18:9-14 and the L parables as a whole are inauthentic. The works of John Drury, Luise Schottroff, and Michael Goulder express similar notions about the inauthenticity of these parables.¹⁰ However, Meier is the latest scholar who uniquely makes his case through the criteria of authenticity and devotes a full volume of his work on this topic. Therefore, this book also dedicates a weighty response to his work. As a result, in this chapter, this book will first take a closer look at Meier's monograph, *A Marginal Jew*. After giving his book a fair hearing, this monograph will, in the next section (and in the footnotes), respond to Meier's propositions and conclusions with critique on unqualified use of the criteria and the form-critical assumptions behind the approach.

---

9. Meier, *Marginal Jew*, 5:200-209.

10. Drury, *Parables*, 130; Goulder, *Luke*, 667-70; Also see: Goulder, "Characteristics," 51-69; Goulder, *Midrash and Lection*; Goulder espouses the position that only Marcan parables go back to Jesus and those from Matthew and Luke were constructed by their evangelists. Part of the rationale is his classification of the parables in which he concludes that the peculiarly Lucan and peculiarly Matthean parables are different enough from the parables in Mark that it is highly likely that they were composed from the minds of the Matthean and Lukan writer. Also: Schottroff, "Die Erzählung", 439-46.

A Marginal Jew Volume 5: Probing the Authenticity of the Parables

Background Overview

Meier's purpose of this fifth volume is to look closely into the authenticity of the synoptic parables of Jesus. He believes that NT scholarship in general has given the parables "a free pass" in that they have not been scrutinized closely using the criteria of authenticity. Instead, many commentators simply presume that the synoptic parables come from Jesus. Meier's book is about disputing that presumption by analyzing the synoptic parables through his application of the criteria for historicity.[11] In the end, Meier can attribute only four parables—the mustard seed, the evil tenants, the talents, and the great supper—as authentic or coming from the historical Jesus.

Volume 5 of *A Marginal Jew* is a continuation of Meier's prior works on the quest for the historical Jesus, which he first started when he published volume one in 1991. This first volume deals with the basic principles about the quest of the historical Jesus and the general historical context in which Jesus lived, including the social, cultural, economic, and familial background. His second volume (1994) focuses on Jesus's development and ministry. In this book, Meier points to John the Baptist as Jesus's mentor who exerted the greatest single influence on him. He asserts that John's end-time perspective affected his formulation of the coming of the "kingdom of God." Jesus then reflects and transforms John's eschatology with the notion that the kingdom is present and yet in the future. Meier also gives his analysis of Jesus's public ministry in terms of its important messages and deeds such as exorcisms, healings, and other miracles. Through his use of the criteria of historicity, his overall starting point or foundation of Jesus is that he was "an eschatological, miracle-working prophet who reflected the traditions and hopes surrounding the prophet Elijah."[12] In the third book, published in 2001, Meier focuses on the people who were

---

11. Meier, *Marginal Jew*, 5:xiii.

12. See Meier, *Marginal Jew*, 5:1. Also, in his notes to the Introduction, Meier stresses the importance of establishing an overall understanding of Jesus that can be used as a lens to interpret the parables. His understanding of Jesus as an Elijah-like eschatological miracle-working prophet is the lens he uses for this purpose. He critiques other authors whom he believes simply import the work of other notable scholars of the historical Jesus quest as their bigger context in their task in finding the "original" meaning of the parables. For example, he critiques Snodgrass whom he says simply follows Jeremias's views. Meier, *Marginal Jew*, 5:21n1.

around Jesus: the crowds, his disciples, the inner circle of the twelve, and some individual members. It looks at Jesus's Jewish competitors such as the Pharisees, the Sadducees, the Essenes, the Samaritans, the Scribes, the Herodians, and the Zealots. This volume concludes with an integrative chapter, with insights coming from Jesus's interactions with these people and their impact on Jesus's Elijah-like prophetic ministry and what sets him and his ministry apart from those surrounding him. Meier's fourth volume (2009) concerns Jesus's attitudes towards the Law. This work takes up the teachings of Jesus on major legal topics such as divorce, oaths, the Sabbath, purity rules, and the various love commandments in the Gospels. It also argues against some misconceptions of the Mosaic Law and points to Jesus's role as an authoritative teacher of the Law, further adding but complicating his broad picture of Jesus as an eschatological prophet and miracle worker. Meier states that this volume regarding the Law is the first part of the final stage of his work that deals with his last four "enigmas" (with the other three being Jesus's parables, Jesus's self-designation and titles, and Jesus's last days and death). His fifth volume concerning the parables was published twenty-four years after his first volume. The problem or issue Meier wants to address in the fifth volume is to figure out if the parables presented in the gospels come from the historical Jesus, if these are creations of the early bearers of the tradition in the first and second generations of Christians, or if these are works of the gospel evangelists as reflected by their style, vocabulary, and theological interest. He argues that through his procedure of applying the criterion of historicity, many of the parables cannot be convincingly attributed to the historical Jesus. Instead, he states that these parables belong to the category of *non liquet*, which means, it is not clear whether they are authentic or not.

Methodology

Throughout his multivolume work, Meier tries to imagine what he calls an "unpapal conclave," which to him is a small group of people comprised of Catholic, Protestant, Jewish, Muslim, and agnostic historians gathered in the basement of the Harvard Divinity School library, engaged in writing a consensus work on the historical Jesus. He believes that if such a group uses strictly the standard criteria of authenticity and other purely historical arguments, it can come up with a consensus document that is able to separate (but not deny) the "theological Jesus" from the historical Jesus. To succeed in this endeavor, each member of the group needs to set aside what he or she believes in terms of faith. From a minimal consensus of this group, Meier believes that a more accurate picture of the historical Jesus will be built through fundamental historical facts.[13] He sees a sharp distinction between the historical Jesus and the Jesus of faith and the necessity of the historian to prescind from the historian's faith beliefs to guard against bias and self-projection. He states that an essential part of his historical Jesus enterprise is: "to distinguish between the quest for the historical Jesus on the one hand and theology (with its subdivision of Christology) on the other."[14]

He selects five main criteria of authenticity for his primary use:[15] (1) the criterion of embarrassment, which assesses for material that would likely not be invented by the early church because it would be "embarrassing" or may cause theological issues;[16] (2) the criterion of discontinuity, which focuses on words and deeds of Jesus that would not have come from Judaism or from the early church;[17] (3) the criterion of multiple attestation, which highlights words and deeds of Jesus that can be derived from more than one independent literary source and/or in more than one literary form or genre;[18] (4) the criterion of coherence, which is used alongside material that has already been deemed authentic through other criteria (i.e., whatever Jesus's words or deeds that fit with the authentic material is also likely to be historical); and, (5) the criterion of Jesus's

---

13. Meier, *Marginal Jew*, 5:11–12, 23–24n10.

14. Meier, *Marginal Jew*, 5:9. An interesting way he describes the distinction is when he states that, on one hand, the quest for the historical Jesus is suitable for the history department of a university, using methods that will work for "sober academic history." On the other hand, Christology needs to be located in the theology department using methods appropriate to theology. Therefore, Meier insists that his task is to erect "a high wall of separation between the historical quest and Christology." Meier, *Marginal Jew*, 5:9. Meier, *Marginal Jew*, 5:22n7, also has no objections to theologians using the results of the quest and incorporating this into contemporary Christology.

15. Meier, *Marginal Jew*, 5:12–17.

16. Examples for this include the baptism of Jesus by John the Baptist and the public crucifixion of Jesus as a criminal by the Romans.

17. Examples include Jesus's use of the phrase "Son of Man" and Jesus's particular use of parables.

18. Examples of independent literary sources include the four Gospels, Paul, and Josephus. An example of multiply attested material is the notion that Jesus taught in parables since this portrayal is in every Synoptic Gospel source.

rejection and execution, which looks at words and deeds that fit and explain his rejection and crucifixion.[19]

Meier offers his critique of "alternative approaches" used by those who are critical or skeptical of the criteria of authenticity. For example, an alternative approach for some is to "muddle through" the process just by using their scholarly knowledge and skill.[20] Meier asserts that there are inherent dangers of using only methods that are unacknowledged and not deliberately contemplated.[21] Next he mentions another major alternative approach that relies on modern studies of communal memory, the oral transmission of traditions in ethnic groups, and the broad patterns preserved in those memories and oral tradition. Meier is not impressed by the findings of those who use these alternative studies.[22] Meier presumes that the re-

---

19. Examples include the triumphal entry and the "cleansing" of the temple.

20. Meier, citing Vermes, *Religion of Jesus*, 7, states that the author Vermes "openly proclaims his disdain for 'methodology' and his preference for muddling through." Meier, *Marginal Jew*, 5:26n27. See also Vermes, *Jesus and the Jew* and Vermes, *Jesus and the World of Judaism*.

21. Meier criticizes Vermes for the following: (1) for instances supposedly not using the criterion of multiple attestation properly; (2) appealing to rabbinic material to comprehend first-century Judaism further, which he thinks is inappropriate, and (3) for finding gaps in Vermes's knowledge of NT outside the Gospels. Meier, *Marginal Jew*, 5:26n27.

22. Meier is skeptical of results attained from analogies drawn from the ethnological studies of the oral transmission of traditions, pointing out that there are key differences between the development of the Jesus tradition and other traditions such as the Homeric epics, medieval epics, and Serbo-Croatian traditions. Meier, *Marginal Jew*, 5:27n28. For specific differences he cites Becker, "Search," 157–89, esp. 75–77. Becker, notes that for research in orality to be valid to the study of Jesus and early Christianity, it needs to meet certain conditions that make it different from the ethnological studies, including "(1) At the beginning of the formation of a tradition, there should be a person whose message has precise contents. (2) This tradition should consist of a 'taciturn' and briefly formulated transmission; it should not have an epic breadth. (3) In general, the transmission should not be addressed to people from a large cultural sphere; it should involve a milieu of small social forms. (4) The group of active transmitters of the tradition should not be too large, and they should remain in contact with one another. (5) The transmission of the tradition should be measured in terms of two (or at most three) generations. (6) Both the group of transmitters and the community must regard the person at the origin of the tradition as an authority whose normative significance is certain; in this way, the tradition will enjoy high respect and will provide an important orientation for the life of the group." Becker, "Search," 76–77. The study of Jesus is more comparable to prophets and teachers of wisdom who had pupils and groups that handed on their teachings. These are more applicable comparisons because of the presence of these students of these teachers who passed on their traditions in rhythmic language and forms that consist of just a few words. Paul is proof that Jesus tradition has special authority (cf. e.g., 1 Cor 7:10–11, 25) and an authoritative tradition "does not necessarily and exclusively lead to a verbatim

sults stemming from this method will be questionable because they involve seeing a pattern or overarching theme out of some individual sayings and deeds that are not necessarily authentic. Therefore, he thinks this method needs to be abandoned.[23] Meier believes that the skepticism against the use of the criteria of authenticity comes from a lack of scholarly agreement with the results, despite their long history of use in scholarship. He attributes this overall skepticism to a misguided understanding of how the criteria of authenticity are defined and how they work.

Meier also expresses his thoughts on studies of the use of memory, eyewitnesses, oral tradition, and oral performances in the ancient world to argue for the historicity of the parables. He doubts that these studies truly add or contribute anything to the assessment of authenticity of any parable. He assumes that the parables were handed down orally and underwent different permutations and that they were delivered in multiple oral performances that he says had either a conservative or creative influence on the parable's structure and content. He assumes that these oral performances and traditions may have influenced the authors of the written Gospels as well, especially if they were a creative influence. Overall,

---

transmission of his words, but the authoritative character ensures a basic tendency to preservation, just as we see in OT prophecy." Becker, "Search," 78.

23. Meier, *Marginal Jew*, 5:27n28, evaluates Allison's method in *Constructing Jesus*, which arises from his use of contemporary cognitive studies of memory. In his assessment, Meier states that although Allison is cynical towards the criteria of authenticity, Allison still uses the criterion of multiple attestation but on general themes and motifs instead of Jesus's sayings and deeds. Meier did not give comments on the studies of memory itself but just the way Allison uses the criteria. Now it is true that Allison is skeptical of using the criteria of authenticity and proposes dismissing their further use. Allison's proposal is that authentic tradition cannot be found at the level of individual sayings, but instead it is found "in themes and motifs—as well as in rhetorical strategies such as the use of parables and hyperbole—that recur across the sources." Allison, "How to Marginalize," 1:25. He believes that is where true memory of the tradition is located. He calls it "recurrent attestation" which means themes and motifs that are repeatedly attested throughout the tradition are the foundational base of authentic memory. It is an emphasis on looking for authentic tradition in the larger patterns of the tradition instead of at the sayings level because of his skepticism in the ability of early Christians to retain detailed memory. Because of his emphasis on deriving good memory out of recurrent themes and motifs, he does agree with the approach (but not the entire theoretical framework) of Theissen and Winter in using "coherence of sources," which focuses on recurrent themes in different streams of tradition. Allison, "How to Marginalize," 1:8. This is in line with the main approach of this book in looking for the theme of justification in authentic Jesus tradition. Please see these comments in Allison, "How to Marginalize," 1:3–30.

Meier does not find these studies helpful because there is no actual record of these performances.²⁴ Only literary sources exist.²⁵ Meier also dismisses the use of social-scientific studies to support claims about eyewitnesses and memory and points to contrary social-scientific studies that offer different opinions.²⁶ Finally, he argues that because there is no way of knowing how these oral performances were done and what the exact contents were, only literary sources can be relied upon including the conclusions that can be derived from source and redaction criticism.²⁷ Therefore, from his perspective, these alternative studies may generally enrich but not necessarily replace form, source, tradition, redaction criticism, and the two-source hypothesis of the Synoptic Gospels.²⁸

---

24. Meier's argument assumes a few things that deserve some responses. Dunn notes that there are those who, perhaps similar to Meier, assume that "oral tradition functioned like written tradition; or that it is no longer possible to say anything about the oral phase of the gospel tradition; or that only written tradition is reliable." Dunn, "Remembering," 191. In other words, there is a bias against oral tradition in favor of a more favorable literary mind-set. But in ancient times, Dunn argues that written material was not as trusted since it could be "easily lost, or destroyed, or corrupted in the copying; much preferable was it to have the teaching or story firmly lodged in one's own mind, retaining the living voice of the teacher." Dunn, "Remembering," 192. Therefore, in agreement with Dunn, this work posits that it is actually more imperative that research takes seriously the oral phase of the history of the Jesus tradition and that it is actually possible to "penetrate back into the oral period of the Jesus tradition" based on the impression or effect that it created already evident in the tradition as we now have it. Dunn, "Remembering," 193. Therefore, this book briefly looks at the research and results of the oral tradition process later in this chapter.

25. Meier, *Marginal Jew*, 5:50. Meier also mentions one author, Richard Bauckham, whom he thinks uses the study of memory and oral testimonies of witnesses to promote a presumption in favor of Gospel reliability. Meier believes that Bauckham has this goal because he has a certain theological agenda Meier thinks makes him unable to do strict historical research. He also questions Bauckham's use of patristic and other early Christian sources, especially Papias on arguing for the reliability of the Gospels. Meier, *Marginal Jew*, 5:77–78n57. See Bauckham, *Jesus*.

26. Meier, *Marginal Jew*, 5:78n57, cites Redman, "How Accurate," 177–97.

27. Meier, *Marginal Jew*, 5:78n57, does refer to counterarguments on the use of memory studies affecting the oral and written sources of the Gospels by citing Kirk, "Orality," 1–22; see also Kirk, "Memory," 1:809–51.

28. Meier, *Marginal Jew*, 5:78n57, agrees with Hurtado that results from oral studies and oral tradition, while important, should not supplant or assign the study of written texts a smaller role. Hurtado questions claims that early Christian groups did not read written texts aloud but instead are delivered or performed from memory and that texts were composed based on those performances. See Hurtado, "Oral Fixation," 321–40.

Meier also expresses his disagreement with another alternative approach, which he describes as the reformulation of the criteria of authenticity. The only example he cites is the criterion of plausibility by Gerd Theissen, which is relevant for this book.[29] He describes its method as having "a number of criteria that are streamlined or consolidated into one or two criteria, while other criteria may quietly and surreptitiously function when they are useful in individual cases."[30] The new criterion breaks down into four sub-criteria. Two fall under contextual plausibility (contextual appropriateness and contextual distinctiveness), and the other two together are called plausibility of effects (source coherence and resistance to the tendencies of the tradition). Meier notes how even with the new criteria, the use of traditional criteria resurfaces in its method.[31] Meier does not agree with Theissen's discontinuing the use of the criterion of double dissimilarity. One of the new criterion's major principles is that the words and deeds of Jesus need to be compatible with first-century Judaism; thus, discontinuity is used more in terms of dissimilarity with early Christianity and not with Judaism.[32] Meier cites his own authenticated results of Jesus's teaching in three topics—voluntary fasting, divorce, and oath swearing—as proof

---

29. Theissen and Winter, *Quest*. Summary of the criterion of plausibility is in Theissen and Merz, *Historical Jesus*, 115–21. See also Theissen, "Historical Scepticism," 549–87.

30. Meier, *Marginal Jew*, 5:18.

31. This observation makes sense as the method is a reformulation, not an elimination of the criteria of authenticity. It is also not to replace the old criteria with a new one, but the old are "rearranged and supplemented by a greater attention to the historical context and the historical impact" as noted in Theissen, "Historical Scepticism," 554. Meier's concerns over the criterion of plausibility are addressed in this book's introduction.

32. In defense of Theissen's discontinuing double dissimilarity, here are a few thoughts from Dunn: He states that the criterion of dissimilarity as originally conceived is a working assumption to find what is distinctive about Jesus. This was originally conceived as the "sure base on which to build a convincing reconstruction of the historical Jesus." Dunn, "Remembering," 200. However, he rightly states that it would be wiser to find out what is characteristic of Jesus instead of what is distinctive. That is because, he says, "any material within the gospels which is characteristic through and across the gospels is likely to reflect characteristic features of Jesus' own mission." Dunn, "Remembering," 202. Also, "motifs, emphases and stylistic features which run throughout the tradition in the various branches which have come down to us or which we can still discern are most obviously to be attributed to a single originating or shaping force. And the only real candidate for that role is Jesus himself." Dunn, "Remembering," 202. Therefore, his point is that "the characteristic emphases and motifs of the Jesus tradition give us a broad, clear and compelling picture of the characteristic Jesus." Dunn, "Remembering," 204. What he is saying is in line with the aim of this book in examining the coherence of themes and motifs in the Jesus tradition.

THE "INAUTHENTICITY" OF LUKE 18:9–14

that the new criterion's principle fails with regard to these topics, especially as he deems them to be authentic but also dissimilar to first-century Jewish thought. Therefore, he thinks objections to double discontinuity are not valid, and the rejection of this double discontinuity criterion is "ill-advised," especially since the results do not conform to Meier's findings in those three topics.[33] Finally, Meier disagrees with the use of the word "plausibility" to describe the criteria as he thinks all reconstructions of Jesus aim to be plausible, and he also disagrees with the emphasis on having Jesus's words and deeds fit with the Jewish-Palestinian environment because the likely bearers of the Christian tradition would all be exposed to and reflect "the same linguistic, cultural, social, political, and economic background that Jesus knew and embodied."[34] Therefore, he argues that having words and deeds fit with the first-century environment will not automatically or necessarily mean they come from the historical Jesus.

Seven "Unfashionable" Theses

In chapter 37, Meier outlines seven propositions about the nature of Jesus's parables, starting with the least controversial and ending with the most. The earlier propositions support and build upon the arguments towards the later ones and ultimately the final proposition. First, he makes sure to define the focus of his quest sharply in volume 5. His quest is about "what the historical Jesus intended when he decided to use parables in general and to speak this or that parable in particular."[35] This purpose is to be examined based on the portrait of the historical Jesus, which he determined in his first four volumes. For him, the parables of the historical Jesus are "comparative short stories used by this Elijah-like eschatological prophet as he seeks to regather a scattered Israel in preparation for the coming kingdom of God." He used the parables as a prophetic tool to communicate with the Israelites during this time in history. The parables are one way he communicated his message among other kinds of speech.[36] He

---

33. Meier, *Marginal Jew*, 5:18–19.
34. Meier, *Marginal Jew*, 5:19.
35. Meier, *Marginal Jew*, 5:33.
36. Meier, *Marginal Jew*, 5:33–34. Other kinds of events that he claims cohere with the parable as a symbolic "word-event" include symbolic healings and exorcisms, and other symbolic actions such as his triumphal entry and temple cleansing. Meier, *Marginal Jew*, 5.33.

makes this preliminary decision to anchor the parable's range of meaning and not just have it mean anything or everything by interpreters who use various hermeneutical approaches.[37]

Thesis 1

> "The fact that scholars widely and wildly disagree on how many parables of Jesus there are in the Synoptic Gospels reveals a still more embarrassing fact: scholars in general do not agree on what constitutes a parable of Jesus."[38]

Meier correctly states that there is general disagreement among scholars on a precise definition of a parable.[39] As a result, it is difficult to distinguish among a parable, similitude, simile, and metaphor. The ultimate reason for this confusion is the wide range of meaning of the Hebrew word מָשָׁל used in the OT and the Greek παραβολη in the NT and in other writings from ancient Greek literature.[40] The main ideas assigned to the Hebrew מָשָׁל are "proverb" and "comparison." Especially in OT wisdom texts, it is defined as "proverb" or "wise saying." Beyond these definitions, the other meanings in the OT fall under the category of "wisdom" such as a "byword," "song of

---

37. Meier states, "Once the parables are detached from the framework of an unusual 1st-century Jew named Jesus, they became capable of bearing almost any meaning that an ingenious interpreter manages to read into them. For those who exalt the text as the locus of meaning, the parables are treated as autonomous pieces of literary art, pulsating with the explosive power of the many meanings inherent in the text. For those who emphasize the reader as the creator of meaning, the parables may be employed as mirrors into which an interpreter can gaze a la Narcissus to ponder his or her existence in their world. Indeed, such mirrors can be custom-designed with a built-in existentialist, psychological, socioeconomic, or theological optic. Hence, no matter the precise approach that modern critics adopt, the parables become, in effect if not in theory, empty and moldable vessels into which interpreters can pour whatever meaning or negation of meaning they consider productive of new insights." Meier, *Marginal Jew*, 5:32.

38. Meier, *Marginal Jew*, 5:35.

39. Meier, *Marginal Jew*, 5:35, 58n6, cites Arland Hultgren, Adolf Jülicher, C. H. Dodd, Joachim Jeremias, Bernard Brandon Scott, Jan Lambrecht, R. Allan Culpepper, Klyne Snodgrass, John Dominic Crossan, T. W. Manson, Ruben Zimmermann, and Birger Gerhardsson.

40. See a list of how the verb māšal and noun māšāl in the MT and parabolē in the LXX are used in Snodgrass, *Stories*, 570–74. See also Koehler and Baumgartner, *HALOT* 1:647.

mockery," "taunts."[41] Meier asserts that the synoptic parables are mistakenly compared with wisdom categories of the OT.

Thesis 2

"The OT wisdom māšāl is not the prime source or analogue of those 'parables' that are most characteristic of and particular to the Synoptic Jesus within the NT corpus."[42]

For this thesis Meier limits his description of parables that are peculiar to the Synoptic Gospels, not in terms of wisdom categories but as comparisons "that have been 'stretched out' into short stories with at least an implicit beginning, middle, and end. In other words, it is a mini-narrative with at least an implicit plot line."[43] He mainly attributes this definition of a narrative parable to Harvey K. McArthur and Robert M. Johnston who compared the NT parables to rabbinic parables of the Tannaitic period.[44] Meier thus describes a synoptic parable of Jesus as "a metaphor or simile stretched out into a whole narrative into which the audience can be drawn, a narrative with a beginning, middle, and end."[45] He states that the noun παραβολη in the Gospels mostly refers to this kind of narrative parable.[46] Meier further notes that this narrative parable is not located in the OT wisdom writings but is, instead, mostly comparable to those found among the literature of the OT Former and Latter Prophets. The general context where these parables are found concerns "argument, rebuke, and even condemnation, usually of a king or some other authority figures."[47]

---

41. Meier, *Marginal Jew*, 5:36.

42. Meier, *Marginal Jew*, 5:36.

43. Meier, *Marginal Jew*, 5:37, 60n14.

44. McArthur and Johnston, *They Also Taught*, 98–99. McArthur and Johnston, *They Also Taught*, 106–7, claim that the by the early first century, the narrative *mashal* was popular among the rabbis. Jesus's parables are earliest narrative *meshalim* attested in literature, making him the first known teacher who used this kind of parable. They assert that Jesus and the rabbis took up and used a popular form they found among common people, although they admit that there is no way to prove this.

45. Meier, *Marginal Jew*, 5:61n14.

46. See a list of occurences of παραβολη in the NT in Snodgrass, *Stories*, 567–69. It refers to a narrative parable in 39 out of 48 total verses (81 percent) where the word occurs.

47. Meier, *Marginal Jew*, 5:37. An example is the parable of Nathan (2 Sam 12:1–2).

Thesis 3

"It is in the 'writing prophets' (alias the Latter Prophets) that we see both (1) a notable expansion of the genre of comparative short story used in argumentation about key events in Israel's history and (2) the use of m-s-l vocabulary to designate this type of speech."[48]

Meier notes that the narrative parables in the Former Prophets are never referred to as מָשָׁל. Instead, it is in the Latter Prophets where texts with comparative narrative are referred to as מָשָׁל. Examples include Ezekiel 15:1–8 and chapters 16 and 17, which have stories with allegories concerning God's dealings with Israel.[49] He claims that מָשָׁל is connected to the prophetic oracle of the future in the allegory of the pot in Ezek 24:1–14. The narrative parable is also used in the context of prophetic oracles in later apocalyptic literature.[50]

Thesis 4

"The Synoptic Jesus who tells narrative parables stands primarily not in the sapiential but in the prophetic tradition of the Jewish Scriptures."[51]

Having described the Synoptic Gospel narrative parable, Meier's fourth thesis moves to limit the kind of tradition to which it is related in the OT. He makes an argument that the Synoptic Gospel parables were used by Jesus's prophetic ministry in the tradition of Elijah, instead of as a wisdom sage. Meier asserts that the historical Jesus presented himself as the "miracle-working, Elijah-like prophet of the end time" and that Jesus used these parables as an eschatological prophet "within the larger context of prophetic conflict with the ruling class at a critical moment in Israel's history."[52] This emphasis on the parables as a form of prophetic rhetoric does contradict the general notion that Jesus's parables were some of the communication tools he used as a wisdom teacher or sage.[53] After defining the parables'

---

48. Meier, *Marginal Jew*, 5:38.

49. See his detailed note on these Ezekiel passages in Meier, *Marginal Jew*, 5:38–39.

50. Ezra 4:13–21; 5:41–53; *Similitudes of Enoch*—1 En. 37–71; "Similitudes" of the Shepherd of Hermas. Meier, *Marginal Jew*, 5:39–40.

51. Meier, *Marginal Jew*, 5:40.

52. Meier, *Marginal Jew*, 5:41.

53. Meier, *Marginal Jew*, 5:67n29, disagrees with Witherington and Crossan in this

main use, he supplies his formal brief definition of the narrative parable of Jesus. A parable is "a striking short story that employs figurative language (i.e., a metaphor or simile stretched out into a narrative) and is meant to be puzzling enough to tease the mind into active thought and personal decision."[54] He notes that his designation of the parable's function as a prophetic tool in the context of the "grand history of God's dealings with Israel or of the Kingdom of God" does not ring true to all the parables in the Gospels such as the good Samaritan and the rich fool. However, in his analysis in later chapters, only the parables he deems authentic fall within the definition and function he describes.

Thesis 5

"Any attempt to define Jesus' parables in greater detail, with a laundry list of supposedly essential characteristics, threatens to introduce qualifications that are true of some but not of all the parables of Jesus as found in the Synoptics."[55]

In this thesis, Meier argues for keeping parable descriptions as general or as vague as possible, unlike other descriptions that delineate so-called "essential characteristics" that may or may not be true. He gives a partial list of questionable characteristics that all parables supposedly have as defined by others and outlines exceptions to these. His list of three questionable characteristics are (1) "Jesus' parables draw upon events of every day peasant life or the cycle of nature in Palestine"; (2) "Jesus' parables are always fictitious narratives"; and, (3) "Jesus' parables are always subversive of traditional religious beliefs, upending them with surprising endings or, alternately,

---

regard. He disagrees less with Witherington as he does state that the narrative parables were not ordinarily used as rhetoric for the sages, but they are more of a prophetic modification of wisdom sayings. See Witherington, *Jesus the Sage*, 158–59. Funk, Hoover, and the Jesus Seminar, *Five Gospels*, 32. Crossan, *Historical Jesus*, 265–302, also places Jesus and his parables in the sapiential tradition, which is understandable because he eliminated eschatology as part of Jesus's message.

54. Part of his definition is derived from C. H. Dodd's definition of a parable: "At its simplest the parable is a metaphor or simile drawn from nature or common life, arresting the hearer by its vividness or strangeness, and leaving the mind in sufficient doubt about its precise application to tease it into active thought." Dodd, *Parables*, 5. Meier admits his dependence on Dodd, but he does outline some distinctions to Dodd's definition: (1) Not every parable deals with common life; (2) not every parable is vivid or strange; (3) Meier only limits his parable to the narrative stretched-out kind. Meier, *Marginal Jew*, 5:68n32.

55. Meier, *Marginal Jew*, 5:41.

posing puzzling stories that resist any specific interpretation."[56] For these characteristics, he cites parables that are exceptions to the rule to justify his claim that these generalizations are not valid in all cases. He does note that parables that portray kings, nobles, rich merchants, and landlords doing extraordinary things tend to be in M and L parables unlike the other parables in Mark and Q that portray common everyday life. He implicitly notes that perhaps this difference reveals a clue to the origins of the parables itself with the Mark and Q parables originating from Jesus and the M and L parables that deal with extraordinary events as not coming from the historical Jesus.[57] Furthermore, he asserts that N.T. Wright's characterization of the parables as "apocalyptic allegory conveying secret messages to his followers while being cryptic to outsiders" is not valid because there are parables that concentrate on themes that are more sapiential and reinforce traditional truth instead of being apocalyptic. Meier wants to invalidate Wright's particular description because Meier claims that Wright uses it to argue for the authenticity of all synoptic parables.[58] Therefore, by setting forth this thesis, Meier is able to use it to strengthen thesis 7 further. It argues for the difficulty of ascertaining the historicity of the parables.

Thesis 6

"The claim that the parables in the Coptic Gospel of Thomas (CGT) represent an independent and indeed earlier and more reliable tradition of the parables of the historical Jesus is highly questionable."[59]

Meier puts up a detailed study of this thesis in a separate chapter (chapter 38). Through a meticulous analysis of a wide cross section of sayings (parabolic and non-parabolic), especially all parables in CGT with parallels in the Synoptics, Meier concludes that CGT is dependent on every synoptic source. CGT exhibits typical features of the second century use of Jesus traditions. It routinely meshes and conflates the sources on which it is dependent just

---

56. Meier, *Marginal Jew*, 5:42–43.

57. Meier, *Marginal Jew*, 5:69n35.

58. Meier, *Marginal Jew*, 5:70n42. See Wright, *Jesus*, 179–80. However, Meier uses the parable of the rich fool as his example of a more sapiential parable to refute Wright, which is a parable he deems as *"non liquet."* It would not be fair for Meier to use a parable he does not deem authentic to refute Wright's characterization of authentic parables as apocalyptic allegories. Meier, *Marginal Jew*, 5:70n42.

59. Meier, *Marginal Jew*, 5:44.

as some second-century writings do (e.g., Didache, Polycarp's Letter to the Philippians, the sayings of Jesus in Justin Martyr). This process of conflating canonical Gospel versions is in lieu of citing the text from a particular Gospel. It places CGT "firmly within the harmonizing stream of mid-second-century Christian writings."[60] There are also sufficient traces of the Synoptic Gospel vocabulary that are in CGT to strengthen the conclusion that it is dependent on the Gospels. Moreover, he shows that CGT reflects many of the redactional techniques of Matthew and Luke, especially the Lukan inclination to add narrative introductions to the parable. Therefore, "in every single case, both inside and outside the parable tradition, no matter what the literary genre or content, we have found it more likely than not that Thomas displays signs of some sort of dependence on the Synoptic material."[61] Therefore, he concludes that CGT cannot be used for the criterion of multiple attestation for any parable because the Thomasine parables should not be counted as independent witnesses.

Thesis 7

"Relatively few of the Synoptic parables can be attributed to the historical Jesus with a good degree of probability."[62]

After concluding that CGT is not an independent source, Meier applies the criteria of authenticity, especially multiple attestation, and explains that only a few would pass the test. He is not saying that the historical Jesus never taught in parables. That is a different claim. The idea that Jesus taught in parables is considered authentic via the criterion of multiple attestation of sources because Mark, Q, M, and L all contain narrative parables attributed to Jesus. Jesus also taught in other ways in addition to teaching in parables, but no one knows for sure the extent to which he taught in parables.

With regards to the criterion of multiple attestation, the only parables that meet the standard are those of the mustard seed, the evil tenants of the vineyard (not multiple attestation but embarrassment), the talents (or pounds), and the great supper, assuming the last two are not simply Q parables that are heavily redacted by Matthew and Luke. None of the M or L parables pass this criterion.

---

60. Meier, *Marginal Jew*, 5:103.
61. Meier, *Marginal Jew*, 5:146.
62. Meier, *Marginal Jew*, 5:48.

With regard to the criterion of discontinuity, Meier does not think this criterion can be used to assess the parables. First, he disagrees with commentators such as Bernard Brandon Scott who argue that Gospel parables are dissimilar to the narrative parables in the OT Scriptures through its use of an introductory formula, such as "it is like." He disagrees because many parables in the Gospels, similar to the OT parables, do not even have introductory formulas.[63] Second, he rejects the idea of those who highlight the subjective, artistic, and romantic argument to differentiate Jesus's parables. This argument proceeds along these lines: "Jesus' parables display much greater literary genius and fresh insight than any Jewish parables before or after him."[64] It is too highly subjective of an argument and it seems anti-Semitic. Third, Meier disagrees with those who claim that discontinuity applies even if parables such the synoptic ones cannot be found in other writings in the NT and other Christian works in the first and second centuries.[65] He does admit that the criterion of dissimilarity works well if the parables of Jesus are compared with the writings of Paul or other NT and later Christian authors. However, Meier states that this comparison does not take into account the work of "oral tradents." Oral tradents are the people whom Meier describes as the "earwitnesses" of Jesus's public ministry who "heard this parable, remembered it, and repeated it in the circle of disciples and in the early church as part of Jesus' teaching."[66] They continue to repeat the parable through various "oral performances" up to the time it was written down in the Gospels or a synoptic written source such as Q. Therefore, these oral tradents absorbed, recited, and repeated the tradition, preserved it and handed it down until the parable was written down. Meier's assumption is that these tradents may have composed parables themselves ("in imitation of the Master") as they learned from being the bearers of the Jesus tradition. Therefore, Meier believes in the possibility that the parables in the Synoptic Gospels include ones that are not authentic because they originated from the tradents instead of the historical Jesus. As a result, this renders the criterion of dissimilarity inapplicable, as the work of these oral

---

63. E.g., parable of the sower, the evil tenants, the two sons (Matthew), the two debtors (Luke), the good Samaritan, the importunate friend at midnight, the rich fool, the barren fig tree, the tower builder and the warring king, the lost coin, the prodigal son, the dishonest steward, the rich man and Lazarus, the widow and the unjust judge, the Pharisee and the tax collector. Meier, *Marginal Jew*, 5:53; Scott, *Hear*, 63–64.

64. Meier, *Marginal Jew*, 5:53.

65. Meier, *Marginal Jew*, 5:53–54.

66. Meier, *Marginal Jew*, 5:54.

tradents cannot be accounted for.⁶⁷ Meier states that no one knows anything about these tradents, especially in terms of their creativity and the extent they composed parables, if ever they did.

With regards to the criterion of coherence, Meier agrees with general scholarship that Jesus's use of parables in his teaching makes sense since various Jewish teachers have used narrative parables like these from Nathan the prophet to the rabbis. However, he claims that the criterion of coherence cannot say anything about the authenticity of any specific individual synoptic parable.⁶⁸

With regards to the criterion of embarrassment, Meier claims that this criterion is not useful to authenticate Jesus's parables. He states that the shock reaction an interpreter might get in reading the parable is very subjective. In addition, a parable that can be interpreted in an embarrassing or shocking way need not be authentic. He gives the example of the good Samaritan as a parable that has shocking and embarrassing features; nevertheless, he claims this parable was composed not by early tradents nor by Jesus but by the author Luke.⁶⁹

Finally, Meier does not believe that the criterion of Jesus's rejection and execution applies for the parables as none of his parables may have directly or likely caused his crucifixion and death.⁷⁰

Therefore, in his analysis in his use of the criteria of authenticity (he uses only multiple attestation; the others he normally uses are dissimilarity, coherence, embarrassment, Jesus's rejection and execution), Meier concludes that most of the synoptic parables cannot be authenticated as

---

67. As mentioned earlier, Meier doubts the usefulness of studies on memory, eyewitnesses, oral tradition, and oral performances in the ancient world in strengthening the case of authenticity, simply because there are no oral record of these traditions. There are no "1st-century DVDs or smartphone downloads that preserve the living voice of such oral performances and transformations. All we have are the carefully composed literary documents called Mark, Matthew, and Luke." Meier, *Marginal Jew*, 5:50. Instead, he argues against the use of the criterion of dissimilarity, because it is possible that the oral tradents may had been creative enough purposefully to make their own parables in deviation from authentic tradition. He states, "It is theoretically possible that all the parables were created by anonymous first-generation bearers of the Jesus tradition and were then added to the authentic words and deeds of Jesus on the way toward the composition of the Synoptic Gospels." Therefore, for him, the burden of proof is on those who argue for conservative transmission by oral tradents or a more carefully guarded transmission of the Jesus tradition. See Meier, *Marginal Jew*, 5:190.

68. Meier, *Marginal Jew*, 5:55.

69. Meier, *Marginal Jew*, 5:52.

70. Meier, *Marginal Jew*, 5:55.

possibly coming from the historical Jesus. Instead, most of them, in terms of authenticity, belong to the category of *non liquet* or not clear whether they are authentic or not. He cannot often prove that a certain parable absolutely does not come from Jesus, and the burden of proof of the parables authenticity or inauthenticity falls upon the person trying to prove one or the other.[71] But he does explicitly state his belief in certain parts of his book that most of the L parables are inauthentic. Again, together with his analysis of the inauthenticity of the good Samaritan he writes, "Creation by the early church or by the evangelists seems a likely explanation, . . . in my view, for most if not all of the L parables."[72]

The rest of this chapter will further show the reasoning behind this book's methodology of using the criterion of plausibility while using Meier's work as a case study. The goal of the next sections is to show the need for the criteria to be qualified and reformulated while also eliminating its negative use. Meier's conclusion of the L parables being "inauthentic" (or created by the early church or evangelists instead of coming from the historical Jesus) will ultimately be judged as questionable. This study will now focus on the following major topics: (1) critique against the unqualified use of the criteria of authenticity, and (2) critique against the underlying assumptions of form criticism (the foundation of the criteria of authenticity) arising from studies in oral tradition, oral transmission, eyewitnesses, and memory. Included within the critique are some current findings on these disciplines. Also, within this second major topic, the current results of studies on ancient biographies and their possible relationship to the Gospels are briefly taken up as further validation for the results of oral tradition studies and memory.

Critique against the Criteria of Authenticity

Meier is a major proponent of the traditional use of the criteria in historical Jesus studies. His stated main goal in his participation in the historical Jesus scholarship is to distinguish what is an accurate picture of the historical Jesus based on historical facts from the "theological Jesus." According to Meier's works, especially in his latest book, he mainly trusts and relies on the assumptions behind form, source, tradition, redaction criticism, and the two-source hypothesis of the Synoptic Gospels. Various statements he

---

71. Meier, *Marginal Jew*, 5:80n63.
72. Meier, *Marginal Jew*, 5:210; also 198–99.

makes in his book lead to that conclusion. Three examples include (1) his overarching goal of separating the "theological Jesus" from the historical Jesus to come up with fundamental historical facts (i.e., peeling off interpretation to get to the kernel of history),[73] (2) his insistence on relying only on literary sources and conclusions from source, form, redaction criticism, and the two-source hypothesis,[74] and (3) the assumption that anonymous creative oral tradents may have composed wholesale many parables of Jesus (i.e., uncontrolled tradition transmission).[75]

The criteria of authenticity did not come out of a vacuum. Chris Keith makes the case that the criteria approach is originally an outgrowth of form criticism despite the fact that practitioners do not agree with form-critical tenets.[76] In his essay he states that the criteria approach is "indebted" or is a "direct outgrowth" of form criticism, and he proceeds to offer a macro-level criticism of the criteria approach.[77] He states that the heart of form criticism is "the separation of the written Gospels by means of identifying the interpretive work of later Christians." This approach assumes that historians can "(a) separate the written Gospels into two different bodies of tradition, one of which reflects the past and the other of which reflects the present of early Christianity, (b) by means of identifying those traditions that reflect early Christian theological interpretations."[78] Keith outlines how these assumptions underlie the work of classic form critics such as Martin Dibelius and Rudolf Bultmann. The major task of the form critic was to figure out which part came from the original tradition and which part did not. By breaking down the units of tradition that were supposedly organized into narratives by "Hellenistic Christianity," which was assumed to be a later version of Christianity, the form critic will, in theory, take off the theological influence of later Christians and be able "to reconstruct the preliterary oral tradition."[79] Then during the period of the New Quest, scholars moved the object of the search from the preliterary oral tradition to the historical figure of Jesus while also retaining form criticism's understanding and methodology for recovering past tradition. In effect, Keith rightly states,

---

73. Meier, *Marginal Jew*, 5:11–12, 23–24n10.
74. Meier, *Marginal Jew*, 5:78n57.
75. Meier, *Marginal Jew*, 5:90.
76. Keith, "Indebtedness," 25–48.
77. Keith, "Indebtedness," 26, 30.
78. Keith, "Indebtedness," 31–32.
79. Keith, "Indebtedness," 32–33.

> The innovation of the New Quest search for authentic Jesus tradition, and their development of criteria in order to do so, was more properly an extension of the form-critical method into the realm of history, much the same as redaction criticism was a literary extension of form-critical methodology—both began with the assumption that the final form of the text represents almost wholly the work of the Gospel authors and their *Sitz-im-Leben*.[80]

The prominence of the criteria of authenticity took off as form-critical scholars paid less attention to the *Sitz im Leben* of forms and turned their "scholarly gaze" towards the remaining tradition while maintaining the methodology and form-critical understanding as they substituted the historical Jesus for the preliterary oral tradition as the object of their search.[81] Using form-critical terms, "authentic" means "does not reflect the theological interpretation of the Gospel authors and their communities."[82] This definition assumes that there is a layer of later Christian interpretation that covered the original layer, which meant Palestinian Christianity. Eventually this movement to find the original or authentic expressed itself more and more in terms of historical positivism.

Keith notes some major issues concerning the use of the criteria approach. Various form-critical assumptions (not all of them) are no longer advocated by scholars who use the criteria who now either dismiss them or modify them.[83] The dichotomy made by form critics between Palestinian and Hellenistic Christianity is no longer accepted.[84] Current research in the areas of oral tradition and social/cultural memory questions the idea of having a discoverable "original form" buried by layers of interpretation. In addition, the notion of "authentic" and "inauthentic" tradition being associated with past and present interpretation or having or lacking interpretive framework is also deemed questionable.[85]

---

80. Keith, "Indebtedness," 33.
81. Keith, "Indebtedness," 34.
82. Keith, "Iindebtedness," 36.

83. Byrskog asserts that form criticism is being challenged on several of its basic tenets and that scholars abandoned it or modified it into an analysis that "looks at forms and literary types from the perspective of mnemonic signs or textual effect rather than their one-dimensional correlation with the *Sitz-im-Leben* of the early church." Byrskog, "Introduction," 19. He did not specify scholars that did so.

84. Hengel, *Judaism and Hellenism*.
85. Keith, "Indebtedness," 37–39.

This book will now expound on some of these findings and, in effect, use these as the rationale for the need to qualify and reformulate the criteria, while using Meier's unqualified and minimalist use of the criteria of authenticity as a negative example. First, the criteria of authenticity (four of them) that Meier primarily uses will be critiqued for their ability to fulfill their intended purpose. Then some recent studies in oral tradition, transmission, eyewitnesses, and memory will be presented that question the form-critical assumptions behind the criteria. These all call for the need to use the criteria more responsibly as in the approach of this study and also support the overall argument that Meier's conclusion of the "inauthenticity" of the L parables is most likely questionable. First are critiques of four criteria in this order: multiple attestation, dissimilarity, coherence, and embarrassment.

Critique of the Criterion of Multiple Attestation

Harvey McArthur calls multiple attestation, while not infallible, the "most objective" among the criteria.[86] The logic of this criterion is the same as the logic of establishing evidence not just from one witness but from two or more witnesses (Matt 18:16).[87] For this criterion, the Synoptic Gospel sources, which are Mark, Q, M, and L, serve as independent witnesses to Jesus's words and deeds. In addition, there is also the Gospel of John. As far as the Gospel of Thomas is concerned, Meier's analysis rightly concludes that it is dependent on the Synoptic Gospels; therefore, CGT does not count as an independent witness.

Although this criterion is helpful, uncontroversial, and a tool that any level-headed historian would use, its common-sense simplicity masks some deficiencies when it is used uncritically to analyze Jesus material. The first deficiency is the presumed reliance on the hypothesis of the two-source solution to the synoptic problem and the existence of Q. If the Griesbach or the two-Gospel hypothesis is considered (i.e., Luke's source is Matthew, Mark used both Matthew and Luke), then the sources that need to be accounted for will change. In this hypothesis, Matthew and the material in Luke not found in Matthew (i.e., L) are the main sources. Therefore, instead of having four synoptic sources, we are left with two plus

---

86. McArthur, "Basic Issues," 48.
87. Stein, "Criteria," 229–30.

5 percent of Mark that is not found in Matthew or Luke.[88] Moreover, an uncertainty rests on the hypothesis's reliance on the existence of Q. Mark Goodacre notes the prominence of Q in historical Jesus research and how historical Jesus scholars simply assume its existence.[89] It is quite ironic that a criterion that relies on existing witnesses uses a witness that is unattested due to its hypothetical nature. Q is somehow a major source assumed to be at par with Mark, which is why Goodacre suggests that Q should always play more of a subsidiary role as compared to Mark when doing historical Jesus work.[90] A second deficiency of the criterion of multiple attestation is the material called "Mark-Q overlaps." This term refers to triple tradition material where Matthew and Luke have major agreements against Mark. It is an issue because it calls into question the existence or independence of Q as a source. In the two-source theory, Matthew and Luke supposedly used Mark independently of one another, so they should not agree with one another against Mark. In reality, passages with major agreements do exist. As an explanation, it is possible that Mark and Q may have occasionally overlapped, but the significance of the overlap leaves the question of Mark and Q's independence to one another.[91] So either the Mark-Q overlaps indicates, for example, that Luke knows Matthew as well as Mark or that Mark and Q are not independent to one another. Either way, it affects the validity of the results that come from multiple attestation as a criterion due to the doubts about the precise relationship of Mark and Q. Third, there are also issues in using John, M, and L as independent sources. No scholarly consensus exists that John is definitively an independent source. As for M and L, some uncertainties in their composition make it difficult to consider each of them as independent sources. For example, how does one distinguish between special M material and Matthean redaction, especially given the presence of unique Matthean style in these texts? The same logic goes for special L material and Lukan redaction. In the end, how plausible is it that material that is only found in either Matthew or Luke each comes from just one discrete source? Fourth, when used in concert with the criterion of embarrassment, the criterion of multiple attestation may cast doubt on whether the tradition is truly embarrassing to the early

---

88. Stein, "Criteria," 230–31.
89. Goodacre, "Criticizing the Criterion," 155.
90. Goodacre, "Criticizing the Criterion," 156.
91. An example given by Goodacre, "Criticizing the Criterion," 160, is Matt 3:16–17// Mark 1:9b–11//Luke 3:21–22.

church. An alleged embarrassing tradition that exists in multiple sources such as the baptism of Jesus conveys the notion that it may not have been that embarrassing. The evangelists had a choice with regard to which material to include and which to exclude. Finally, most things Jesus said and did are not really attested in the extant traditions.[92] A Gospel writer would not have been able to include every single tradition possible concerning Jesus (John 20:30; 21:25). Furthermore, the Gospel of Mark also indicates that Jesus spoke more parables than what is portrayed in the Gospel. For instance, Mark 4:33 makes this statement: "With many such parables he spoke the word to them, as they were able to hear it." Mark 12:1 reads, "And he began to speak to them in parables [plural]." However, only the parable of the tenants comes after the phrase, which probably means Mark has only a limited number of parables included in this Gospel.[93] Meier rightly notes, "The 'historical Jesus' is not coterminous with the 'real Jesus.' The latter Jesus would, at least in principle, involve everything Jesus of Nazareth said, did, and experienced in the thirty-plus years of his life in the first half of the first century CE. A good deal of that total reality of who Jesus was is lost to us and will never be recovered."[94] Therefore, that important notion specifically makes using multiple attestation in a negative manner to render traditions "inauthentic" quite precarious. In summary, all these considerations mark some difficulties in using the criterion of multiple attestation in an uncritical manner to assign traditions as authentic or not. It is not that this highly useful criterion should not be utilized. A key part of this monograph effectively involves using multiple attestation of themes. It is more about using it critically and being honest about its limitations. It is about qualifying it and not using it in a negative sense. Based on Meier's minimalist use of this criterion, his analysis and conclusions based on his use of this method is flawed.

Critique on the Criterion of Dissimilarity

The criterion of dissimilarity originally specifies double-dissimilarity in which it assigns the likelihood of authenticity to a tradition if it may not have been derived from Judaism or from the early Christian church. Dissimilarity with early Christianity is determined when the tradition appears to be

---

92. Keener, *Historical Jesus*, 155.
93. Theissen and Merz, *Historical Jesus*, 338–39.
94. Meier, *Marginal Jew*, 5:10.

disadvantageous or embarrassing for the early Christians. By itself only, it is called the criterion of embarrassment. Dissimilarity to Judaism assumes that there is a full distinction between Jesus and Judaism.

Dagmar Winter briefly outlines the history of this criterion.[95] The need to determine a unique Jesus was already present in the eighteenth century when the Deists desired a distinct religious champion for a "rational religion who was opposed to the superstitions of his religious contemporaries, be they Jews or the early Christian tradents." What is seen as authentic is devoid of "prejudices and false religions opinions."[96] The theory behind this concept was supported further by the philosophy of history of Georg Friedrich Hegel, using his outline of the shape of history as bearing the pattern of "thesis-antithesis-synthesis." Applied to the historical Jesus, the pattern is "Israel-Judaism-Christianity" where Jesus is derived in part from Israel but is antithetical to Judaism. Judaism in Jesus's time is considered as the late form of Judaism that is supposedly being superseded by early Christianity. Also, in the nineteenth century, Jesus was understood as the "romantic ideal of the hero in history." He was, as Winter notes, "the genius beyond compare, the great independent heroic individual who arises at crisis time, repudiates Jewish legalism and ushers in a new historical era, before being crucified because he is dangerously new."[97] In the early twentieth century, Bultmann's dialectical theology emphasized the otherness of God, which resulted in the de-emphasis of Jesus's life that reflects his Jewish context. Instead, what was upheld was his message as the risen Christ. This concept of the otherness of God was promoted further in the New Quest, and Jesus's uniqueness was historicized.[98] The result was the promotion of the criterion of dissimilarity with Käsemann's well-known definition of the criterion: "In only one case do we have more or less safe ground under our feet; when there are no grounds either for deriving a tradition from Judaism or for ascribing it to primitive Christianity."[99] The arrival of the Third Quest with its emphasis on finding Jesus in his Jewish context led to sustained criticism of the criterion of dissimilarity. In its place, the notion of Jesus's continuity with Judaism and early Christianity starts to take shape.

---

95. Winter, "Saving the Quest," 115–31.
96. Winter, "Saving the Quest," 119.
97. Winter, "Saving the Quest," 120.
98. Winter, "Saving the Quest," 120–21.
99. Winter, "Saving the Quest," 122, quoting Käsemann, "Problem," 37.

Therefore, based on its history, the criterion of dissimilarity is founded on faulty presuppositions, including an incorrect notion of the Judaism during Jesus's time, a measure of anti-Semitism, and the promotion of the theologians' own perspectives of what Jesus must have been like as determined in various phases of the Quest. Therefore, the use of the criterion of dissimilarity is inherently problematic.

But other than incorrect presuppositions, there are also serious methodological flaws that come with the use of this criterion. First, this criterion gives a tradition or saying that reflects what is most distinctive about Jesus instead of what is characteristic of him. If used or misused in a negative sense, this criterion leaves just a fraction of Jesus's teaching and deeds as authentic. This serious distortion delineates a historical Jesus that is defined based on his more peripheral characteristics. Second, the result of this method is "a Jesus cut off from both his Jewish predecessors and his Christian followers."[100] It focuses more on a "thinly veiled historicized Christology than on a critically reflected appreciation of an individual's impact in history."[101] Third, the method presupposes that enough is known about Jesus, first-century Judaism, and early Christianity to assess with good accuracy what is dissimilar and what is not when looking at any material. But that is not the case. Hooker notes, "It could be that if we know the whole truth about Judaism and the early church, our small quantity of 'distinctive' teaching would wither away altogether."[102] In other words, with more knowledge, what could be assessed as distinctive or unique may be an established characteristic of the Jesus tradition.[103] Fourth, even if perfect knowledge of Judaism and early Christianity could be achieved, the method's results deny the possibility of overlapping characteristics. The method itself drives its own conclusions in giving only a Jesus that is distinct from all his contemporaries.[104] Fifth, the criterion, if it is exclusively used and in isolation, "denies the principle of correlation, a fundamental principle of historical scholarship."[105] Sixth, when used in tandem with the criterion of

---

100. Allison, "How to Marginalize," 1:5.
101. Winter, "Saving the Quest," 124.
102. Hooker, "Christology and Methodology," 482.
103. Winter, "Saving the Quest," 124.
104. Hooker, "Christology and Methodology," 482.
105. Winter, "Saving the Quest," 124.

coherence, the mistakes that may be made through the use of dissimilarity will be magnified even more by the results of coherence.[106]

Meier states that he did not technically use this criterion for the parables. He gives three reasons why he believes the criterion of dissimilarity is inoperable for the L parables. Out of the three reasons, only one is significant: he emphasizes the possibility that creative oral tradents could have composed their own Lucan parables and attributed them to Jesus. For him, even if the Lukan parables can be proven to be dissimilar enough to other Jewish parables or credibly viewed as unique only to Luke and the Gospels when compared to other writings of the NT and the early church, they still would not pass the criterion because of the possibility that creative oral tradents may have written some or most of the singly attested parables.[107] If that assumption is the case, one cannot determine if the parables are authentic or not. Therefore, he concludes it would be futile to use the dissimilarity criterion with these parables. In reality, Meier is implicitly using the dissimilarity criterion but in a negative manner against the L parables. He employs, in a sense, an argument from silence that is used not only to invalidate a criterion but also to render a tradition inauthentic. Implicit in his assumption is that the transmission of the L parables cannot be trusted to guard authentic Jesus tradition. Therefore, his reasoning centers on some form-critical assumptions concerning the nature of oral transmission.[108] A critique of these assumptions will be addressed further in the section regarding oral tradition and transmission. But aside from considering Meier's use (or non-use) of this criterion, this study does not recommend the use of the double-dissimilarity criterion at all based on the many reasons just given.

Critique on the Criterion of Coherence

Anthony Le Donne notes two ways in which the criterion is used.[109] The first is how Norman Perrin describes coherence: "Material from the earlier strata of tradition may be accepted as authentic if it can be shown to cohere with material established as authentic by means of the criterion of dissimilarity."[110]

106. Hooker, "Christology and Methodology," 483.
107. Meier, *Marginal Jew*, 5:53–54.
108. Meier, *Marginal Jew*, 5:53–54.
109. Le Donne, "Criterion," 95–114.
110. Perrin, *Rediscovering*, 43.

In this case, coherence is a sub-criterion of the criterion of dissimilarity. There are two assumptions regarding the use of this criteria: The original parts of the Gospels can be stripped from their unhistorical parts, and what is original coheres with Jesus's eschatological vocation.[111]

Le Donne traced the concept of coherence from Johannes Weiss who envisioned that the tradition cohered either with the preaching of Jesus or the early church. What is eschatological is deemed to be from Jesus while the more ethical aspects are from the church.[112] Le Donne attributes to Paul Schmiedel the general notion of coherence as the tradition that agrees in character with "absolutely credible passages."[113] Rudolf Bultmann applied this criterion as a sub-criterion of double dissimilarity and especially advocated for coherence with the more eschatological oriented tradition for a material to be authentic. C. H. Dodd distinguishes a dichotomy between the "original" parts of Jesus's teaching and its redactional frameworks.[114] Noticeable overall is the presupposition of an authentic core by which other traditions are measured. This presupposition is a form-critical assumption that is hard to defend given the current state of studies in oral tradition and memory theory.

Another way coherence is applied is as a sub-criterion not of dissimilarity but of anything the historian finds to be foundational material. For example, through criteria such as embarrassment, discontinuity, and multiple attestation, Meier establishes this foundational database first as established tradition. Whatever coheres with this information is authentic.[115].

In terms of critique, in looking at coherence in general, its basic principle holds that material content needs to cohere with tradition that is undisputed. Unfortunately, not much is undisputed, making the results of this criterion difficult to assess. In applying the first kind of coherence (as a sub-criterion of dissimilarity), its problems are derived from the issues of applying the criterion of dissimilarity. For example, the findings of coherence applied in this type would emphasize what is peripheral instead of what is characteristic of Jesus. So overall, coherence applied this way is just as useful as dissimilarity. The second way to apply coherence still has some flaws. First, the charge of being too subjective is mentioned as this

---

111. Le Donne, "Criterion," 97.
112. Le Donne, "Criterion," 98.
113. Le Donne, "Criterion," 99.
114. Le Donne, "Criterion," 103.
115. Le Donne, "Criterion," 105.

presupposes an ability to sort out what seems coherent or not, despite historians coming from many perspectives. For example, Hooker asks how can anyone be sure that what someone counts as coherent is coherent from the first century perspective.[116] Allison notes, "There is nothing objective about coherence."[117] Second, this criterion assumes that Jesus is always coherent and that Jesus did nothing random or unrelated to his general pattern of sayings and deeds. That is hard to defend. Instead, in agreement with Le Donne, Jesus must have been generally coherent but also possibly displayed some characteristics of randomness.[118] Finally, a flaw in this criterion is that it assumes binary thinking, that tradition can be divided into two categories: traditions that cohere with the historian's reconstruction of Jesus and traditions that cohere with the historian's reconstruction of the early Christian church. Other expressions of these binary divisions include those traditions that cohere with the eschatological preaching of Jesus and those of the early church, those that cohere with the life-setting of Jesus as opposed to the setting of the early Palestinian communities and early Christianity, those that refer to Jesus's career, and those that pertain to theological reflection about Jesus by the early church. Le Donne asserts that historical memory cannot be neatly classified into binary units. Instead he proposes looking at it from the perspective of a continuum. Memories that have been coherently framed for the earliest followers would also be coherently framed for future followers and each would have a certain affinity with each other. Le Donne asserts that the memory of Jesus's words and deeds would have been coherent "within every mnemonic frame along the way."[119] In a sense these memories become all interconnected such that they cohere with the whole tradition with varying levels of coherence. Therefore, the criterion of coherence is difficult to apply to the traditional notion of authenticating some traditions and rendering others inauthentic. This does not mean that this criterion should not be used. It just means that there is a need to reformulate it and qualify its use in a manner similar in how it is done in the continuum approach that this monograph supports.

---

116. Hooker, "Christology and Methodology," 483.
117. Allison, "How to Marginalize," 1:3.
118. Le Donne, "Criterion," 110.
119. Le Donne, "Criterion," 112.

THE "INAUTHENTICITY" OF LUKE 18:9–14

Critique on the Criterion of Embarrassment

The criterion of embarrassment "focuses on actions or sayings of Jesus that would have embarrassed or created difficulty for the early church."[120] This definition assumes that the dissimilarity did not originate from the evangelist's redaction as determined by redaction-critical analysis and source criticism. The goal is to arrive at a tradition not introduced by the evangelist but from an older and well-known tradition that may go back to the historical Jesus. This criterion is the same as the criterion of dissimilarity from early Christianity. Examples include (1) the baptism of Jesus by John the Baptist as Jesus was supposedly sinless and above being baptized by his inferior contemporary, (2) the accusation that Jesus was demon-possessed (Mark 3:22—"having Beelzebul"), (3) the reaction of his family to his ministry, and (4) Jesus's ignorance of the timing of the last day.

Rafael Rodriguez states that the problem of this criterion mainly lies with its view of the Gospels and the Jesus tradition from the point of view of form criticism. It assumes that what must be embarrassing to the early church must not have originated with the church but with the historical Jesus. This assumption can never be a certainty. All the writings we have from the Gospels are from the early Christians, and, as Hooker correctly asserts, "probably it bears its mark to a lesser or greater extent."[121] The material "has been handed on, shaped, molded, used, and perhaps created by the early Christian communities."[122] All the tradition's features, including the seemingly embarrassing ones, served and functioned within the overall tradition itself. These already belong as part of the tradition, and if the evangelists had so desired they would have not included these features if they were that embarrassing.[123] In addition, similar to the argument made against the criterion of dissimilarity, this criterion also assumes full knowledge of Jesus and the early church to make an accurate judgment of what is an embarrassing tradition. Obviously, no one knows enough about Jesus or the early church to make a good assessment. Perhaps given the probable plurality of the early church, some of them may find matters embarrassing and others may not. As Rodriguez correctly states, "The criterion of embarrassment

---

120. Rodriguez, "Embarrassing Truth," 134, quoting Meier, *Roots*, 168.
121. Hooker, "Christology and Methodology," 486.
122. Hooker, "Christology and Methodology," 485.
123. Rodriguez, "Embarrassing Truth," 147.

renders a historical datum embarrassing; it does not authenticate already-embarrassing historical data."[124]

Therefore, this study simply calls for the use of this criterion in a more critical and responsible manner.

Conclusions regarding the Critique of the Criteria for Authenticity

This critique on the traditional use of the criteria of authenticity reflects two major issues that call for a qualified and responsible manner regarding their use: (1) The criteria approach is indebted to form criticism and its questionable form-critical assumptions, and (2) there are flaws in the methodology itself no matter which criteria one chooses, and one criterion (double-dissimilarity) need not be used at all. To put the criteria in service to segregate what is "authentic" from what is "inauthentic" requires the use of tools that need to be carefully and critically handled (qualified and reformulated) while laboring under the conditions of questionable assumptions. These questionable assumptions will be expounded on even more in the next section concerning the findings on the studies on oral tradition, transmission, and memory. But overall, just this critique on the unqualified and traditional use of the criteria of authenticity calls for a more responsible application of the criteria and casts serious doubts on the assertions that Meier makes concerning the "inauthenticity" of the L parables.

Studies on Oral Tradition, Transmission, Eyewitnesses, Memory

Meier expresses that he does not put much stock in studies in orality, memory, oral tradition, and transmission.[125] Unfortunately, the assumptions he uses that come from form criticism do not provide an adequate model for oral tradition and transmission and give an incorrect or undeveloped view on the role of memory. Meier's reliance on faulty form-critical assumptions materially affects his analysis and conclusions on the biblical texts. This next section will be a brief survey on the various models of oral tradition and its transmission, the role of eyewitnesses, and the role of memory. Meier's

---

124. Rodriguez, "Embarrassing Truth," 146.
125. Meier, *Marginal Jew*, 5:50.

form-critical model of oral tradition and its deficiencies will be outlined first, and then other alternative models and aspects that affect oral tradition and transmission, as well as eyewitnesses and memory, will follow.

Form Criticism

Form criticism assumes that the Gospels are composed of short units of tradition or pericopae that were transmitted orally until these were put together by the evangelists in writing within an overall framework.[126] It asserts that many anonymous individuals orally passed on the Jesus tradition not only by handing down the tradition but also by making creative modifications to it. According to Martin Dibelius, these anonymous individuals who handled the tradition came from the community, such as preachers, teachers, and others. The changes that took place in the tradition operate not because of the high influence of certain individuals but because of certain "laws" of transmission. These laws operate uncontrollably and impersonally, depending on the type of form of the tradition, and, in general, these were thought to bring expansion and further elaboration of the tradition with some borrowing of other elements such as external motifs, myth, and others. The presence of these laws mostly reduces the role of the evangelists as collectors or editors of the tradition.[127] According to Bultmann, the collection of the tradition started in the early Palestinian church. The main purpose why this tradition is collected is for the use of the church in specific situations such as apologetic, preaching, or other purposes. Each form is collected, takes shape, and is adapted or even actually created based on its specific *Sitz im Leben* or typical life situation just mentioned.[128] Therefore, the traditions tell more about the life of the early Christians than the historical life of Jesus as these originated in the context of the early church, although some have argued that these traditions may also have conceivably originated from a *Sitz im Leben Jesu*.[129] The early church possibly creating some gospel traditions partly fuels the notion that some traditions originated from Jesus and others came from the community. As a result, some criteria of authenticity

---

126. Classical works of form criticism include Schmidt, *Rahmen der Geshichte*; Dibelius, *From Tradition*; Bultmann, *History*.

127. Dibelius, *From Tradition*, 1–17.

128. Bultmann, *History*, 368.

129. Bauckham, *Jesus*, 244, cites Easton, *Gospel before the Gospels*; Taylor, *Formation*; Lightfoot, *St. Mark*, 102.

are needed to distinguish between the two and come up with an explanation of the origin of inauthentic material.[130]

With regard to oral tradition, form criticism models it after parallels in folklore.[131] The community in general or groups within it shaped and transmitted the tradition in such an impersonal way that it seems as if there are "laws" of transmission in operation. This notion comes from a so-called "romantic" view of folk tradition where an anonymous collective creates folk tales.[132] In this type of community there is no interest in the past and no notion of preserving historical accounts. The laws of transmission operated within this free system in the community through anonymous individuals until the tradition reached its written version. For example, in form criticism, the Gospel of Mark is considered the end product of the process of oral tradition. There is supposedly a "pure form" underneath layers of accretion that have taken place in the tradition, and that it is possible to get to a reconstruction of this "pure form." This is not a plausible assumption if, for example, the oral tradition process is viewed instead as a series of oral performances rather than something that resembles an editable printed text that can be analyzed and investigated. But according to Eric Eve, for Bultmann "there was no essential difference between the oral and written stages of the tradition, a highly questionable assertion that effectively led Bultmann into treating orality as a kind of writing."[133]

As for parables, according to Bultmann the applications attached to them and the overall contexts that are included with them are secondary.[134] Also, since the early church created the traditions, many prophetic and apocalyptic sayings were adopted and ascribed to Jesus. It did not matter whether these sayings came from Jesus or from Christian prophets who spoke for the risen Jesus.[135] There is no interest or importance given to eyewitnesses.

Form criticism is inadequate and unable to show a plausible understanding of oral tradition. A few major reasons include the following: First,

---

130. Bauckham, *Jesus*, 244.

131. Dibelius refers to Johann Gottfried Herder's view on folk poetry and Franz Overbeck's work of primitive Christian literature. Dibelius, *From Tradition*, 5.

132. Eve, *Behind the Gospels*, 20, cites Güttgemanns, *Candid Questions*, 127, as stating that this notion is not from empirical research but from a metaphysical viewpoint that asserts a divine origin of folk poetry.

133. Eve, *Behind the Gospels*, 26–27. See also Bultmann, *History*, 6, 87, 239, 321.

134. Bultmann, *History*, 166–205.

135. Bultmann, *History*, 108–28.

THE "INAUTHENTICITY" OF LUKE 18:9-14

using the model of folklore to understand the oral tradition of the Gospels is questionable. The nature of the traditions, the time span between Jesus and the Gospels, and the validity of the "romantic" idea of the folks as collective anonymous authors make this overall model problematic.[136] Second, form critics disregard the difference between oral and written media. A literary model is incorrectly used to analyze the process of oral transmission. Other conclusions such as the notion of an original or pure form of a pericope does not stand because material transmitted orally has no original form based on the more plausible notion of oral transmission as varied performances. Related to this idea is that traditions are assumed to be transmitted "purely" in an oral way instead of a more accurate setting of a mainly oral society supplemented with written texts. Third, the laws of transmission are speculative, and the purported tendencies do not come out the way it is described to go. E. P. Sanders makes the valid case that no laws of transmission function consistently throughout the gospel tradition.[137]

For these few reasons among others, alternative models other than form criticism came about to account for oral tradition and address areas that form criticism overlooked, including matters such as media differences, eyewitnesses, and social memory. But just by simply relying on form critical assumption concerning oral tradition and transmission, Meier's ideas on these issues are already on shaky ground. The introduction of other models or oral tradition and transmission expands on this point even further.

Rabbinic Model

A second model for oral tradition can be considered a radical alternative to the form critical approach. Instead of a theory that assumes uncontrolled growth of traditions created by an informal community (from its impersonal laws of transmission within anonymous people in the community), the rabbinic model assumes that the oral tradition of the Gospels underwent a process similar in the methods and practices carried out in rabbinic Judaism. The rabbinic practice is considered the nearest available analogue to the Jesus tradition. This theory espouses a highly controlled practice in contrast with the uncontrolled process delineated by form criticism.[138]

---

136. Bauckham, *Jesus*, 247; Eve, *Behind the Gospels*, 28.
137. Sanders, *Tendencies*, 272, 275.
138. Two notable authors and works for the "Scandinavian School" method are

Birger Gerhardsson and Harald Riesenfeld note that in the New Testament, the writings employ the technical language of "receiving, handling, and holding fast to a tradition" (e.g., 1 Cor 11:2, 23; 15:1, 3; Gal 1:9; Phil 4:9; 1 Thess 2:13; 4:1; 2 Thess 2:15; 3:6). This language in its context was used in the sense of deliberately handing over a tradition from someone with authority to another who is supposed to learn this by memory. Gerhardsson asserts that this is the way the oral Torah was passed on in rabbinic schools and this model is the most comparable way to how Jesus and his disciples may have handled the tradition.[139] The disciples of the rabbis memorized their teacher's material using techniques that were used to make sure deviation was minimal. They had to memorize much material with various methods to aid memory, but it was mostly learned by constant repetition.[140] The shape of the material also aids in memory by being expressed concisely like a proverb or aphorism that stands out in the mind. Likewise, Gerhardsson believes that Jesus, as the disciples' teacher, taught his students to handle his teachings and pass them on in an analogous manner.[141] Development and change did take place in this highly controlled mode of transmission, but it was done in a deliberate manner by those with authority to allow it. Also, while form critics believe that the traditions were transmitted and used by the early church within the community's various functions, this rabbinic model separates the occasion of the tradition's transmission to its use in the early church. Instead, transmission was mainly done independently in a setting where a teacher handed over the tradition to the students.[142]

This model of oral tradition is vastly different from that of form criticism and is criticized on a few major points. First, there is the criticism of anachronism, given that rabbinic techniques of a later time period are being applied to the situation in the first century. Gerhardsson assumes that the ancient world was conservative in its methods, which means the rabbinic techniques may have originated way back. Also, memorization was the common educational method of the ancient Greco-Roman world at the time, including the elementary level. Second, the assumed controlled precise transmission of tradition cannot explain the level of variation in the Jesus tradition. In other words, the transmission delineated by the rabbinical model seems

---

Gerhardsson, *Memory*; Riesenfeld, *Gospel Tradition*.

    139. Gerhardsson, *Memory*, 281–83, 288–91; Riesenfeld, *Gospel Tradition*, 1–22.

    140. Gerhardsson, *Memory*, 113–36, 142–86, 163–69.

    141. Gerhardsson, *Memory*, 136–42.

    142. Bauckham, *Jesus*, 250.

too controlled to explain the divergences between the traditions.[143] Third, the Gospels do not portray Jesus as teaching by repetition, nor is there evidence that "the apostolic college in Jerusalem" controlled the tradition as Gerhardsson asserts.[144] Therefore, it is less rigid and controlled than the model prescribes. Fourth, the model, like the form-critical model, does not account for the difference between oral and written media, and it assumes inaccurately that the transmission of the tradition was purely oral, with no use of writing. Finally, it is difficult to assume uniform handling of tradition throughout the church and in various regions (Galilee, Jerusalem, gentile cities) from 30 CE until 70 CE when the first Gospel was written.[145]

Although it is also an inadequate model, the rabbinic approach does address some of the deficiencies of the form-critical approach to oral tradition especially as it introduces the importance of memory, the careful handling of the tradition (instead of the tradition being subject to speculative laws of transmission), and the notion of authoritative tradents (instead of anonymous community individuals).

Informal Controlled Model

Kenneth Bailey considers this model[146] as halfway between the "informal uncontrolled" model of form criticism and the "formal controlled" one of the rabbinic method.[147] The model of form criticism is informal in the sense that there is no specific teacher nor student nor structure within the community in which the tradition passed on from one to another. The tradition is uncontrolled in the sense that it can develop and change in any kind of unrestricted fashion. For the most part, the tradition that comes from Jesus disappears. Therefore, form criticism's transmission is unreliable and unable to preserve the tradition in its earlier forms.[148] The rabbinic method, on the other hand, is formal in the sense that there is an identified teacher, student, and material that is passed on from one to the other. It is controlled in that the material is memorized and strictly preserved.[149] However, this

---

143. Dunn, *Jesus Remembered*, 198.
144. Davids, "Gospels," 76–81.
145. Eve, *Behind the Gospels*, 39–46.
146. Bailey, "Informal Controlled," 34–54; "Middle Eastern Oral," 363–67.
147. Bailey, "Informal Controlled," 38.
148. Bailey, "Informal Controlled," 36.
149. Bailey, "Informal Controlled," 37.

model cannot plausibly explain the variation in the Jesus traditions in their current form. Therefore, Bailey espouses a model of "informal controlled" tradition as a halfway measure. What makes his theory unique is that it is based on anecdotal evidence from his time spent of more than thirty years working as a teacher and missionary in the Middle East. This theory has the advantage of benefitting from data from a more culturally relevant part of the world as well as being able to verify in practice these types of oral transmission. He claims that his observations of how transmission is done is from the *haflat samar*, which is a gathering of people who told and handed down tales. In this setting the community gathers and retells stories that are relevant for the identity of the community. It is informal in the sense that the retelling tends to be done not by a formal teacher but by the community through its elders and dominant individuals while the others listen.[150] It is controlled since the community overall exerts what is necessary to make sure the traditions are faithfully preserved, especially through correcting the person who serves as the oral tradent. There are varying degrees of flexibility with regard to the preservation of the tradition depending on the type of material transmitted. For example, there is not much control over jokes, casual news, or any other news irrelevant to the identity of the community or information not judged with high value, while material such as poems and proverbs are to be strictly preserved and controlled. In terms of material such as parables and historical events that are relevant to the identity of the community, there is both flexibility and control. There is flexibility over the stories' style and details while making sure the core point of the story is preserved.[151] Bailey asserts that these principles are analogous to the oral tradition process of the Gospels and believes this model accounts for the variations found in the Gospels while preserving key features and structures.

He has several advantages to his theory. First, it has the ability to address some deficiencies of both form criticism and the rabbinic method. In particular, per Dunn, "the paradigm of literary editing is confirmed as wholly inappropriate; in oral tradition one telling of a story is in no sense an editing of a previous telling; rather, each telling starts with the same subject and theme, but the retellings are different; each telling is a performance of the tradition itself."[152] Second, it validates the theory of oral tradition and

---

150. Bailey, "Informal Controlled," 40.
151. Bailey, "Informal Controlled," 42.
152. Dunn, *Jesus Remembered*, 209.

transmission espoused by Werner Kelber's media contrast model, which means it accounts for the difference between oral and written media. Third, it is developed from a culture with a more relevant social context for first-century Christians.[153] Finally, it accounts for the actual picture of stability and variability expressed in the Gospels.[154]

For the model's deficiencies, the theory behind it has some issues. *Haflat samar* may not have been a gathering to preserve tradition but rather a nightly gathering for hearing stories for the purposes of entertainment,[155] but the process of an informal controlled model of oral tradition operates outside of the *haflat samar* setting, as well.[156] While Bailey may seem to claim that the essential core of the tradition that is preserved may contain accurate historical information, it is not the main purpose of preserving the tradition. Rather, as Theodore Weeden argues, it is "for the efficacious purpose of preserving and faithfully articulating stories which are congruent with and validate the social identity of an oral society in any given period of time" (not that Weeden denies that there may be historical information in the tradition).[157]

Validation of Informal Controlled Model from Genre Studies

While there are deficiencies behind the theoretical background of Bailey's findings, his idea of traditions that are controlled but with varying degrees of flexibility is also supported by findings in recent studies on ancient biographies and their relationship to the character of the Gospels. This topic is beyond the scope of this book, but a few notes from these studies to validate Bailey's model are helpful.

Craig Keener states that a majority of scholars currently regard the Gospels' genre as ancient biography.[158] He writes, "A biography was understood as a basically factual narrative about a real individual. Biography thus offers the closest available analogy for how audiences would initially

---

153. Eve, *Behind the Gospels*, 79–85.

154. Dunn, *Jesus Remembered*, 210–49, shows examples of Gospel texts illustrating the variability and stability of the tradition as delineated by Bailey's method.

155. Weeden, "Kenneth Bailey's Theory," 38–42.

156. Eve, *Behind the Gospels*, 80–81.

157. Weeden, "Kenneth Bailey's Theory," 33.

158. Keener, "Chapter 1," 3.

approach the narrative first-century Gospels."¹⁵⁹ Studies done on ancient biographies and ancient historiography (Luke is a mixture of ancient historiography and biography) reveal an expectation of "historical intention and significant use of prior information in biographies" that are not present in ancient novels.¹⁶⁰ For ancient biographies such as the Gospels where the major character subject is a very recent figure, "a default expectation that much of the information is accurate is usually likelier than are a priori skeptical assumptions."¹⁶¹ Therefore, this matches Bailey's model for the need of the Christian community to preserve and transmit the substance of the tradition they possess faithfully. In addition, the character of ancient biography also allows for flexibility that is seen in the Gospel accounts. The convention of ancient biography allows for "considerable flexibility in how biographies recounted their information."¹⁶² Keener further notes that "ancient audiences did not expect biographers to invent events but did allow them to flesh out scenes and discourse for the purpose of what they considered narrative verisimilitude."¹⁶³ These findings likely correspond to the flexibility for which Bailey's model calls in terms of the information content in the preserved tradition. As to the degree of flexibility involved, it depended on the sources and biographers, but what studies show is that biographies of figures from the recent past, such as the Gospels, have a lesser degree of flexibility or variation compared to biographies on figures of the distant past.¹⁶⁴ These findings are not intended to show that there is an essential continuity between the production of the Gospels and the earlier oral tradition, which is a form critical assumption that effectively disregards the differences between oral and written media. What it does show is that the quality of the factual information in the Gospels assumed in Bailey's model possibly corresponds with the substance of the information reflected in an ancient biography.

One more important issue is that in terms of sources, ancient writers used a variety of oral and written sources of which most material is no longer extant. Accounts of stories or parables, such as the unique Lukan

---

159. Keener, "Chapter 1," 4. The groundbreaking work that provides a lot of detailed evidence for this is Burridge, *What are the Gospels?*

160. Keener, "Chapter 1," 5.

161. Keener, "Chapter 1," 5.

162. Keener, "Chapter 1," 6.

163. Keener, "Chapter 1," 44.

164. Keener, "Chapter 1," 8.

parables, that cannot be multiply attested need not be assumed to have originated from fabrication. Keener rightly states, "It is logical to generally expect the same degree of accuracy or imprecision in their unique accounts as in their parallel ones, insofar as these accounts reflect the same general character."[165]

Oral and Written Media Contrast Model[166]

Form criticism and the rabbinic model do not account for the differences between oral and written media. This is one aspect where the models are inadequate in describing the possible oral tradition process. Werner Kelber is prominently credited for taking the difference between the two seriously. His work is aided by the works of folklorists, anthropologists, and contemporary experts on orality. He defines oral transmission as "a process of social identification and preventive censorship."[167] In his first chapter entitled "Pre-Canonical Synoptic Transmission," he outlines some of the differences between the two media. For instance, a speaker who delivers a speech accounts for the audience in front of him or her, which may affect his or her performance. Therefore, the speaker addresses a certain social context. The author of written material does not have to deal with an audience as it is composed without the reader present and is, therefore, detached, thus enabling the writer to have more control over his or her work. An oral performer also needs to make his or her speech memorable, which means the speaker is bound to use devices such as formulaic speech and mnemonic patterning.[168] If a saying in the Jesus tradition was to survive, it needed to be expressed in patterns including "heavily patterned speech forms, abounding in alliteration, paronomasia, appositional equivalence, proverbial and aphoristic diction, contrasts and antitheses, synonymous, antithetical, synthetic, and tautologic parallelism and the like."[169] In terms of limitations, unlike written texts, the audience and social context influence speeches. Oral transmission is a process of social identification because the tradition would have been preserved depending on whether the particular message finds an audience that has "social relevancy and

---

165. Keener, "Chapter 1," 15, 21, 23.
166. See Kelber, *Oral*; Güttgemanns, *Candid Questions*.
167. Kelber, *Oral*, 14.
168. Kelber, *Oral*, 14–15.
169. Kelber, *Oral*, 27.

acceptability," or the message finds "an echo in people's hearts and minds" so the audience identifies with it.[170] This theory is different from assuming that a transmission is merely done through rote memorization espoused by the rabbinic model. On the other hand, oral transmission is also a process of preventive censorship in the sense that it also eliminates tradition that the bearers find not useful or not socially approved. Therefore, changes take place in the performance that may look different, affecting such things as themes, varying sequences, or differences in details.[171] An original or pure form of the tradition does not really exist because each oral performance is unique and can be considered more as recreations with no linear process of development. This idea goes up against the form critical assumption of a pure form underneath layers of accretions. Instead, the result is a process where the tradition (Kelber here is writing on the pre-Markan oral tradition) "diverges into a plurality of forms and directions. Variability and stability, conservatism and creativity, evanescence and unpredictability all mark the pattern of oral transmission."[172]

Kelber has been accused of pushing the differences too far between orality and writing, given the conclusions of his analysis of Mark and Paul's letters.[173] Gerhardsson also critiques Kelber's model of oral tradition in terms of how he may have used A. B. Lord's work on Yugoslavian epic poets as normative for all oral tradition and points out that what he deemed as normative may not be the most comparable for Jesus and the early church.[174] Regardless of the shortcomings of his model and assumptions, his most important point concerns the nature of oral tradition. Eric Eve remarks that for Kelber,

> Oral tradition is not a series of strata that can be uncovered by archaeological digging, nor does it follow inexorable laws of development that can be reverse-engineered to arrive at some putative "original form." Oral tradition consists in a series of individual performances . . . . To survive, oral tradition needs to be memorable, and it achieves memorability by adopting standard patterns and motifs, by focusing on the striking and extraordinary, by making its heroes larger than life and pitting them in black-and-white contests, and by focusing on essentials. In doing so, it manifests

---

170. Kelber, *Oral*, 24.
171. Kelber, *Oral*, 28–30.
172. Kelber, *Oral*, 33.
173. Dunn, *Jesus Remembered*, 203.
174. Gerhardsson, *Reliability*, 85n86.

both stability and variability, . . . [that is] stability in the core with almost infinite variability in the details of performance.[175]

Therefore, the nature of oral tradition as depicted by Kelber is quite incompatible with the notion of oral tradition espoused by form criticism.

Eyewitnesses to the Tradition

Other than accounting for the nature of oral tradition and transmission, the differences in media, and oral performance theory, studies have also been done to assess the possible impact of ancient eyewitnesses to the origination and transmission of the Jesus tradition. While it is recognized that certain individuals in the community performed oral tradition, not much is known of the role played by the original eyewitnesses, either as the original authoritative performers or as sources for the performers, and the nature of their witness or what they remember. Examples of authors who deal with these issues are Samuel Byrskog and Richard Bauckham.[176]

Byrskog offers some informative and pertinent points about the role of eyewitnesses. In ancient times, eyewitness testimony was very important. Heraclitus, the well-known pre-Socratic philosopher states, "Eyes are surer witnesses than ears."[177] Byrskog defines "autopsy" as "a visual means to gather information concerning a certain object, a means of inquiry, and thus also a way of relating to that object (whether that is a place, an event or archaeological item)."[178] In ancient times ancient historians performed autopsies through questioning those who were eyewitnesses. In these times, writing was just as an aid to memory and for preservation and did not serve as a substitute for memory. Therefore, there was a tendency to prefer oral tradition.

An important point Byrskog makes is that eyewitnesses interpret events while considering their own interests and conceptual framework. They construct narratives of these events based on their interests without necessarily lacking concern with the core historical truth. From his survey of ancient historiographical techniques, Byrskog asserts that there was interest for historical truth, and the method of autopsy was the means to find it. Although

---

175. Eve, *Behind the Gospels*, 64.
176. Byrskog, *Story as History*; Bauckham, *Jesus*.
177. Byrskog, *Story as History*, 49.
178. Byrskog, *Story as History*, 48.

Byrskog claims that the revealed historical truth was, in effect, interpreted truth, this understanding allows for comprehending the heavy theological interpretations in the Gospel as based on autopsy.[179] This notion questions the validity of discarding outright the theological interpretations as elaborations and accretions of the early church or the evangelists as assumed in form criticism, but as to how closely the evangelists practiced autopsy compared to other ancient historians is unknown.

Byrskog argues that early Christians who were eyewitnesses (e.g., Peter, the women, the family of Jesus) also served as informants of what they witnessed. Byrskog claims that they were the primary oral tradents of the Jesus tradition.[180] He also surmises that the early Christians exhibited the same pattern of Greco-Roman social groups in terms of the importance of preserving traditions of the past for their self-identity.[181] He also identified examples of autopsy that are incorporated in a variety of Christian texts.[182]

In summary, Byrskog's work expounds on the importance and consideration of eyewitnesses, which is an aspect that form criticism neglects. It asserts that all remembering occurs in a social context (in line also with social memory theory) as communities were able to supply conceptual frameworks through which the past is interpreted. It does not mean that only the present concerns totally define the past but that the factual core of what is believed to have happened is still there and continues to influence the present. The role of the authoritative individual eyewitness or oral tradent may be considered and illumined against the anonymous collective of tradents assumed by form criticism.

Richard Bauckham's monograph further explains the major importance of eyewitness testimony in the early church. He claims that the inclusion of personal names in the Gospels as recent historical tradition within an oral tradition-oriented context signals the presence of eyewitnesses. Bauckham sees that later extracanonical gospels invent names in place of those that are anonymous in the synoptic tradition. But in the Gospels themselves, these operate in reverse order in that they work towards the elimination of names instead of invention. Therefore, he concludes, the names belong to the original form of the tradition. The reason the names disappear from the tradition over time is that there

---

179. Eve, *Behind the Gospels*, 138.
180. Eddy and Boyd, *Jesus Legend*, 289n73.
181. Byrskog, *Story as History*, 91.
182. Byrskog, *Story as History*, 223–53.

is no reason to keep the name of the witness if the witness died or if the person is not known anymore to a certain community. Therefore, details such as names in the Gospels testify to actual eyewitness tradents such as Cleopas in Luke 24:18, Simon of Cyrene and his sons, and recipients of Jesus's healings such as Lazarus.[183]

Bauckham asserts that the eyewitness testimony of the Gospels displays an inside interpretation of events, which approaches a certain degree of historical accuracy even if some narrative freedoms are present in eyewitness testimony not for the purpose of embellishment but to make the facts more intelligible and significant.[184] Bauckham also asserts that the named eyewitnesses in the Gospels originated and remained guardians and guarantors of the tradition, as opposed to the form critical view of anonymous community transmission. His work overall argues for the transmission and control of the tradition by authorized individuals instead of an anonymous collective assumed in form criticism.[185]

Social Memory

Alan Kirk states that memory theory "supplies the grounds for a comprehensively revised account of the history of the Jesus tradition, one capable of displacing the moribund form-critical model while incorporating—indeed, giving a better account of—the latter's enduring insights."[186] Meier's reliance on the form-critical approach to memory, which means not accounting for it at all, neglects one of the most important aspects to consider when studying the Jesus tradition. This next section will concentrate on the difference memory theory makes in analyzing the gospel tradition. In the process of discussing memory theory, some important works will also be underscored.

A major premise built into form criticism is to ignore the concept of memory as an essential feature to consider with regards to the Jesus

---

183. Bauckham, *Jesus*, 35, 42, 44, 47, 49. Eddy and Boyd, *Jesus Legend*, 417–19.

184. Eve, *Behind the Gospels*, 149.

185. Eve, *Behind the Gospels*, 157–58.

186. Kirk cites as enduring insights (1) the mediation of tradition in a "repertoire of small-scale cultural genres"; (2) "the powerful effects of present community realities and concerns—*the Sitz im Leben*—upon the tradition and its representation of the past"; and, (3) "the autonomy of the tradition, that is, its remarkable tendency to run its own course as it interacted with the contingent historical and social realities of its tradent communities." Kirk, *Memory*, 1.

tradition.[187] The remembered past has nothing to do with how the tradition is formed or transmitted; instead, the major drivers are sociological forces from the early Christian communities and the laws of transmission. Kirk asserts that no one really defends anymore the notion that "tradition's development is controlled by any of Bultmann's posited laws of development."[188] This is a notion that espouses a development trajectory from simple and pure forms to complex structures.[189]

The form-critical approach misunderstands the relationship between memory and the tradition. It makes a total distinction between the two. Form criticism is not concerned with any historical interest but simply that the tradition serves the needs of the Christian community.[190] Tradition is a product of the present. Also, a major paradigm in form criticism is that memory is individual in nature; it is "an individual faculty of recollection."[191] The consensus in the past in biblical scholarship was that there was not much of a connection between memory and tradition. In this perspective, memory is viewed as "a filing cabinet for past experience," and to remember is to retrieve the data "like retrieving checked baggage from storage."[192] What is deemed as memory concerning Jesus is limited to the reminiscence of the original disciples and associates, and this memory terminated when the eyewitnesses no longer existed. Then second-generation Christians remembering and repeating information in stories about Jesus became the Jesus tradition.[193] Bultmann did acknowledge that memory may have been a factor in the literary production of the early church. This memory is responsible for "residual traces" of historically authentic elements in the tradition.[194] But tradition again is mainly a sociological and theological product of the church community. It was mostly invented and projected back into the past. Traditions supposedly morphed and grew while memories are either "preserved intact, suppressed, or replaced."[195] Both memory and tradition as distinct entities can then be found in the

---

187. Kirk, *Memory*, 3.
188. Kirk, *Memory*, 4.
189. Kirk, *Memory*, 3–4.
190. Kirk, *Memory*, 1–2.
191. Kirk and Thatcher, "Jesus Tradition," 25.
192. Kirk and Thatcher, "Jesus Tradition," 26.
193. Kirk and Thatcher, "Jesus Tradition," 26.
194. Kirk, *Memory*, 2.
195. Kirk and Thatcher, "Jesus Tradition," 26.

Gospel, and the quests for the historical Jesus became involved in methods and criteria "designed to sift nuggets of genuine memory out of the mass of tradition in which the evangelists have embedded them."[196] Kirk and Thatcher further note that because "these nuggets are [allegedly] so few and so small, 'memory' has, for all practical purposes, disappeared as an analytical category in Jesus research."[197] Incidentally, the "criterion of dissimilarity" was a natural result of this notion of tradition and memory. If elements that are specifically Christian, as well as Jewish and Greco-Roman were peeled away, the original historical core may be exposed in the form of "pithy, memorable sayings that represented the point at which remembrances of Jesus were most likely to be found, because they were uniquely able to perdure through oral storytelling."[198]

To summarize, from the form-critical perspective, memory is of an individual character comprised of the reminiscences of the person that need to be retrieved. From the perspective of the Jesus material, memory comes from the original eyewitnesses of Jesus. This memory forms a small trace within the overall Jesus tradition (tradition being the reminiscence of second-generation Christians) and may be derived by peeling off the outer tradition to get to the core memory.

A lot can be said about memory to address the form-critical perspective; however, that goes beyond the scope of this monograph. Nevertheless, some highlights of memory theory need to be made to show how memory is much more complex and involved than the inadequate form-critical assumptions of memory that Meier espouses. He neglects to account for them in his work.

Memory is essential for oral tradition to endure, but the kind of memory needed for oral tradition is not just the memory of one individual person. The bearer is part of a community to which the tradition circulates.

196. Kirk and Thatcher, "Jesus Tradition," 27.

197. Kirk and Thatcher, "Jesus Tradition," 27. Kirk and Thatcher reviews this notion from three sources: Käsemann; Perrin; the Jesus Seminar. Käsemann notably characterizes tradition as a replacement of memory with *kerygma*. Perrin asserts that the evangelists have no interest of past recollections of Jesus but the interest is simply to have Jesus speak to the needs of the community. For the Jesus Seminar, especially for Robert Funk and Roy Hoover, there is a sharp differentiation between authentic memory and fabricated tradition. The memory of Jesus is suppressed by the early Christians and it is up to applying certain criteria that the memory can be distinguished from the accretions of tradition. In all cases, memory becomes an insignificant factor in Jesus studies. Kirk and Thatcher, "Jesus Tradition," 27–28.

198. Kirk and Thatcher, "Jesus Tradition," 30.

To remember anything, the recollection needs to be located, per Eve, "in a stable temporal and conceptual framework, which, far from being our own individual creation, is supplied by the social groups to which we belong, as in the very language in which we frame our thoughts and perceptions."[199] In other words, memory is a social act. The Jesus tradition was not handed down from one individual to another or to others outside of a social context.[200] Therefore, social or collective memory depends on the memory of the group. From a broader perspective, oral tradition is only one aspect of social memory. Social memory comprises other aspects, such as "communicative rituals, monuments, ceremonies, habitual practices, and written texts."[201] Since the Jesus tradition is not purely oral but a mixture of "intertwined" oral and written material (while form criticism assumes a purely oral phase of tradition until it is written down), social memory, which contains the aspect of both written and oral material, is actually the better description overall for pre-gospel tradition.[202]

In ancient times the use of memory was significant. Eve outlines the importance of memory in the ancient context. Memorization played a great role in ancient education as part of enculturating its recipients, assisted by mnemonic aids and training. Ancient texts were read aloud often as a part of the process of internalizing them. Verbatim rote memorization was the basis of all education even at an early level. Memory was also employed in writing and in the composition of texts. Eve states, "The connection between reading, writing, composing, and memory, the memorization of texts and reliance on memory in composition . . . were constant features of the educated culture from ancient Mesopotamia until at least the end of the European Middle Ages as attested in Roman writers."[203] Thus, it is likely that memory also played an important role in the eventual composition of first-century

---

199. Eve, *Behind the Gospels*, 93, refers to the pioneer of the study of social memory, Maurice Halbwachs, who promoted the notion that memory is necessarily social. See Halbwachs, *On Collective Memory*.

200. Eve notes that the passing on of social memory may have been done in informal settings and formal settings such as worship, teaching, commemorative ceremonies such as the Lord's Supper (1 Cor 11:23–26), and other gatherings that provided a context for rehearsal of traditions in the form of "hymns, prophecy, preaching and teaching, as well as, presumably, in the reading of Scripture or, on occasion, Paul's letters (1 Corinthians 12:28; 14:6, 19, 26; 2 Corinthians 10:10; Ephesians 4:11; 5:19; Colossians 3:16)." Eve, *Behind the Gospels*, 92–93.

201. Eve, *Behind the Gospels*, 86.

202. Eve, *Behind the Gospels*, 87.

203. Eve, *Writing the Gospels*, 86.

texts such as the Gospels. The concept of memory deserves far more attention than what is given by form criticism.

Eve also outlines the way memory works in general.[204] To communicate memory, one must use a language learned from a specific social culture. To have people understand the memory, narrative patterns need to be employed. Some kind of "framework" (i.e., the ways in which society works) needs to be in place. This framework is used to encode memories as well as to retrieve and interpret them. Memory being socially embedded works well but is not perfect. Human brains tend to forget what is deemed unnecessary to remember. A specific memory is also summarized to get the gist or main idea of the matter at hand. But memory is not a mental activity of retrieving something from the brains as if retrieving a file from a hard drive. Memory is "a process of reconstruction based on memory traces."[205] The reconstruction in the brain pulls together the memory traces in a certain way to meet current needs. Gaps will be filled with the perceived notion of what should be remembered. A *schemata* assists in the reconstruction by providing a model to be able to make sense of things. One type of schemata called the "script" is "the sequence of actions that typically goes to make up an event."[206] Eve's example of a script describes the events that take place when a person visits a dental office, including reporting to the receptionist, being in the waiting area, being summoned by the dentist, and other actions. Knowing a script such as this one for different events aids in memory reconstruction. Another type of schemata is called the frame, which is "a piece of structural knowledge about some aspect of the world, for example that a car generally has wheels, seats, a chassis, a body and an engine."[207] This kind of knowledge can be added to help encode and reconstruct memory. Memory reconstruction may be guided or misled by schemata, especially if the schemata are erroneous, or these can help guide comprehension, fill gaps, and make sense of anything oral or written.[208] Overall, in terms of reliability, memory is variable in that it is neither infallible nor terribly inefficient.[209] In addition, repeated acts of

---

204. Eve, *Writing the Gospels*, 87–91.
205. Eve, *Writing the Gospels*, 87.
206. Eve, *Writing the Gospels*, 88.
207. Eve, *Writing the Gospels*, 88.
208. Eve, *Writing the Gospels*, 90.
209. Eve, *Writing the Gospels*, 89.

remembering also influence the way something is recalled. Either they fix the incidence more in memory or they may add distortions.[210]

The reconstruction of collective memory serves the present needs of the society or group that possesses it. Halbwachs believes that the function of collective memory was "to maintain the identity, values and cohesion of the group."[211] As a result, groups reshape memories to meet present needs and forget things that will not serve the groups' purpose. There are those who believe in the "constructivist," "presentist," or "invention of traditions" notion that sees groups totally invent or reinterpret the past to suit their current needs. Barry Schwartz correctly argues against this constructivist notion and asserts that "social memory is preserved by witnesses, and the content of the tradition they convey is more than a mere reflection of their needs and troubles. Without the stabilizing force of tradition, Jesus' image would become blurred as new generations replace one another and would eventually cease to be recognizable."[212] It would have been easy for early Christians to make statements that address current needs in the Gospels such as the issue about circumcision, speaking in tongues, and the role of women, but these are not taken up. Therefore, it is not all about meeting present issues. Schwartz argues that while the tradition does undergo changes, most of the knowledge remains, which is why Jesus is recognizable across generations. A more credible model includes various "continuity" approaches that do appreciate how the present needs reshape or give interpretation of the past but hold to the notion of the past as still influencing the present. This model provides templates and frames for understanding the present. While memories can and are reshaped, there are limits to how reshaping can be done without forgetting or misremembering everything from the past. In addition, interpretation of the past can be contested. Most likely not everyone in the early Christian communities remembered Jesus in the exact same way. Therefore, there is an element of negotiation that must have taken place within the collective memory.

Also important for the collective memory of the followers of Jesus are the collective memory of some versions of Israelite traditions and cultural background that are significant for their specific circumstances.[213]

---

210. Eve, *Writing the Gospels*, 90–91.
211. Eve, *Writing the Gospels*, 93.
212. Schwartz, "Christian Origins," 55.
213. Eve, *Behind the Gospels*, 98.

In terms of communicating social memory, stories are often the most effective and memorable to enable societies to provide order and explanation to the events that need to be remembered. Oral tradition preserves certain kinds of memory, but these need to be encapsulated in memorable form. Other studies from the psychology of memory also illuminate how oral tradition can be relatively stable over time. For example, David Rubin's work generalizes the oral-formulaic theory of Parry and Lord and agrees with them that oral tradition is not generally made stable by rote memorization but uses "multiple constraints or cues."[214] A number of cues or serial cues are implemented for one to remember what comes next in the material that needed to be remembered. Examples of these cues for oral tradition as cited by Eve include "an overall plot and intermediate structures such as the standard scripts for various kinds of scene." They have features such as vivid concrete imagery, "rhyme, alliteration, assonance, rhythm and melody" in addition to other factors such as "meaning, gist, imagery and structure."[215] These constraints not only make the tradition stable but also allow for changes within the constraints if things change. In the Jesus tradition, these constraints are there to support the stability of the tradition in the process of transmission. Memory in oral tradition is also affected by oral performance. John Miles Foley derives his theory of memory's link to oral performance by what oral practitioners say about the role of memory in their performance. Foley states, "Memory in oral tradition is emphatically not a static retrieval mechanism for data ... [but a] kinetic, emergent creative activity" linked to performance where it derives its meaning. Foley notes that it involves "an oral/aural communication requiring an auditor or audience."[216] These factors make memory in oral tradition different from our normal conception of memory. Eve further highlights Foley's findings and concepts, which reveal how the social memory of a tradition that is performed with its "certain terms and themes and structures take on a special meaning that is far more than is implied by the literal surface meaning of the words actually employed."[217] Eve writes that these insights are potentially applicable to the Jesus tradition on at least three levels: "the Gospels (and other

---

214. Rubin, *Memory*, 39–193.
215. Eve, *Behind the Gospels*, 100.
216. Eve, *Behind the Gospels*, 102, cites Foley, "Memory," 83–96 (84).
217. Eve, *Behind the Gospels*, 107.

early Christian documents) as oral-derived texts, the oral tradition behind the Gospels, and the historical Jesus as an oral performer."[218]

For the collective memory of a figure such as Jesus, a large part of the collective memory has to do with the person's reputation. Rafael Rodriguez promotes the notion that the social memory of the past contains "a stable core around which peripheral elements are added or subtracted to meet current interests."[219] Jesus's persistent historical reputation forms part of this stable core. Rodriguez defines reputation as a "socially constructed and shared persona" employed in social interaction.[220] This reputation, as Rodriguez puts it, is not a pure invention but needs "to resonate with existing shared values, even while it makes selective use of the past."[221] It depends not totally on the words and actions of the person but also on factors in the social context and the work of "reputational entrepreneurs" who promote the subject person's reputation based on the interest of a society or group. Instead of understanding the Gospels as "records of facts drawn from some pool of collective memory," it is better to see them as products of the evangelists who are reputational entrepreneurs as they have the interest to promote a particular image of Jesus and have the position to shape the narratives appropriate to their particular context.[222] It does not mean the reputation is a purely invented construct as it has to resonate with the communities' shared values as it uses aspects of the past to do so.

There are also other works and authors that provide much insight into the notion of memory and its implications. For example, James Dunn, in *Jesus Remembered*, asserts that the only way one can know Jesus as he actually was is through the impact he made on his first followers as expressed in the synoptic tradition. In effect, he states that there is no way to get an objective depiction of Jesus and one is left to rely on how he was remembered by his followers and eyewitnesses and the impact he made on them.[223] Dunn's view on oral tradition necessitates the need of Jesus's followers for a story that can explain to them and others their distinct group identity, and this story is done through oral traditions regarding the memory of Jesus.

---

218. Eve, *Behind the Gospels*, 107.
219. Eve, *Behind the Gospels*, 125.
220. Eve, *Behind the Gospels*, 125.
221. Eve, *Behind the Gospels*, 125. See Rodriguez, *Structuring*.
222. Eve, *Writing the Gospels*, 120.
223. Dunn, *Jesus Remembered*, 125–32, 335–36.

THE "INAUTHENTICITY" OF LUKE 18:9-14

The work of Richard Horsley and Jonathan Draper contributes much in the aspect of oral tradition.[224] Among the significant insights as cited and summarized by Eve are (1) the need to move from a print-culture literary mind-set when looking at ancient texts like the Gospels; (2) the necessity of working with social memory theory and the construction of a model of oral tradition; (3) the need to account for "social, economic, and cultural conditions of the early Christians to aid in the reconstruction of the Jesus tradition;" and, (4) "the importance of Israelite cultural traditions as the metonymic referent of much of the Jesus tradition, and the identification of certain cultural scripts as key to their interpretation."[225]

In terms of what can be done to proceed further with or without the criteria of authenticity and its form critical assumptions, Rodriguez believes, "Jesus historiography ought to approach the Gospels as memorial artifacts, coherent instances of the performance of the Jesus tradition that present images of the historical Jesus in terms that either were plausible or could be rendered plausible in first-century C.E. contexts."[226] He argues that "multiple (and sometimes contradictory) interpretations of Jesus found in the Gospels allow the historian to chart trajectories of memory refraction that have been propelled forward by the initial perceptions of Jesus by his contemporaries."[227] Dunn offers to find "the remembered Jesus" by looking for the impact Jesus made on his followers. His methodological proposals assume that whatever is characteristic of the synoptic tradition comes from the impact Jesus made on his first followers without dealing with any notion of authenticity or lack of authenticity in specific passages.[228] Le Donne proposes to identify "the development of various mnemonic traditions by means of placing them in a trajectory and triangulating backwards to approximate earlier forms of refracted memories of Jesus."[229]

Finally, as a closing summary, here are a few statements that cite the impact of studies on oral tradition and memory to form critical assumptions. Dunn states that from the perspective of oral tradition, one cannot simply "peel through the layers of faith to an "original": "We can never succeed in stripping away that faith from the tradition, as though to leave

---

224. See Horsley and Draper, *Whoever Hears You*; Horsley, *Jesus in Context*.
225. Eve, *Behind the Gospels*, 122.
226. Rodriguez, "Embarrassing," 150.
227. Rodriguez, *Structuring*, 13.
228. Dunn, *Jesus Remembered*, 327–36.
229. Per Rodriguez, "Embarrassing," 150n78. See Le Donne, *Historiographical Jesus*.

a nonfaith core. When we strip away faith, we strip away everything and leave nothing."[230] Chris Keith writes that various scholars and their findings in memory studies render the classification of "authentic" and "inauthentic" (and its further representation of "past" and "present," "with interpretation" or "without interpretation") as inaccurate when memory is considered. The past is always packaged in an interpretive framework that came from the present. Therefore, scholars cannot simply take out the interpretation and arrive at tradition. Instead of eliminating the interpretations, perhaps a better approach is to account for them.[231]

Conclusion

This section of the chapter on the studies of oral tradition, eyewitnesses, and memory is a progressive and sustained argument that the form-critical assumptions that underlie the criteria approach are no longer plausible. Adding these findings to the critique of the methodology of the criteria of authenticity, it is hard not to question Meier's adherence to form-critical assumptions and the findings from his application of the criteria of authenticity reasonably.

The findings of this chapter are the following. First, the criteria of authenticity are the "wrong tools" if they are to be used in an unqualified, traditional sense as their methodological flaws and underlying form critical assumptions thwart the criteria from achieving their intended purpose. Therefore, the criteria need to be qualified and reformulated and critically applied to be useful. Second, studies in oral tradition, transmission, eyewitnesses, and social memory reveal that the model of what a tradition is as espoused by form criticism is inaccurate. For example, because of these studies, it is questionable that the tradition has an "original form" that can be excavated from layers of interpretive accretions. The notion of tradition being "authentic" and "inauthentic" is most likely a false dichotomy. Therefore, using the criteria in a negative sense to find what is "inauthentic" is questionable. In effect, that makes Meier's conclusions about the "inauthenticity" of the L parables, including the parable of the Pharisee and tax collector, also questionable.

Overall, this chapter contributes to the reasoning that changes need to be made to the traditional criteria to make them more useful. The flaws

230. Keith, "Indebtedness," 38, quotes Dunn, *New Perspective*, 30.
231. Keith, "Indebtedness," 39–40.

of the criteria, the invalid form-critical presuppositions behind them, and the contribution of recent studies in relevant areas such as oral tradition, transmission, eyewitnesses, and social memory show that reform in methods is needed. Instead of using the criteria to separate what is authentic from what is not, it is possibly more appropriate to use the criteria critically to determine possible characteristics of the Jesus tradition and ultimately his impact on early Christianity. This chapter, in effect, further lends support for the continuum approach and its emphasis on locating Jesus within early Judaism and Christianity.

Conclusion

DID LUKE THE EVANGELIST co-opt or recast this theme of justification from Paul? Or is there a better likelihood that Luke derived the theme from sources within the Jesus tradition?

Through the criterion of coherence, the results of this study help make the case that the theme of justification as determined in Luke 18:9–14 may be plausibly regarded as a theme that originated from the Jesus tradition. In other words, this theme as expressed in this parable is not so incongruent or incompatible with the Jesus tradition that one needs to explain its presence in the Gospels as a product of Paul's theology. This study finds that justification's related themes and motifs in the parable of the Pharisee and tax collector cohere with themes and motifs found in various synoptic sources (i.e., L, Mark, Q) as well as in different forms (e.g., parables, pronouncement stories, passion narrative, miracle stories, minatory sayings).

Theissen and Winter state, "Plausibility is a matter of probability that illuminates in various degrees; it is not religious certainty. That which is plausible is always only relatively plausible."[1] This study does not conclusively determine whether the evangelist derived his theme of justification from Paul or from the Jesus tradition, but if the findings of this book are accepted, it offers more supporting evidence of the likelihood that Luke derived the notion of justification in Luke 18:9–14 from sources that already exist in the Jesus tradition.

As further support for this finding, Luke 18:9–14 is also determined to be a plausible fit in the first-century Jewish Palestinian context. Furthermore,

---

1. Theissen and Winter, *Quest*, 226.

this book also summarizes some current findings in other areas of historical Jesus research such as oral tradition, transmission and memory, and criteria approach critique. These explain the reasons why the criteria approach needs to be qualified and reformulated and not used in a negative sense. In other words, the criteria need to be used in a more critical manner than the way they are traditionally used by scholars such as John Meier in his latest book. In effect, these findings explain some of the rationale behind the methodology of this monograph in its use of the continuum approach.

There are many possible prospective areas for future research. If it is in the area of justification in the Gospels and the use of the continuum approach, the criterion of coherence can be extended to look for the theme of justification in more Gospel sources such as John and Matthew. The findings in that study can supplement and add further support to the thesis of this book. Another way to solidify the findings here is by using all the sub-criteria that is called for in the criterion of plausibility. These sub-criteria are the criterion of resistance to tendencies of the tradition which measures the plausibility of historical impact and also the sub-criterion of contextual distinctiveness which identifies elements distinctive to Jesus in his Jewish and early Christian context. Another direction is in using the memory approach. Using the available models from scholars such as Rafael Rodriguez, Anthony Le Donne, and Chris Keith, perhaps there is a way to trace "justification" in memory. Perhaps, if possible, there is a way to find out how early the notion of "justification" goes back in the social memory of Jesus's followers. Therefore, future research options are available that can vary in terms of topic or approach.

Bibliography

Allison, Dale C., Jr. *Constructing Jesus: Memory, Imagination, and History.* Grand Rapids: Baker Academic, 2013.
———. "How to Marginalize the Traditional Criteria of Authenticity." In *Handbook for the Study of the Historical Jesus,* edited by Tom Holmen and Stanley E. Porter, 1:3–30. Leiden: Brill, 2010.
Apocrypha and Pseudepigrapha of the Old Testament. Edited by R. H. Charles. Oxford: Clarendon, 1913.
The Apostolic Fathers: Greek Texts and English Translations. Edited by Michael W. Holmes. 3rd ed. Grand Rapids: Baker Academic, 2007.
Arndt, William F. *The Gospel According to St. Luke.* Concordia Classic Commentary Series. St. Louis: Concordia, 1956.
The Babylonian Talmud. Edited by I. Epstein. 35 vols. London: Soncino, 1935–1952.
Bailey, Kenneth Ewing. "Informal Controlled Oral Tradition and the Synoptic Gospels." *Asia Journal of Theology* 5 (1991) 34–54.
———. *Jesus through Middle Eastern Eyes: Cultural Studies in the Gospels.* Downers Grove, IL: InterVarsity, 2008.
———. "Middle Eastern Oral Tradition and the Synoptic Gospels." *ExpTim* 106 (1995) 363–67.
———. *Poet and Peasant: A Literary Cultural Approach to the Parables in Luke.* Grand Rapids: Eerdmans, 1976.
———. *Through Peasant Eyes: More Lucan Parables, Their Culture and Style.* Grand Rapids: Eerdmans, 1980.
Barclay, John M. G. *Paul and the Gift.* Grand Rapids: Eerdmans, 2015.
Barrett, Kyle Scott. "Justification in Lukan Theology." PhD diss., Southern Baptist Theological Seminary, 2012. Ann Arbor, MI: University Microfilms International, 2012.
Bauckham, Richard. *Jesus and the Eyewitnesses: The Gospels as Eyewitness Testimony.* Grand Rapids: Eerdmans, 2006.
Bauer, David R., and Robert A. Traina. *Inductive Bible Study: A Comprehensive Guide to the Practice of Hermeneutics.* Grand Rapids: Baker Academic, 2011.
Bauer, Walter, et al. *Greek-English Lexicon of the New Testament and Other Early Christian Literature.* 3rd rev. ed. Chicago: University of Chicago Press, 2000.

BIBLIOGRAPHY

Beale, Gregory K. *A New Testament Biblical Theology: The Unfolding of the Old Testament in the New.* Grand Rapids: Baker Academic, 2011.
Becker, Jürgen. "The Search for Jesus' Special Profile." In *Handbook for the Study of the Historical Jesus,* edited by Tom Holmen and Stanley E. Porter, 1:57–89. Leiden: Brill, 2011.
Best, Ernest. *Disciples and Discipleship: Studies in the Gospel of Mark.* Edinburgh: T. & T. Clark, 1986.
———. *Following Jesus: Discipleship in the Gospel of Mark.* JSNTSup 4. Sheffield: JSOT, 1981.
Biblia Hebraica Stuttgartensia. Edited by K. Ellinger et al. 5th ed. Stuttgart: Deutsche Bibelgesellschaft, 1997.
Blomberg, Craig L. *Interpreting the Parables.* 2nd ed. Downers Grove, IL: InterVarsity, 2012.
———. *Jesus and the Gospels: An Introduction and Survey.* Nashville: Broadman & Holman, 1997.
———. "The Tradition History of the Parables Peculiar to Luke's Central Section." PhD diss., University of Aberdeen, 1982.
Bock, Darrell L. *Luke 9:51—24:53.* Baker Exegetical Commentary on the New Testament 3AB vol. 2. Grand Rapids: Baker Academic, 1996.
———. *Luke 1:1—9:50.* Baker Exegetical Commentary on the New Testament 3A vol. 1. Grand Rapids: Baker, 1994.
Bovon, François. *Luke the Theologian: Fifty-Five Years of Research (1950-2005).* 2nd rev. ed. Waco, TX: Baylor University Press, 2006.
———. *Luke 2: A Commentary on the Gospel of Luke 9:51—19:27.* Hermeneia. Minneapolis: Fortress, 2013.
Brown, Colin, ed. *New International Dictionary of New Testament Theology.* 4 vols. Grand Rapids: Zondervan, 1975-1978.
Bruce, F. F. "Justification by Faith in the Non-Pauline Writings of the New Testament." *EvQ* 24 (1952) 66–77.
Bultmann, Rudolf. *The History of the Synoptic Tradition.* Translated by J. Marsh. 2nd ed. Oxford: Blackwell, 1968.
Burridge, Richard A. *What Are the Gospels? A Comparison with Graeco-Roman Biography.* SNTSMS 70. Cambridge: Cambridge University Press, 1992.
Byrskog, Samuel. "Introduction." In *Jesus in Memory: Traditions in Oral and Scribal Perspectives,* edited by Werner H. Kelber and Samuel Byrskog, 1–20. Waco, TX: Baylor University Press, 2009.
———. *Story as History—History as Story: The Gospel Tradition in the Context of Ancient Oral History.* Tübingen: Mohr Siebeck, 2000.
Carroll, John T. *Luke: A Commentary.* The New Testament Library. Louisville: Westminster John Knox, 2012.
———. "Luke's Portrayal of the Pharisees." *CBQ* 50 (1988) 604–21.
Carson, D. A., ed. *Right with God: Justification in the Bible and the World.* Grand Rapids: Baker, 1992.
Carson, D. A., et al., eds. *Justification and Variegated Nomism.* 2 vols. Grand Rapids: Baker Academic, 2001, 2004.
Chilton, Bruce. "Mamzerut and Jesus." In *Jesus from Judaism to Christianity: Continuum Approaches to the Historical Jesus,* edited by Tom Holmen, 17–33. London: T. & T. Clark, 2007.

Chilton, Bruce, and Craig A. Evans. *Jesus in Context: Temple, Purity and Restoration*. Leiden: Brill, 1997.

Cicero. *De officiis*. Translated by Walter Miller. LCL. Cambridge: Harvard University Press, 1913.

Cook, Donald E. "A Gospel Portrait of the Pharisees." *RevExp* 84 (1987) 221–33.

Crossan, John Dominic. *The Historical Jesus*. San Francisco: Harper, 1991.

———. *In Parable: The Challenge of the Historical Jesus*. Sonoma, CA: Polebridge, 1992.

———. "Parable and Example in the Teaching of Jesus." *NTS* 18 (1972) 287–307.

Culy, Martin M., et al. *Luke: A Handbook on the Greek Text*. Waco, TX: Baylor University Press, 2010.

Darr, John A. *On Character Building: The Reader and the Rhetoric of Characterization in Luke-Acts*. Louisville: Westminster John Knox, 1992.

Davids, Peter H. "The Gospels and Jewish Tradition: Twenty Years after Gerhardsson." In *Gospel Perspectives. Studies in History and Tradition in the Four Gospels*, edited by R.T. France and D. Wenham, 1:75–100. Sheffield: JSOT, 1980.

Dibelius, Martin. *From Tradition to Gospel*. Translated by Bertram Lee Woolf. London: Nicholson and Watson, 1934.

Dio Chrysostom. *Dio Chrysostom*. Translated by J. W. Cohoon and H. Lamar Crosby. 5 vols. London: Heinemann, 1932–1951.

Dodd, C. H. *The Parables of the Kingdom*. New York: Scribner's Sons, 1961.

Donahue, John R. "Tax Collectors and Sinners: An Attempt at Identification." *CBQ* 33 (1971) 39–61.

Downing, F. Gerald. "The Ambiguity of 'The Pharisee and the Toll-Collector' (Luke 18:9-14) in the Greco-Roman World of Late Antiquity." *CBQ* 54 (1992) 80–99.

Drury, John. *The Parables in the Gospels: History and Allegory*. London: Society for Promoting Christian Knowledge, 1985.

Dunn, James D. G. *Beginning from Jerusalem*. Vol. 2 of *Christianity in the Making*. Grand Rapids: Eerdmans, 2009.

———. *Jesus Remembered*. Vol. 1 of *Christianity in the Making*. Grand Rapids: Eerdmans, 2003.

———. *A New Perspective on Jesus: What the Quest for the Historical Jesus Missed*. London: Society for Promoting Christian Knowledge, 2005.

———. "Remembering Jesus: How the Quest of the Historical Jesus Lost its Way." In *Handbook for the Study of the Historical Jesus*, edited by Tom Holmen and Stanley E. Porter, 1:183–205. Leiden: Brill, 2011.

Easton, B. S. *The Gospel before the Gospels*. London: Allen and Unwin, 1928.

Eddy, Paul Rhodes, and Gregory A. Boyd. *The Jesus Legend: A Case for the Historical Reliability of the Synoptic Jesus Tradition*. Grand Rapids: Baker Academic, 2007.

Edwards, James R. *The Gospel According to Luke*. PNTC. Grand Rapids: Eerdmans, 2015.

———. *The Gospel According to Mark*. PNTC. Grand Rapids: Eerdmans, 2002.

Ellis, E. Earle. *The Gospel of Luke*. Rev. ed. NCB. Grand Rapids: Eerdmans, 1974.

Esler, Philip Francis. *Community and Gospel in Luke-Acts: The Social and Political Motivations of Lucan Theology*. SNTSMS 57. Cambridge: Cambridge University Press, 1987.

Evans, Craig A. *Mark 8:27—16:20*. WBC 34B. Nashville: Nelson, 2001.

Evans, Craig A., and Stanley E. Porter, eds. *Dictionary of New Testament Background*. Downers Grove, IL: InterVarsity, 2000.

Eve, Eric. *Behind the Gospels*. Minneapolis: Fortress, 2014.

———. *Writing the Gospels: Composition and Memory*. London: Society for Promoting Christian Knowledge, 2016.

Farris, Michael. "A Tale of Two Taxations (Luke 18:10–14b)." In *Jesus and His Parables: Interpreting the Parables of Jesus Today*, edited by V. George Shillington, 23–34. Edinburgh: T. & T. Clark, 1997.

Feldman, Louis H. *Jew and Gentile in the Ancient World*. Princeton: Princeton University, 1993.

Fitzmyer, Joseph A. *The Gospel of Luke X–XXIV*. Anchor Bible 28A. Garden City, NY: Doubleday, 1985.

———. *The Gospel of Luke I–IX*. Anchor Bible 28. Garden City, NY: Doubleday, 1981.

———. "Pauline Justification as Presented by Luke in Acts 13." In *Transcending Boundaries: Contemporary Readings of the New Testament: Essays in Honour of Francis J. Moloney*, edited by Rekha M. Chennattu and Mary L. Coloe, 249–63. Rome: LAS, 2005.

Foley, John Miles. "Memory in Oral Tradition." In *Performing the Gospel: Orality, Memory and Mark*, edited by Richard A. Horsley et al., 83–96. Minneapolis: Fortress, 2006.

Forbes, Greg W. *The God of Old: The Role of Lukan Parables in the Purpose of Luke's Gospel*. JSNTSup 198. Sheffield: Sheffield Academic, 2000.

France, R. T. *The Gospel of Mark*. NIGTC. Grand Rapids: Eerdmans, 2002.

Freedman, David Noel, ed. *Anchor Bible Dictionary*. 6 vols. New York: Doubleday, 1992.

Freyne, Sean. *Jesus a Jewish Galilean: A New Reading of the Jesus-Story*. London: T. & T. Clark, 2004.

Friedrichsen, Timothy A. "The Temple, a Pharisee, a Tax Collector, and the Kingdom of God: Rereading a Jesus Parable (Luke 18:10–14A)." *JBL* 124 (2005) 89–119.

Funk, Robert W., et al. *The Parables of Jesus: Red Letter Edition*. Sonoma, CA: Polebridge, 1988.

Funk, Robert W., et al., eds. *The Five Gospels*. New York: Macmillan, 1993.

Gaffin, Richard B. "Justification in Luke-Acts." In *Right with God: Justification in the Bible and the World*, edited by D. A. Carson, 106–25. Grand Rapids: Baker, 1992.

Gathercole, Simon J. "The Justification of Wisdom (Matt 11.19b/Luke 7.35)." *NTS* 49 (2003) 476–88.

———. *Where Is Boasting: Early Jewish Soteriology and Paul's Response in Romans 1–5*. Grand Rapids: Eerdmans, 2002.

Gerhardsson, Birger. *Memory and Manuscript: Oral Transmission and Written Transmission in Rabbinic Judaism and Early Christianity*. Lund: Gleerup, 1961.

———. *The Reliability of the Gospel Tradition*. Peabody, MA: Hendrickson, 2001.

Goodacre, Mark. "Criticizing the Criterion of Multiple Attestation: The Historical Jesus and the Question of Sources." In *Jesus, Criteria, and the Demise of Authenticity*, edited by Chris Keith and Anthony Le Donne, 152–69. New York: T. & T. Clark, 2012.

Goulder, Michael D. "Characteristics of the Parables in the Several Gospels." *JTS* 19 (1968) 51–69.

———. "Did Luke Know any of the Pauline Letters?" *PRSt* 13 (1986) 97–112.

———. *Luke: A New Paradigm*. JSNTSup 20. 2 vols. Sheffield: JSOT, 1989.

———. *Midrash and Lection in Matthew*. Eugene, OR: Wipf & Stock, 2004.

Green, Joel B. *The Gospel of Luke*. NICNT. Grand Rapids: Eerdmans, 1997.

———. "The Message of Salvation in Luke-Acts." *ExAud* 5 (1989) 21–34.

———. *Salvation*. St. Louis: Chalice, 2003.

———. *The Theology of the Gospel of Luke*. Cambridge: Cambridge University Press, 1995.

Green, Joel B., et al., eds. *Dictionary of Jesus and the Gospels*. Downers Grove, IL: InterVarsity, 1992.

———. *Dictionary of Jesus and the Gospels*. 2nd ed. Downers Grove, IL: InterVarsity, 2013.

Gundry, Robert H. *Mark: A Commentary on His Apology for the Cross*. Grand Rapids: Eerdmans, 1993.

Güttgemanns, Erhardt. *Candid Questions Concerning Gospel Form Criticism: A Methodological Sketch of the Fundamental Problems of Form and Redaction Criticism*. Edited by Dikran Y. Hadidian. Translated by William G. Doty. Pittsburgh Theological Monograph Series 26. Pittsburgh: Pickwick, 1979.

Hagner, Donald A. *Matthew*. 2 vols. WBC. Dallas: Word, 1993, 1995.

Halbwachs, Maurice. *On Collective Memory*. Edited by D. N. Levine. Translated by Lewis A. Coser. The Heritage of Sociology. Chicago: University of Chicago Press, 1992.

Hamel, Gildas. *Poverty and Charity in Roman Palestine, First Three Centuries CE*. Berkeley: University of California Press, 1990.

Hamm, Dennis. "The Tamid Service in Luke-Acts: The Cultic Background behind Luke's Theology of Worship (Luke 1:5–25; 18:9–14; 24:50–53; Acts 3:1; 10:3, 30)." *CBQ* 25 (2003) 215–31.

Harrison, Stephanie. "The Case of the Pharisee and the Tax Collector: Justification and Social Location in Luke's Gospel." *CurTM* 32 (2005) 99–111.

Hays, J. Daniel. "'Sell Everything You Have and Give to the Poor': The Old Testament Prophetic Theme of Justice as the Connecting Motif of Luke 18:1—19:10." *JETS* 55 (2012) 43–63.

Hendrick, Charles. *Parables as Poetic Fictions: The Creative Voice of Jesus*. Peabody, MA: Hendrickson, 1994.

Hendrickx, Herman. *The Parables of Jesus*. San Francisco: Harper & Row, 1986.

Hengel, Martin. *Judaism and Hellenism: Studies in Their Encounter in Palestine in the Early Hellenistic Period*. Translated by John Bowden. 2 vols. Philadelphia: Fortress, 1974.

Herodotus. Translated by A. D. Godley. 4 vols. LCL. Cambridge: Harvard University Press, 1926–1938.

Herzog, William R. *Parables as Subversive Speech: Jesus as Pedagogue of the Oppressed*. Louisville: Westminster John Knox, 1994.

Hesiod. *Hesiod, the Homeric Hymns and Homerica*. Translated by Hugh G. Evelyn-White. LCL. Cambridge: Harvard University Press, 1914.

Hill, David. *Greek Words and Hebrew Meanings: Studies in the Semantics of Soteriological Terms*. Cambridge: Cambridge University Press, 1967.

Hoffman, Paul. "πάντες ἐργάται ἀδικίας: Redaktion und Tradition in Lc 13, 22–30." *ZNW* 58 (1967) 188–214.

Holmen, Tom. "An Introduction to the Continuum Approach." In *Jesus from Judaism to Christianity: Continuum Approaches to the Historical Jesus*, edited by Tom Holmen, 1–16. London: T. & T. Clark, 2007.

———, ed. *Jesus from Judaism to Christianity: Continuum Approaches to the Historical Jesus*. London: T. & T. Clark, 2007.

Holmgren, Frederick C. "The Pharisee and the Tax-Collector: Luke 18:9-14 and Deuteronomy 26:1–15." *Int* 48 (1994) 252–61.

Hooker, Morna D. "Christology and Methodology." *NTS* 17 (1970) 480–87.

———. *The Gospel According to Saint Mark*. Black's New Testament Commentary. London: Black, 1991.

———. "On Using the Wrong Tool." *Theology* 75 (1972) 570–81.
Horsley, Richard A. *Jesus in Context: Power, People, and Performance.* Minneapolis: Fortress, 2008.
Horsley, Richard A., and Jonathan A. Draper. *Whoever Hears You Hears Me: Prophets, Performance and Tradition in Q.* Harrisburg, PA: Trinity Press International, 1999.
Hultgren, Arland J. *The Parables of Jesus: A Commentary.* Grand Rapids: Eerdmans, 2000.
Hurtado, Larry W. "Oral Fixation and New Testament Studies? 'Orality,' 'Performance' and Reading Texts in Early Christianity." *NTS* 60 (2014) 321–40.
Jeffrey, David Lyle. *Luke.* Grand Rapids: Brazos, 2012.
Jeremias, Joachim. *Jerusalem in the Time of Jesus.* Philadelphia: Fortress, 1969.
———. *The Parables of Jesus.* Translated by S. H. Hooke. 3rd ed. Zürich: Zwingli Verlag, 1954. Reprint. London: SCM, 1958.
Johnson, Luke Timothy. *The Gospel of Luke.* SP 3. Collegeville, MN: Liturgical, 1991.
———. "The Social Dimensions of *Soteria* in Luke-Acts and Paul." *Society of Biblical Literature Seminar Papers* 32 (1993) 520–36.
———. *Sharing Possessions: Mandate and Symbol of Faith.* Overtures to Biblical Theology. Philadelphia: Fortress, 1981.
Johnston, Robert Morris. "Parabolic Interpretations Attributed to Tannaim." PhD diss., Hartford Seminary Foundation, 1977.
Jones, Peter. *Studying the Parables of Jesus.* Macon, GA: Smyth & Helwys, 1999.
Josephus. Translated by H. St. J. Thackeray et al. 10 vols. LCL. Cambridge: Harvard University Press, 1926–1965.
Jülicher, Adolf. *Die Gleichnisreden Jesu.* Zwei Teile in einem Band. Nachdruck der Ausgabe Tübingen, 1910. Darmstadt: Wissenschaftliche Buchgesellschaft, 1963.
Käsemann, Ernst. "The Problem of the Historical Jesus." In *Essays on New Testament Themes,* 15–47. SBT 41. London: SCM, 1964.
Kazen, Thomas. "Son of Man as Kingdom Imagery: Jesus between Corporate Symbol and Individual Redeemer Figure." In *Jesus from Judaism to Christianity: Continuum Approaches to the Historical Jesus,* edited by Tom Holmen, 87–108. London: T. & T. Clark, 2007.
Keener, Craig S. *Acts: An Exegetical Commentary.* 4 vols. Grand Rapids: Baker Academic, 2012–2015.
———. "Chapter 1: Ancient Biography and the Gospels: Introduction." In *Biographies and Jesus: What Does it Mean for the Gospels to Be Biographies?* edited by Craig S. Keener and Edward T. Wright, 1–43. Lexington, KY: Emeth, 2016.
———. *The Historical Jesus of the Gospels.* Grand Rapids: Eerdmans, 2009.
———. "Some Ancient Context for Luke 15:11–32." In *Biblical Parables: Essays in Honor of Robert M. Johnston,* edited by Thomas R. Shepherd and Ranko Stefanovic, 155–67. Berrien Springs, MI: Andrews University Press, 2016.
Keith, Chris. "The Fall of the Quest for an Authentic Jesus: Concluding Remarks." In *Jesus, Criteria, and the Demise of Authenticity,* edited by Chris Keith and Anthony Le Donne, 200–205. New York: T. & T. Clark, 2012.
———. "The Indebtedness of the Criteria Approach to Form Criticism and Recent Attempts to Rehabilitate the Search for an Authentic Jesus." In *Jesus, Criteria, and the Demise of Authenticity,* edited by Christ Keith and Anthony Le Donne, 25–48. New York: T. & T. Clark, 2012.

Kelber, Werner H. *The Oral and the Written Gospel: The Hermeneutics of Speaking and Writing in the Synoptic Tradition, Mark, Paul and Q.* Voices in Performance and Text. Bloomington: Indiana University Press, 1997.

Kingsbury, Jack Dean. *Conflict in Luke: Jesus, Authorities, Disciples.* Minneapolis: Fortress, 1991.

———. *Jesus Christ in Matthew, Mark, and Luke.* Proclamation Commentaries: The New Testament Witnesses for Preaching. Philadelphia: Fortress, 1981.

Kirk, Alan. *Memory and the Jesus Tradition.* New York: Bloomsbury T. & T. Clark, 2018.

———. "Memory Theory and Jesus Research." In *Handbook for the Study of the Historical Jesus,* edited by Tom Holmen and Stanley E. Porter, 1:809–51. Leiden: Brill, 2011.

———. "Orality, Writing and Phantom Sources: Appeals to Ancient Media in Some Recent Challenges to the Two Document Hypothesis." *NTS* 58 (2012) 1–22.

Kirk, Alan, and Tom Thatcher. "Jesus Tradition as Social Memory." In *Memory, Tradition and Text: Uses of the Past in Early Christianity,* edited by Allen Kirk and Tom Thatcher, 25–42. SBL Semeia Studies, 52. Atlanta: Society of Biblical Literature, 2005.

Kittel, G., and G. Friedrich, eds. *TDNT.* 10 vols. Grand Rapids: Eerdmans, 1964.

Koehler, Ludwig and Walter Baumgartner. *HALOT.* Study ed. 2 vols. London: Brill, 2001.

Ladd, George E. *A Theology of the New Testament.* Edited by Donald A. Hagner. Rev. ed. Grand Rapids: Eerdmans, 1993.

Le Donne, Anthony. "The Criterion of Coherence: Its Development, Inevitability, and Historiographical Limitations." In *Jesus, Criteria, and the Demise of Authenticity,* edited by Chris Keith and Anthony Le Donne, 95–114. New York: T. & T. Clark, 2012.

———. *The Historiographical Jesus: Memory, Typology, and the Son of David.* Waco, TX: Baylor University Press, 2009.

Legasse, Simon. *Jesus et L'Enfant. Enfants, Petits et Simples dans la Tradition Synoptique.* EBib. Paris: Gabalda, 1969.

Lehtipuu, Outi. *The Afterlife Imagery in Luke's Story of the Rich Man and Lazarus.* NovTSup 123. Leiden: Brill, 2007.

Levine, Amy-Jill. "Luke's Pharisees." In *Quest of the Historical Pharisees,* edited by Jacob Neusner and Bruce D. Chilton, 113–30. Waco, TX: Baylor University Press, 2007.

———. *Short Stories by Jesus.* New York: Harper Collins, 2014.

Lightfoot, Robert Henry. *The Gospel Message of St. Mark.* Oxford: Clarendon, 1950.

Loader, William. "Sexuality and the Historical Jesus." In *Jesus from Judaism to Christianity: Continuum Approaches to the Historical Jesus,* edited by Tom Holmen, 34–48. London: T. & T. Clark, 2007.

Lord, Albert B. *The Singer of Tales.* Cambridge: Harvard University Press, 1960.

Lucian. *Lucian.* Translated by A. M. Harmon. 8 vols. LCL. Cambridge: Harvard University Press, 1913–1967.

Maddox, Robert. *The Purpose of Luke-Acts.* Gottingen: Vandenhoeck & Ruprecht, 1982.

Manson, T. W. *The Sayings of Jesus.* Study ed. London: SCM, 1957.

Marshall, I. Howard. *The Acts of the Apostles: An Introduction and Commentary.* TNTC. Grand Rapids: Eerdmans, 1980.

———. *The Gospel of Luke: A Commentary on the Greek Text.* NIGTC. Grand Rapids: Eerdmans, 1978.

———. *Luke: Historian and Theologian.* New Testament Profiles. 3rd ed. Downers Grove, IL: InterVarsity, 1998.

———. "Luke's View of Paul." *SwJT* 33 (1990) 41–51.

———. *New Testament Theology: Many Witnesses, One Gospel.* Downers Grove, IL: InterVarsity, 2004.

Martin, Ralph P. "Salvation and Discipleship in Luke's Gospel." *Int* 29 (1976) 366–80.

Martinez, Florentino Garcia, ed. *The Dead Sea Scrolls Translated: The Qumran Texts in English.* 2nd ed. Leiden: Brill; Grand Rapids: Eerdmans, 1996.

Martinez, Florentino Garcia, and Eibert J. C. Tigchelaar, eds. *The Dead Sea Scrolls Study Edition.* 2 vols. Leiden: Brill; Grand Rapids: Eerdmans, 2000.

Mattill, A. J., Jr. "The Jesus-Paul Parallels and the Purpose of Luke-Acts: H. H. Evans Reconsidered." *NovT* 18 (1975) 15–46.

McArthur, Harvey K. "Basic Issues: A Survey of Recent Gospel Research." *Int* 18 (1964) 39–55.

McArthur, Harvey K., and Robert M. Johnston. *They Also Taught in Parables: Rabbinic Parables from the First Centuries of the Christian Era.* Grand Rapids: Zondervan, 1990.

McKnight, Scot, and Grant R. Osborne, eds. *A New Vision for Israel: The Teachings of Jesus in National Context.* Grand Rapids: Eerdmans, 1999.

Meier, John P., *A Marginal Jew: Rethinking the Historical Jesus.* 5 vols. Anchor Bible Reference Library. New York: Doubleday, 1991–2016.

Menoud, Philippe H. "Justification by Faith According to the Book of Acts." In *Jesus Christ and the Faith: A Collection of Studies,* 202–27. Pittsburgh: Pickwick, 1978.

Merz, Annette. "How a Woman Who Fought Back and Demanded Her Rights Became an Importunate Widow: The Transformations of a Parable of Jesus." In *Jesus from Judaism to Christianity: Continuum Approaches to the Historical Jesus,* edited by Tom Holmen, 49–86. London: T. & T. Clark, 2007.

Metzger, Bruce M. *A Textual Commentary on the Greek New Testament: A Companion Volume to the United Bible Societies' Greek New Testament. Fourth Revised Edition.* 2nd ed. Stuttgart: Deutsche Bibelgesellschaft/German Bible Society, 1994.

Midrash Rabbah: Translated into English with Notes, Glossary and Indices. Edited by H. Freedman and Maurice Simon. 10 vols. London: Soncino, 1939.

The Mishnah: Translated from the Hebrew with Introduction and Brief Explanatory Notes. Translated by Herbert Danby. Oxford: Clarendon, 1933.

Moore, George Foot. *Judaism in the First Centuries of the Christian Era.* 3 vols. Cambridge: Harvard University Press, 1927.

Morris, Leon. *Luke: An Introduction and Commentary,* rev. ed. TNTC. Grand Rapids: Eerdmans, 1988.

Moxnes, Halvor. *The Economy of the Kingdom: Social Conflict and Economic Relations in Luke's Gospel.* Overtures to Biblical Theology. Philadelphia: Fortress, 1988.

Myers, Ched. *Binding the Strong Man: A Political Reading of Mark's Story of Jesus.* Maryknoll, NY: Orbis, 1988.

Neale, David A. *None but the Sinners: Religious Categories in the Gospel of Luke.* JSNTSup 58. Sheffield: Sheffield Academic, 1991.

The New Oxford Annotated Bible with the Apocryphal/Deuterocanonical Books. Edited by Bruce M. Metzger and Roland E. Murphy. New Revised Standard Version. New York: Oxford University Press, 1991.

New Testament Apocrypha. Edited by Wilhelm Schneemelcher. Translated by R. McL. Wilson. Rev. ed. 2 vols. Cambridge: James Clarke/Louisville: Westminster John Knox, 1991–1992.

Noel, Timothy. "The Parable of the Wedding Guest: A Narrative-Critical Interpretation." *PRSt* 16 (1989) 17–28.
Nolland, John. *Luke 1–9:20*. Word Biblical Commentary 35A. Dallas: Word, 1989.
———. *Luke 9:21—18:34*. Word Biblical Commentary 35B. Dallas: Word, 1993.
Novum Testamentum Graece. Edited by E. Nestle and K. Aland. 27th ed. Stuttgart: Deutsche Bibelstiftung, 1993.
The Old Testament Pseudepigrapha. Edited by James H. Charlesworth. 2 vols. ABRL. New York: Doubleday, 1983–1985.
Paffenroth, Kim. *The Story of Jesus According to L*. JSNTSup 147. Sheffield: Sheffield Academic, 1998.
Parsons, Mikeal C. "Landmarks along the Way: The Function of the 'L' Parables in the Lukan Travel Narrative." *SwJT* 40 (1997) 33–47.
———. "Short in Stature: Luke's Physical Description of Zacchaeus." *NTS* 47 (2001) 50–57.
Perrin, Norman. *Rediscovering the Teaching of Jesus*. London: SCM, 1967.
Philo. Translated by F. H. Colson and G. H. Whitaker. 10 vols. LCL. Cambridge: Harvard University Press, 1929–1962.
Redman, Judith C. S. "How Accurate Are Eyewitnesses? Bauckham and Eyewitnesses in the Light of Psychological Research." *JBL* 129 (2010) 177–97.
Resseguie, James L. *Narrative Criticism of the New Testament: An Introduction*. Grand Rapids: Baker, 2005.
———. *Spiritual Landscape: Images of the Spiritual Life in the Gospel of Luke*. Peabody, MA: Hendrickson, 2004.
Reumann, J. H. P., et al. *Righteousness in the New Testament: Justification in the United States Lutheran-Roman Catholic Dialogue*. Philadelphia: Fortress, 1982.
Riesenfeld, Harald. *The Gospel Tradition and Its Beginnings: A Study in the Limits of 'Formgeschichte.'* London: Mowbrays, 1957.
Rodriguez, Rafael. "Authenticating Criteria: The Use and Misuse of a Critical Method," *JSHJ* 7 (2009) 152–67.
———. "The Embarrassing Truth about Jesus: The Criterion of Embarrassment and the Failure of Historical Authenticity." In *Jesus, Criteria, and the Demise of Authenticity*, edited by Chris Keith and Anthony Le Donne, 132–51. New York: T. & T. Clark, 2012.
———. *Structuring Early Christian Memory: Jesus in Tradition, Performance and Text*. LNTS 407. London: T. & T. Clark, 2010.
Rohrbaugh, Richard L. *The Biblical Interpreter*. Philadelphia: Fortress, 1995.
Rubin, David C. *Memory in Oral Traditions: The Cognitive Psychology of Epic, Ballads, and Counting-out Rhymes*. Oxford: Oxford University Press, 1995.
Safrai, Shemuel, and Menahem Stern, eds. *The Jewish People in the First Century: Historical Geography, Political History, Social, Cultural and Religious Life and Institutions*. 2 vols. CRINT. Philadelphia: Fortress, 1976.
Sanders, E. P. *Jesus and Judaism*. Minneapolis: Fortress, 1985.
———. "Jesus and the Sinners." *JSNT* 19 (1983) 5–36.
———. *The Tendencies of the Synoptic Tradition*. SNTSMS 9. Cambridge: Cambridge University Press, 1969.
Sandmel, Samuel. *Philo's Place in Judaism: A Study of Conceptions of Abraham in Jewish Literature*. New York: KTAV, 1971.
Scaer, Peter J. "Resurrection as Justification in the Book of Acts." *CTQ* 70 (2006) 219–31.

BIBLIOGRAPHY

Schmidt, Karl Ludwig. *Der Rahmen Der Geshichte Jesu: Literarkritische Untersuchungen Zur ältesten Jesusuberlieferung.* Berlin: Trowizsch & Sohn, 1919.

Schottroff, Luise. "Die Erzählung vom Pharisäer und Zöllner als Beispiel für die theologische Kunst des Uberredens." In *Neues Testament und christliche Existenz,* edited by FS H. Braun et al., 439–61. Tübingen: Mohr-Siebeck, 1973.

———. *The Parables of Jesus.* Minneapolis: Fortress, 2006.

Schreiner, Thomas R. *New Testament Theology: Magnifying God in Christ.* Grand Rapids: Baker Academic, 2008.

———. *Paul, Apostle of God's Glory in Christ: A Pauline Theology.* Downers Grove, IL: InterVarsity, 2001.

Schwartz, Barry. "Christian Origins: Historical Truth and Social Memory." In *Memory, Tradition and Text: Uses of the Past in Early Christianity,* edited by A. Kirk and T. Thatcher, 43–56. SBL Semeia Studies 52. Atlanta: Society of Biblical Literature, 2005.

Scott, Bernard Brandon. *Hear Then the Parable.* Minneapolis: Fortress, 1989.

Seccombe, David P. "Luke and Isaiah." *NTS* 27 (1981) 252–59.

———. *Possessions and the Poor in Luke-Acts.* Studien zum Neuen Testament und seiner Umwelt. Linz: Studien zum Neuen Testament und seiner Umwelt, 1983.

Seifrid, Mark A. *Christ, Our Righteousness: Paul's Theology of Justification.* Vol. 9 of *New Studies in Biblical Theology,* edited by D. A. Carson. Downers Grove, IL: InterVarsity, 2000.

———. *Justification by Faith: The Origin and Development of a Central Pauline Theme.* Leiden: Brill, 1992.

Select Papyri. Translated by A. S. Hunt and C. C. Edgar. 2 vols. LCL. Cambridge: Harvard University Press, 1932–1934.

Sider, John W. *Interpreting the Parables: A Hermeneutical Guide to their Meaning.* Grand Rapids: Zondervan, 1995.

Snodgrass, Klyne R. *Stories with Intent: A Comprehensive Guide to the Parables of Jesus.* Grand Rapids: Eerdmans, 2008.

Stein, Robert H. "The 'Criteria' for Authenticity." In *Studies of History and Tradition in the Four Gospels,* edited by R. T. France and David Wenham, 225–63. Sheffield: JSOT, 1980–1981.

———. *The Gospel of Luke.* The New American Commentary 24. Nashville: Broadman & Holman, 1992.

———. *Mark.* Baker Exegetical Commentary on the New Testament. Grand Rapids: Baker Academic, 2008.

Stegemann, Ekkehard W., and Wolfgang Stegemann. *The Jesus Movement: A Social History of Its First Century.* Translated by O. C. Dean, Jr. Minneapolis: Fortress, 1995.

Stuhlmacher, Peter. *Reconciliation, Law & Righteousness: Essays in Biblical Theology.* Philadelphia: Fortress, 1986.

Talbert, Charles H. *Reading Luke: A Literary and Theological Commentary on the Third Gospel.* New York: Crossroad, 1982.

Tannehill, Robert C. "A Study in the Theology of Luke-Acts." *AThR* 43 (1961) 195–203.

Taylor, Vincent. *The Formation of the Gospel Tradition.* 2nd ed. London: Macmillan, 1935.

Theissen, Gerd. "Historical Scepticism and the Criteria of Jesus Research: My Attempt to Leap over Lessing's Ugly Wide Ditch." In *Handbook for the Study of the Historical Jesus,* edited by Tom Holmen and Stanley E. Porter, 1:549–87. Leiden: Brill, 2011.

Theissen, Gerd, and Annette Merz. "The Delay of the Parousia as a Test Case for the Criterion of Coherence." *LS* 32 (2007) 49–66.

———. *The Historical Jesus: A Comprehensive Guide*. Minneapolis: Fortress, 1998. Translated by John Bowden from *Der historische Jesus: Ein Lehrbuch*. Göttingen: Vandenhoeck & Ruprecht, 1996.

Theissen, Gerd, and Dagmar Winter. *The Quest for the Plausible Jesus: The Question of Criteria*. Translated by M. Eugene Boring. Louisville: John Knox, 2002.

The Tosefta: Translated from the Hebrew with a New Introduction. Translated by Jacob Neusner. 2 vols. Peabody, MA: Hendrickson, 2002.

Tucker, Jeffrey T. *Example Stories: Perspectives on Four Parables in the Gospel of Luke*. JSNTSup 162. Sheffield: Sheffield Academic, 1998.

Van Elderen, Bastiaan. "Another Look at the Parable of the Good Samaritan." In *Saved by Hope*, edited by James I. Cook, 109–19. Grand Rapids: Eerdmans, 1978.

Van Unnik, W. C. "Luke-Acts, a Storm Center in Contemporary Scholarship." In *Studies in Luke-Acts*, edited by Leander E. Keck and J. Louis Martyn, 15–32. Nashville: Abingdon, 1966.

Vermes, Geza. *Jesus and the Jew*. Philadelphia: Fortress, 1973.

———. *Jesus and the World of Judaism*. Philadelphia: Fortress, 1983.

———. *The Religion of Jesus the Jew*. Minneapolis: Fortress, 1993.

Wallace, Daniel B. *Greek Grammar Beyond the Basics*. Grand Rapids: Zondervan, 1996.

Weeden, Theodore J., Sr. "Kenneth Bailey's Theory of Oral Tradition: A Theory Contested by Its Evidence." *JSHJ* 7 (2009) 3–43.

Winter, Dagmar. "Saving the Quest for Authenticity from the Criterion of Dissimilarity: History and Plausibility." In *Jesus, Criteria, and the Demise of Authenticity*, edited by Chris Keith and Anthony Le Donne, 115–31. New York: T. & T. Clark, 2012.

Witherington, Ben, III. *The Gospel of Mark: A Socio-Rhetorical Commentary*. Grand Rapids: Eerdmans, 2001.

———. *Jesus the Sage: The Pilgrimage of Wisdom*. Minneapolis: Fortress, 1994.

Wright, N. T. *Jesus and the Victory of God*. Minneapolis: Fortress, 1996.

———. *Luke for Everyone*. London: Society for Promoting Christian Knowledge, 2004.

———. *The New Testament and the People of God*. Vol. 1 of *Christian Origins and the Question of God*. Minneapolis: Fortress, 1992.

Wright, Stephen I. "Parables on Poverty and Riches (Luke 12:13–21; 16:1–13; 16:19–31)." In *The Challenge of Jesus' Parables*, edited by Richard N. Longenecker, 230–33. Grand Rapids: Eerdmans, 2000.

York, John O. *The Last Shall Be First: The Rhetoric of Reversal*. JSNTSup 46. Sheffield: Sheffield Academic, 1991.

Young, Brad H. *Jesus and His Jewish Parables: Rediscovering the Roots of Jesus' Teaching*. New York: Paulist, 1989.

———. *The Parables: Jewish Tradition and Christian Interpretation*. Peabody, MA: Hendrickson, 1998.

Zeisler, J. A. "Luke and the Pharisees." *NTS* 25 (1979) 146–57.

Ancient Document Index

Old Testament/Hebrew Bible

Genesis

1:28	81
6:5	35
6:9–13	71n77
6:22	71n77
12:3	81
13:2	65
13:13	71n77
14:13–24	65
18:4–8	66n60
38:8–10	81
48:14	80n3

Exodus

14:13	89n43
20:14–15	32n77
21:22–25	81
22:21–22	65n57
23:9	65n57
23:20	48n7
25:17–22	36
32:9	49n10
33:3	49n10
33:5	49n10
38:5–8	36

Leviticus

6:1–5	39n119, 112
16	36
16:19–31	33
16:29	109
16:31	109
18:5	54n20
19:9–10	65n57
19:13	32n78
19:18	55, 55n24
19:33–34	55n24
19:33	65n57
23:22	65n57
23:27	109
23:29	109
23:32	109
27:30	110

Numbers

18:27	110
29:7	109

Deuteronomy

5:17–18	32n77
10:16	49n10
10:17–19	65n57
12:17	110
14:13	110

ANCIENT DOCUMENT INDEX

Deuteronomy (continued)

14:22–23	34
15:7	65n57
24:15	65n57
24:17–18	65n57
24:19–21	65n57
26:1–15	109
26:12–14	109

1 Samuel

1:10–11	81
1:13	32n75, 108n48
1:26	31, 106n37, 111n67
7:6	34n82, 109

2 Samuel

7:11–14	90
12:1–2	127n47
12:15b–23	72n82

1 Kings

8:14	31, 106n37, 111n67
8:22	31, 106n37, 111n67

2 Chronicles

20:17	89n43

Ezra

4:13–21	128n50
5:41–53	128n50
9:1–2	35
9:5–6	35
9:6	35, 111, 114

Psalms

5	114
7	114
14:1	35
17	114
24:3–5	114
26	114
30	32
35:13	34n82, 109
50:23	89n43
51	39, 114
51:1–4	112
51:19	114
79:9	114
89:4–5	90n48
91:16	89n43
92	32
95:10	35
118	32
119:123	89n43
122	104n26
123:1	35
127:3–5	81
134	104n26
135	104n26
136	32
138	32
141:2	105

Proverbs

3:34	40n123, 113n77, 114
27:2	114
29:23	114

Isaiah

11:1	90n48
11:10	90n48
25:6–8	92n59
25:6	60n38, 96n68
29:18–19	48
32:6	35
35:5–6	48
40:5	89n43
42:1–4	74n90
42:16–17	89n43
42:18	48
49:1–6	74n90
50:4–9	74n90
52:12–53:12	76n92
52:13–53:12	74n90

53	74n90
53:7	76n92
53:9	76n92
53:11	74, 74n90, 77
53:12	76
55:1–2	92n59
56:7	104
56:10–12	67n65
58:7	65n57
58:10	65n57
59:11	89n43
61	74n90
61:1–2	74n90
61:1	48
65:13–14	92n59

Jeremiah

23:5	90n48
33:15	90n48

Ezekiel

2	49n10
15:1–8	128
16	128
17	128
21:26	40n124
24:1–14	128
33:13	24n54
34	74

Daniel

7	74n88
7:13	74

Hosea

6:6	110n64

Amos

5:11–15	65n56
5:11	65n56
5:12	65n56
5:13	65n56
5:15	65n56

Micah

6:7–8	110n64

Zephaniah

1:7	92n59

Zechariah

7:3	33, 33n81
7:5	33, 33n81, 34n82, 109
7:9–10	65n57
8:19	33, 33n81

Malachi

3:1	48n7

Apocrypha

1 Esdras (1 Esd)

4:45	35

2 Esdras (2 Esd)

12:7	114

Judith (Jdt)

9:1	105, 105n32

Prayer of Manasseh (Pr Man)

1:8–9	112n73

Sirach (Sir)

50:1–21	105n30
50:5–18	105n32
50:19	105n30

Pseudepigrapha

Apocalypse of Abraham
(Apoc. Ab.)

9–32	65n59

Assumption of Moses
(As. Mos.)

7:9–10	107n41

1 Enoch (1 En.)

13:5	35, 111n69
37–71	128n50

4 Ezra

8:47–50	113n78
12:7	114
12:32	90n48

Joseph and Aseneth
(Jos. Asen.)

10:15	43n141
10.2–13:15	111n70

Psalms of Solomon
(Pss. Sol.)

17:21–40	90n48
17:21	90

Testament of Gad
(T. Gad)

5:7	89n43

Testament of Abraham
(T. Ab.)

10–15	65n59
A 1:1–25	66n60
A 2:2	66n60
A 4:6	66n60
A 17:7	66n60
A 20:15	66n60
B 4:10	66n60
B 13:5	66n60

Nag Hammadi texts

Coptic Gospel of Thomas
(CGT)

	64

New Testament

Matthew

2:2–10	93n60
3:16–17	138n91
5:3–7	113
5:46	103n21
6:5	31, 106n37, 111n67
6:16–18	34n82, 109
7:13–14	80, 91, 92n57, 99
7:22–23	80, 91, 99
8:5–13	80, 95, 99
8:5–6	96
8:5	96
8:6	67
8:7	96
8:8–10	96
8:11–12	80, 91, 96, 99
8:13	96
9:2	67
9:10	103n19
9:27–31	80, 88, 99
11:1–5	90
11:19	103n19
13:55–56	33n79
14:19	111n68
14:23	104
15:19	111
15:24	11
18:4	44n143, 113n76
18:16	137
18:17	103n21
18:21–35	113
19:3	99

ANCIENT DOCUMENT INDEX

19:13–25	80, 99	8:27—10:45	83n18
19:13–15	80	8:29	88
19:16–30	80, 83, 95, 99	8:35	89n45
19:16	84	9:33–37	83n18
19:21	85n26	9:36–37	81, 81n11
19:22	83n20	10:1–31	80
19:30	80, 91	10:1	80
20:29–34	80, 88, 99	10:2–12	80
21:10	33n79	10:13–17	83
21:31–32	28n62	10:13–16	80, 83n18, 86, 88, 90, 99
21:31	103n20		
22:1–14	80, 93, 99	10:13	80, 90n50
22:1–10	93n60	10:14	82n15
22:1–4	96n68	10:15	82, 83
22:8	95	10:16	82
22:11–14	93n60	10:17–31	80, 83, 88, 95, 99
22:34–40	53	10:17–22	83, 90
23:12	40, 44n143, 113n76	10:17	84, 84n22, 86
23:23	110n64	10:18	84
25:10	96n68	10:19	84n23
26:6–13	47n5	10:20	85, 87
26:6	26, 47n5	10:21	84n23, 85, 85n26, 86–87
26:36	104		
27:43	23	10:22	85, 90–91
27:57	24n54	10:23–27	83
		10:23	85–86
Mark		10:24b	83n18
		10:25	85–86
1:9b–11	138n91	10:26	86, 89n45
1:15	87n35	10:27	87
2:15–17	11	10:28–31	84, 86
2:15	103n19	10:28	86–87, 90
2:18–20	34n82, 109	10:29–30	86–87
3:4	89n45	10:30	80, 84n22, 87
3:22	145	10:31	86–87
4:33	139	10:45	85n25
5:23	89n45	10:46–52	80, 88, 90, 99
5:28	89n45	10:46	88
5:34	89n45	10:47–48	88, 90
6:2–3	33n79	10:47	88, 91n52
6:41	35, 111n68	10:48	88–89
6:46	104	10:49–50	88
6:56	89n45	10:49	89
7:21–23	35	10:50	89
7:34	35, 111n68	10:51–52	88
8:22—10:52	90n46	10:51	89
8:22–26	88, 90	10:52	89–90

Mark (continued)

11:25	31, 106n37, 111n67
12:1	139
12:28–34	53
13:13	89n45
13:20	89n45
14:3–9	47n5
14:3	26, 47n5
14:24	85n25
15:14	76
15:30–31	89n45
15:43	24n54

Luke

1:9–10	104
1:10	30n68, 105
1:5–25	30n68, 106n36
1:14–17	72
1:25	81
1:46–55	67
1:51–53	40n124, 44n143
1:52	67
1:53	68, 72n81
2:10	72, 73n83
2:11	73n87
2:16	73n83
2:22	30n67
2:24	40n124
2:36–38	34n82, 109
2:42	30n67
2:51	30n67
3:3	48, 52
3:8–14	73
3:10–14	40n122
3:11–12	103
3:12–13	28
3:12	29
3:21–22	138n91
4:1–13	55, 75
4:2	75
4:13	75
4:16–30	95–96
4:16–27	74n90
4:16–21	90
4:18–19	48, 96
4:18	67
4:21	17n10, 73n87
4:25–26	96
4:27	95
4:33–37	75
4:43	17n10
5:10	17n10
5:11	68
5:16	104
5:17—6:11	27
5:17–26	25
5:21	33n79
5:26	27
5:27–31	28
5:27–30	29
5:28–32	25
5:28	68
5:29–32	77
5:29	73n83
5:30	25, 27–28, 73
5:32	24n50, 28, 40n122
5:33	34n83
6:1–11	27
6:1–5	56n26
6:2	25
6:3	17n10
6:6–11	56n26
6:7	25, 58n30
6:11	27
6:12	104
6:18	75
6:20–26	40n124, 67
6:20–21	113
6:20	63
6:23	72
6:24	63, 67, 72n81
6:25	67
6:27–38	97n71
6:45	35
6:46–49	68
7	47, 74n88
7:1	96
7:1–16	47
7:1–10	80, 95, 98–99
7:2–3	96
7:2	95
7:4–6	96

7:5	97n70	8:19–21	94n62
7:6–9	96	8:26–39	75
7:9	97n70, 98	8:48	52
7:10	96	9:3	17n10
7:11–17	95–96	9:13	17n10
7:16	47	9:14	17n10
7:18–35	48, 52	9:16	111n68
7:18–23	90, 95	9:37–43	75, 81n11
7:18	48	9:46–50	24
7:20	48	9:51—19:27	16
7:22	48, 53, 95	9:59–62	94n62
7:23	48, 48n6, 53	10:1–37	98
7:24–28	48	10:1–20	54
7:24	17n10	10:1–9	54
7:25	67n64	10:8–12	54
7:26–27	48	10:16	55
7:28–29	53	10:17–18	75
7:28	48, 53	10:17	55
7:29	28, 48, 49, 49n11, 51–52	10:18–19	55
7:30	25, 27, 52	10:20	72
7:31–35	49	10:21–24	54
7:33–34	49	10:25–37	20, 47, 53–54, 54n20, 77–78, 101n2
7:34–35	81n11		
7:34	28–29, 74, 103n19	10:25	55, 57
7:35	49, 49n11, 52, 53, 77	10:28	54n20, 57
		10:29–37	40n124
7:36–50	25–27, 47–50, 73, 76–78, 87n37, 95–96, 98, 101n2, 113	10:29	24, 24n50, 54
		10:30–35	15, 53
		10:36–37	53
		10:37	54n20, 57
7:36–38	50	10:38–42	40n124
7:39–40	47n5	11:1	17n10
7:39	33n79, 50–51, 76	11:5–8	69n71
7:40–42	50	11:14	75
7:41–42	27, 50n15	11:22	17n11, 23
7:41	17n15	11:28	68
7:43	50	11:37–44	24, 58n30
7:44–46	27, 50–51	11:37–41	26, 40n124
7:47–48	52, 77	11:39–43	64n55
7:47	50	11:39	27
7:48–50	50	11:42	26–27, 34–35, 38
7:48	52–53	11:43	26–27
7:49	33n79	11:53–54	27
7:50	50, 52, 78	11:53	26
8:2	75	11:54	58n30
8:4–15	68	12:1–2	24

ANCIENT DOCUMENT INDEX

Luke *(continued)*

12:1	17n10, 26
12:13–21	72n81
12:16–20	15
12:19	67
12:21	40n124
12:32–34	68
12:49—13:9	91
13:3	40n122
13:5	40n122
13:10–17	91
13:11	75
13:16	75
13:18–19	91
13:20–21	91
13:22–30	80, 91, 91n54, 93n60, 96n67, 99
13:23	92
13:24–29	91n54
13:24	92
13:25	92
13:26	92
13:28–29	92n55
13:28	92
13:29	92
13:30	92–93
13:31–33	26
13:32	75
14	62
14:1–24	57, 93
14:1–14	24, 78, 98
14:1–6	27, 57, 94
14:1–4	58
14:1	26, 57
14:3–4	58n31
14:3	17n10
14:5–6	58
14:7–14	47, 57, 64n55, 77, 94
14:7–11	27
14:7	58
14:8–10	59
14:10	77, 95
14:11	40, 40n124, 44n143, 55, 59, 67, 76, 113n76
14:12–14	27, 72n81, 94
14:12–13	59
14:13	62
14:14	55, 59n35, 60, 77
14:15–24	27, 57, 62, 80, 93, 93n60, 98–99
14:15–16	96n68
14:15	93n60, 94–95
14:16–23	94
14:16–21	93n60
14:18	94n62
14:19	94n62
14:20	94n62
14:21	62, 68
14:24	95
14:26	94n62
14:30	33n79
15	60
15:1–32	11, 25, 27, 47, 60, 74, 77–78, 98
15:1–2	24, 28, 60–62
15:1	28–29, 61
15:2	25, 33, 61, 73, 103n19, 109
15:3	17n10, 60
15:4–7	60
15:5–7	72
15:6	61
15:7	28, 61, 77
15:8–10	60
15:9	61
15:10	28, 61, 72, 77
15:11–32	39, 40n122, 40n124, 66, 81n11, 101n2
15:11–31	61
15:20	61
15:21–24	61
15:23	61, 67
15:24	61
15:28	61
15:30	33n79
15:32	61, 72–73, 77
16	16
16:1–31	27
16:1–9	63
16:1	16, 17n10

ANCIENT DOCUMENT INDEX

16:10–13	63		70, 76, 78, 91n51,
16:14–31	47, 62, 78, 98		97, 98
16:14–18	63, 64n52	18:1	16, 23n45, 69,
16:14–17	24, 24n50		69n71
16:14–15	16, 65	18:2	70
16:14	24, 26, 38, 58n30,	18:3–4	71
	62, 75n91	18:3	1, 22, 69n70
16:15	35, 38, 55, 64	18:4–5	57, 71
16:16–18	68n69	18:4	70
16:16–17	38, 68	18:4a	70
16:19–31	15, 20, 40n124, 62,	18:5–8	1, 22
	72n81, 77	18:5	69n70, 70–71, 77,
16:19–26	63		97n71
16:19	67	18:6	69n70
16:20	65n56, 67	18:7	69n70, 70
16:21	67, 67n62	18:8	22, 22n41, 40, 43,
16:22	78		57, 69n70, 71, 78
16:23–24	67	18:9—19:27	22
16:23	67	18:9–14	1–2, 6, 8–10, 13–
16:24	65, 105		14, 17, 22–23, 27,
16:24–31	65		41, 44, 46, 50–53,
16:25	67		55, 59, 64, 66, 69,
16:27–31	63		70, 74, 76–79,
16:27–28	65		86–89, 89n44, 90,
16:29	68		93, 97–100, 108,
16:30	40n122, 65, 68		114–17, 170
16:31	68, 78	18:9	1, 16, 17, 19,
17	16		22n41, 23, 23n45,
17:1	16, 17n10		25, 32–33, 37–38,
17:3–4	40n122		43, 55, 59, 61, 70,
17:11	69		72, 75, 107, 109
17:12–19	69	18:10–14a	16, 20
17:13	105	18:10–13	19
17:19	52	18:10	17, 19, 20, 25,
17:20—18:8	22		25n56, 104
17:20–21	69	18:10a	21n34
17:20	22, 24, 69n71,	18:10b	21n34
	107n45	18:11–12	19, 21n34, 55, 87
17:22–37	16	18:11	18, 18n20, 23, 24,
17:22	24, 69, 107n45		31, 33n79, 38, 70,
17:24	69		73, 75–76, 97, 106
17:25	69	18:11a	20
17:26–32	71n77	18:11b	20
17:34	17n15	18:12	18, 18n20, 20, 33,
18	1, 1n3, 28, 81		38, 73n86, 108n49,
18:1–8	1, 13, 13n54, 16,		109
	22, 47, 55, 66, 69,		

Luke (continued)

18:13	18, 18n16, 19, 21n34, 31, 35, 36, 43, 51, 70–71, 76, 91, 105
18:13a	20
18:13b	20
18:14–15	61
18:14	1, 18n20, 19, 22, 30, 32n76, 44, 51, 53–55, 60–61, 67, 76, 83n21, 86–87, 91, 95, 104
18:14a	19–21, 21n34, 25, 37, 40, 70n75, 71, 73, 113
18:14b	19, 21, 21n34, 22, 23n45, 40, 44, 59, 81, 109, 113
18:14c	21n34
18:14d	21n34
18:15–17	22, 40, 80, 83n21, 97–99
18:15	71, 97n71
18:17	98
18:18	83n20, 84, 98
18:18—19:10	22
18:18–30	54, 72n81, 80, 83, 83n21, 95, 98–99
18:22	68, 85n26
18:23–25	72
18:23	72
18:28	57
18:35–43	54, 66, 80, 88, 98–99
18:38–39	43, 105
18:39	71, 97, 97n71
18:42	43, 52
19:1–10	40n122, 43n140, 47, 71, 77–78, 97–98
19:1–3	71
19:2	72
19:3	72
19:4	71
19:5	71, 77
19:6	71–73, 78
19:6–7	62
19:7	28, 60n39, 71–72, 74, 76
19:8–10	72
19:8	39n118, 73, 73n86, 78, 103
19:9	71, 73
19:10	28, 35, 61, 73–74
19:11	23n45
19:39	27
19:46	104
20:26	58n31
20:45—21:4	72n81
22:3–4	75
22:31–32	75
22:37	76
22:40–45	75
22:53	75
22:59	33n79
22:63–65	75
22:67	75
22:70	75
23:4	76, 76n92
23:9	76n92
23:11	24
23:14–15	76n92
23:14	76
23:15	76
23:22	76, 76n92
23:25	76
23:33	76n92
23:35	64n53, 75–76
23:36–37	75
23:37	76
23:39–43	76–77
23:39	75–76, 76n92
23:45–47	106n36
23:47	74, 76
23:48	35, 111
23:50–54	24n54
23:50–51	76n92
24:18	159
24:47	40n122
24:50–53	30n68, 106n36

John

4:46–54	95n64
6:42	33n79
6:52	33n79
9:2	72n82
11:41	35, 111n68
12:1–3	47n5
12:3	47n5
17:1	35, 111n68
19:38–42	24n54
19:39–40	24n54
20:30	139
21:25	139

Acts

2:15	105n34
2:37–39	40n122
2:42	104
3:1	30n67, 30n68, 104, 105n34, 106n36
3:13	74n90
3:19	40n122, 52n17
3:26	52n17, 74n90
4:11	24
5:31	40n122, 52n17
7:51–53	49n10
10	106n36
10:3	30n68
10:28	97n72
10:30	30n68
10:43	52n17
11:3	97n72
11:18	40n122, 58n31
13	1n3, 6
13:2–3	34n82, 110
13:13–41	1
13:38	52n17
15:5	26
16:13	104
16:16	104
17:18	33, 109
17:30	40n122
20:21	40n122
20:33–34	64n54
22:16	52n17
23	26
26:18	52n17
26:20	40n122

Romans

3:25	112

1 Corinthians

5:10–11	32n77
6:9–10	32n77
6:9	32n78
7:10–11	121n22
7:25	121n22
11:2	150
11:23–26	162n200
11:23	150
12:28	162n200
14:6	162n200
14:19	162n200
14:26	162n200
15:1	150
15:3	150

2 Corinthians

1:9	17n11, 17n12, 23
10:10	162n200
11:27	34n82, 110

Galatians

1:9	150

Ephesians

4:11	162n200
5:19	162n200

Philippians

3:4–6	34
4:9	150

Colossians

3:16	162n200

1 Thessalonians

2:5–6	64n54
2:13	150
4:1	150

2 Thessalonians

2:15	150
3:6	150

1 Timothy

4:10	92n56
6:5	64n54
6:11–12	92n56

2 Timothy

3:2	64n54
4:7–8	92n56

Titus

1:11	64n54

Hebrews

2:13	23
2:17	36
9:5	112

James

4:6–10	113n77
4:6	40n123
4:10	40n123

1 Peter

5:5–6	40n123, 113n77

1 John

2:2	112
4:10	112

Revelation

19:9	60n38, 96n68

Dead Sea Scrolls

CD (Damascus Document)

20:34	89n43

IQH (Hodayot or Thanksgiving Hymnal)

7.34	34, 109
15.34–35	31n73, 109

1QS (Rule of Community, Manual of Discipline)

112–13	89n43

1QSa (Appendix A, to 1QS, Rule of the Congregation)

2:15–22	92n59

1 QSb (Appendix B to 1QS, Rule of the Blessings)

4:22	114

4QFlor (Florilegium (or Eschatological Midrashim) from Qumran Cave 4)

1:11–13	90n48

Ancient Document Index

Rabbinic Writings

Mishnah

m. 'Abot ('Abot)

3.17	104n25

m. B. Qam. (Baba Qamma)

10.2	103n22

m. Demai

2.3	106n39

m. Hag. (Hagigah)

2.7	106n38

m. Ma'as. (Ma'aserot)

1:1	110n59

m. Ned. 3.4 (Nedarim)

3.4	103n22, 104n25

m. Pirke Aboth

2.5	107n43

m. Seb. (Shevi'it)

9.1	110n60

m. Ta'an. (Ta'anit)

1.6	110n57

m. Tamid

5.1	105n32
5.6	106n40

m. Tehar. (Teharot)

7.4–6	106n39
7.6	103n22
8.3	106n39

Babylonian Talmud

b. B. Qam.

94b	103n24, 112n74

b. Ber. (Berakot)

17a	113n79
28b	31n73, 34, 108n50
31a	108n47

b. 'Erub. (Erubin)

13b	113n78

b. Sanh (Sanhedrin)

4b	70n72
25b	103n23, 104n25

b. Sotah (Sotah)

22b	34n88

b. Suk. (Sukkah)

45b	34

b. Ta'an. (Ta'anit)

12a	110n57

Palestinian Talmud

y. Ber.

4.2	108n50
14b	102n12

y. Sotah

20c	102n12

Other Rabbinic Works

'Abot de Rabbi Nathan ('*Abot R. Nat.*)

13	66n60

Rabbah

Ruth Rab.

6.4	72n82

m. Eccl. Rab.

7.2	35, 111
7.5	111n66

Ancient Document Index

Greco-Roman Writings

Cicero

Off. (De officiis)

15–51	103n18

Dio Chrysostom

Discourses (Disc.)

32:9–11	64n54
35:1	64n54
54:1–3	64n54

Orations (Or.)

14.14	103n18

Herodotus

Hist. (Historiae)

1.105	72n82
4.67	72n82

Hesiod

Op. (Opera et dies)

1.235	72n82

Josephus

Jewish War (J.W.)

1.5.2 110	25n57
1.110–12	101n4
2.162	101n5

Jewish Antiquities (Ant.)

7.10.5	35
11.143	111n71
13.289	101n6
12.154–59	103n17
12.175–86	103n17
12.164	104n26
18.15	101n3
297–98	101n7, 108n49

Lucian

Timon (Tim.)

56	64n54

Philo

Praem. (De praemiis et poenis)

127	64n54

Spec. (De specialibus legibus)

3.1110–19	81

Tacitus

Hist (Historiae)

5.5	81

Papyri

Select Papyri

2:286	103n17
2:358	103n17
2:382	103n17
2:420	103n17

Early Christian Writings

2 Clement (2 Clem.)

1:6–7	89n43
9:2	89n43

Didache (Did.)

8:1	34n83, 110n57

www.ingramcontent.com/pod-product-compliance
Lightning Source LLC
Chambersburg PA
CBHW070324230426
4366 3CB0001 1B/2214